Teachers Leading Change

About the Authors

Judy Durrant works within the Centre for Education Leadership and School Improvement (CELSI), part of the Faculty of Education at Canterbury Christ Church University. She leads a Masters programme and consultancy supporting leadership of learning and school-based enquiry. Her current research focuses on teacher leadership, professionalism and school improvement.

Dr. Gary Holden is a Secondary Link Advisor for Kent Local Education Authority. He is an experienced teacher and deputy headteacher and a Masters tutor for Canterbury Christ Church University and University of Cambridge. His doctoral studies explored the impact of teacher-led development work on teacher, school and student learning.

Judy Durrant and Gary Holden are co-authors (with David Frost and Michael Head) of *Teacher-Led School Improvement* (RoutledgeFalmer, 2000). Judy Durrant is co-author (with David Frost) of *Teacher-Led Development Work: Guidance and Support* (David Fulton, 2003).

Teachers Leading Change

Doing Research for School Improvement

Judy Durrant
and
Gary Holden

Paul Chapman Publishing

P-E
D937
2006

Paul Chapman Publishing
A SAGE Publications Company
1 Oliver's Yard
55 City Road
London EC1Y 1SP

SAGE Publications Inc
2455 Teller Road
Thousand Oaks, California 91320

SAGE Publications India Pvt Ltd
B-42, Panchsheel Enclave
Post Box 4109
New Delhi 110 017

Library of Congress Control Number: 2005926681
A catalogue record for this book is available from the British Library

ISBN 1-4129-0066-2
ISBN 1-4129-0067-0 (pbk)

Typeset by Pantek Arts Ltd, Maidstone, Kent
Printed on paper from sustainable resources
Printed in Great Britain by T. J. International, Padstow, Cornwall

For David

Contents

Resources available online:
www.paulchapmanpublishing.co.uk/resource/durrant.pdf

Appendix 1 An audit of professional development activity
Appendix 2 Some definitions of leadership
Appendix 3 The impact of teacher-led development work
Appendix 4 How can headteachers support teachers leading change?
Appendix 5 What can teacher leaders do to build capacity?
Appendix 6 Has your research taken full account of ethical issues?

Publisher's Note

The authors and publisher are grateful for permission to reproduce the following material in this book :

Figure 2.1 from Hargreaves, D.H. (1999) 'Helping Practitioners Explore Their School's Culture', in J. Prosser (ed.) *School Culture*. London: Paul Chapman Publishing.

Figure 2.2 from Stoll, L., and Fink, D. (1996) Changing Our Schools: *linking school effectiveness and school improvement*. Buckingham: OUP.

Figure 2.3 from Hargreaves, D.H. (2003) *Working Laterally: how innovation networks make an education epidemic*; p. 6, figure 1, (ref DfES/0825/2003). Crown copyright material is reproduced with the permission of the Controller of HMSO and the Queen's Printer for Scotland.

Table 2.1 from Sammons, P., Hillman, J. and Mortimore, P. (1997) 'Key characteristics of effective schools : A review of school effectiveness research', in J. White and M. Barber (eds), *Perspectives on School Effectiveness and School Improvement*. London : Institute of Education .

Every effort has been made to trace and acknowledge all the copyright owners of the material reprinted herein. However, if any copyright owners have not been located and contacted at the time of publication, the publishers will be pleased to make the necessary arrangements at the first opportunity.

Preface

In this book, we invite readers to consider a theoretical and practical perspective on school improvement in which teachers' leadership of learning is seen as the key to school change. We draw on the valuable and well-established traditions of 'teachers as researchers' and action research, setting these in the contemporary context of school improvement, emphasising collaborative and strategic approaches in leading learning and building capacity for learning. This requires teachers to use methodological techniques in particular ways to support their leadership of change. It also requires them to use strategies for improvement to guide their methodology, in order to ensure maximum impact upon individuals and institutions. We invite a wide perspective on school-based enquiry that requires teachers, headteachers and those supporting school improvement to conceptualise beyond the 'research project', towards enquiry as the driving force for change, through which they can engage and motivate other members of the school community to work and learn collaboratively. This embraces both intrinsic and extrinsic values and motivation, from helping schools to investigate how to improve students' achievement through to emancipatory influences on teachers, students and other participants.

This book bridges theory and practice quite deliberately in the knowledge that there is much work to be done to improve communication and understanding between teachers and others working in schools, policymakers and the academic and research communities. It provides both a theoretical and a practical rationale for teachers' leadership of change through enquiry. We offer opportunities for teachers and headteachers to engage with the interacting school improvement, school leadership and methodological discourses. Equally importantly, we provide insights into the world of schools and classrooms through our experience as teachers, tutors, advisors and consultants. The intention is to show how these ideas about leadership, enquiry and school improvement are worked out in practice and to offer frameworks for activities that we already know to be effective in both motivating teachers and structuring support for their enquiry and leadership. We offer these as learners ourselves, engaged in journeys encompassing multiple roles; one of us is an experienced deputy headteacher, school-based academic tutor and doctoral scholar now working as a Local Education Authority advisor and School Improvement Partner, while the other moved from teaching and subject leadership in a secondary school into an academic role that involves direct support for teacher leadership and school improvement through school-based consultancy, teaching and research.

In England, we are currently working within the context of a range of new policy initiatives. 'The New CPD' (Continuing Professional Development) is characterised by teachers taking responsibility for their own and each other's learning, within and between schools, and developing innovative practice through classroom research (DfES, 2005a). A more open and invitational approach than hitherto is being supported through provision of an exciting range of materials based on current research whereby teachers can experiment, supplemented by reflection (DfES, 2004b). At the same time, the 'New Relationship with Schools' (DfES, 2004a) has been introduced in which every school has been allocated a School Improvement Partner. Although these developments are extremely encouraging and provide important touchstones, our argument is not tied to current policy initiatives. It is important that teachers and headteachers are able to see their way through current rhetoric, to consider the real dilemmas and conflicts facing schools and their implications and to develop the knowledge, skills and understanding necessary in order to work effectively in rapidly changing professional environments, which include inevitable changes in policy and funding arrangements. We therefore need to consider approaches that harness yet transcend the latest initiatives. How can schools find direction? How can headteachers and teachers prioritise development and work with coherence? What can we expect of teachers? How can they use, and discriminate between, the enormous wealth of materials and strategies available to them? How can teachers find professional fulfilment and move collectively towards desired outcomes, as the political pendulum swings back and forth?

We need to take a fresh look at purposes and processes in schools and consider what will help them to move and grow, nurturing the people within as leaders and learners in order to foster creative and committed communities of learning. To be able to do this, we need to be clear about what we mean by 'school improvement'. While this book emphasises our advocacy of teachers and their all-important work, we must not forget that at the heart of these endeavours are children and young people and in particular their learning. Some would define 'improvement' quite narrowly in terms of making the teaching and learning process and conditions within schools better in order to raise student achievement, including an improvement in the capacity of a school to manage change in this regard. We would join with others in taking a broader view to encompass enhancement of pupils' progress, development and achievement. This is underpinned by the capacity of the school to develop and maintain the culture, strategies and conditions that enable it to define a direction for change, set its own goals, maintain stability and momentum and engage in self-evaluation (Stoll, 1999). We think of empowerment not as a tool of implementation, which seems to be a contradiction in terms, but as a means to enhance agency. In our work with teachers and headteachers, we are pushing notions of teacher leadership and shared leadership into new dimensions, building on collaborative work initiated by our colleague Dr David Frost, now at the University of Cambridge. This work is based on the premise that teachers must exercise leadership in the complex processes of school improvement principally because leadership and agency are fundamental to people's humanity.

Schools need sustainable approaches that build internal capacity for improvement. 'Capacity' is a well-worn term; we take it to mean the ability within schools to learn continuously in order to respond creatively to rapidly changing and unpredictable socio-political environments and local variables and vicissitudes, while holding fast to shared principles and values. This requires schools to have confidence in their own values and purposes and to develop ways of working that celebrate human diversity whilst being inclusive of everyone's needs and promoting learning for all. It requires knowledge about the complex relationship between student, professional and organisational learning and also about processes of change. This learning and change depend ultimately on teachers, supported in turn by their headteachers, drawing on a web of internal and external support. Schools aspiring to be learning communities must therefore include 'collegial decision making' (Frost and Durrant, 2003: 2) in notions of capacity building. In other words, where we talk about 'the school', we must ensure that this means 'the individuals in the school', not just the headteacher, an elite group or those with the most powerful voices.

Our exploration involves delving into some dark corners, becoming involved with some mess and confusion, acknowledging that there are problems that defy quick, slick solutions and that there are questions that are open-ended and have no right answers. It also requires an understanding of each school's uniqueness and people's idiosyncrasies. Rather than offering answers, we explore how to address the questions and work with the dilemmas, recognising that both the substance of the questions and the processes by which they are addressed are different for every school and for the individuals involved. Whilst there is a continually developing body of knowledge about learning, pedagogy and organisational development, it is no easy matter for teachers to access, assimilate, adapt and apply that knowledge. There may be many different routes to changing practice and there is certainly no blueprint for practice in situations that are infinitely complex. Nevertheless, wherever theory, research, experience and excellent practice exist upon which to draw, there are also ways to move forward and make progress, as long as the overall purpose remains clear. Therefore we need practical processes that engage teachers in the day-to-day work that makes improvement happen. This book is an attempt to acknowledge the reality of relationships and structures, cultures and communities to be found in schools and, through our research and experience in a range of contexts, to offer ways of working that energise teachers. This includes revisiting their original purposes, if necessary rekindling their passion for learning and also nurturing their leadership, helping to create the kind of schools that we would want for all children and for diverse communities.

At the heart of this book is a particular set of ideas about school improvement. We suggest that:

- the core purpose of schools is to engage everyone in learning
- teachers play a central role in the leadership of learning
- headteachers play a key role in supporting teachers' leadership of learning
- the foundation and catalyst for this leadership of learning is school-based enquiry, connecting evidence generated in school with the wider educational discourse

● through teachers' collaboration, enquiry and leadership of learning, there is potential to unlock school cultures in order to build and sustain capacity for school improvement.

Chapter 1 considers some current perspectives on school improvement and argues that we need a more holistic approach that demands nothing less than a reculturing of schools, a change of mindset, a new way of working. Teachers' leadership of learning through enquiry provides a focus for such an approach.

In Chapter 2, we consider how to unlock school cultures by adopting the principles suggested above. We argue that the current discourse on school improvement and effectiveness has taken some schools further along the road but that transformation remains elusive; many schools reach a plateau where they are left tinkering around the edges of entrenched structures and ways of working. We argue for transformation through teachers' engagement in dialogue, enquiry and leadership of change, with the common purpose of fostering true learning communities.

In Chapter 3, we show how school-based enquiry can be used not simply to provide 'findings' upon which to base school change, but as a powerful engine for improvement in its own right. It is a vehicle for the development of teachers' personal and interpersonal capacity to lead change and can drive organisational development. This requires us to revisit extended concepts of professionalism, with the caution that whilst trying to find manageable and practical ways of invigorating teachers' busy lives with enquiry, they should not be further burdened with greater responsibility and intensification of their day-to-day work.

Chapter 4 is broken down into a series of sections that explore aspects of teacher research related to leadership of learning and school improvement. These offer various rationales, ideas and strategies to inspire teacher leaders to adopt fresh approaches to their own and others' learning. Activities are suggested for facilitators fostering these ways of working; most can also be used by teachers working individually. The sections examine the process of enquiry, from finding a focus through evidence gathering and analysis through to changing practice. Teacher-led research is presented as integral to improvement and as a source of inspiration, understanding, involvement and growth.

Chapter 5 explores relationships and structures within schools through the experiences and dilemmas of three teachers who have used an enquiry approach to their leadership of change. These stories show that power and authority used inappropriately can lead to people's incapacity to lead change and the stifling of learning at every level of an organisation, whilst active support for teachers' leadership can lead to improvements in practice and significant cultural change. Internal and external opportunities and constraints are examined. The chapter concludes with a suggested model for shared leadership of mutual learning inside schools and across school boundaries.

In Chapter 6 we conclude that it is not usually realistic to remove what is there already and start again. In the vast majority of cases we have to find ways of building upon what is good in each school. We do not usually need bulldozers, but where individuals continue to cultivate their own small plots, there will only be infinitesimal change. We need landscape gardening, but not of the

'Ground Force' variety, where a handful of celebrities create a sensation in the course of two days, presided over by a film crew, and then leave. That is merely cosmetic change; it does not build capacity. In order to instil capacity for improvement that is sustainable, those for whom the garden is part of their everyday lives have to learn to be the landscape gardeners, designing, cultivating, nurturing and appreciating the environment in which they live and learn. They not only learn *in* this environment, but can also learn *about* it and *from* it, so that they can understand how to shape and use it to meet their needs. Teachers and headteachers, working with students and other members of the school community, can transform the landscape of their schools. In order to do this, we must move towards school cultures that foster more consistent support for shared leadership, inclusive learning relationships and human affirmation within a community working and growing together.

This book is not a manual or a textbook for teacher research. There are many contemporary and seminal texts that fulfil that purpose admirably and we have not attempted a synthesis of these or tried to offer a replacement. We draw upon the teacher research and action research traditions that have been developed since the 1970s through the work of Lawrence Stenhouse, John Elliott, Bridget Somekh, Helen Simons and others. We include references to some well-established texts that we have found helpful, providing a rich source of inspiration and reassurance. Connecting with the language of self-discovery and emancipation is always refreshing. However, we would emphasise the connections that need to be made between this work, often applied to individuals or small collaborative groups, and the broader understandings about school improvement explained above which involve capacity building to enable schools to maintain momentum and enact their values and purposes.

As we suggest in Chapter 3, schools that learn to work with evidence can become more effective self-critical learning communities. If enquiry is an engine for change, evidence fuels the fire. Teachers working with evidence are confronted with the direct questions and challenges that motivate them to make improvements; amidst high-stakes external accountability they themselves are often the most self-critical. Evidence indicates directions for change but also, through involvement in research and leadership, individuals grow and learn. They develop confidence extending beyond their research theme or project, leading them to increase their influence, their contribution to decision making and the shaping of school structures and cultures. Headteachers and teacher leaders working in parallel can use evidence and enquiry formatively and powerfully to build capacity for institutional and systemic change.

Teacher leadership through enquiry is a means by which commitment to children and young people and their learning finds passionate expression. The teachers, headteachers and colleagues with whom we work are enthusiastically involved, highly motivated, extremely hard working and provide much inspiration to us as we endeavour to offer support through Higher Education and the Local Education Authority. Many overlapping contacts and networks with individual colleagues, agencies and institutions across the national and international education community are helping us to shape our ideas and investigate our own practice. This book represents the learning we have enjoyed and the approaches we are currently using and continuing to develop.

While improvement may be achieved slowly on a small scale, a reculturing of schools along with a reconceptualisation of external support are needed if the notion of teacher leadership is to be taken seriously. Teachers leading change need the scope to be creative with curriculum and pedagogy; they benefit from having time to collaborate; they work best in a climate that permits risk-taking; they need frameworks and structures of support; they need critical friendship. Teachers should not appear as token practitioners or outsiders within the school improvement discourse – their evidence matters and their voices should be heard as equal participants. At the same time, advisors and external supporters of school improvement, including consultants, academics, policymakers and researchers, should not be awkward guests in the school environment. We need to be working together. But it is teachers, supported primarily by headteachers, who make schools into places vibrant with learning.

A note on the supporting materials in this book

Throughout this book we offer discussion and workshop activities and ideas for planning and action to support teachers leading change. We suggest specific tasks, such as action planning for leaders involved with a particular initiative, ideas for nurturing personal professional learning and broader activities to address whole-school issues, such as analysing and discussing the school culture and the extent to which it is supportive of teacher leadership and enquiry. The ideas, activities and examples throughout the chapters are not by any means intended as a 'training course' or a set of exercises through which schools will improve. They are offered as illustrations of a particular approach which has, in some schools and through some teachers, resulted in improved learning for students, teachers and organisations and is also beginning to have impact in networks and clusters of schools. The activities have been developed and used with groups of teachers and the examples are real, or drawn from real-life situations. Teachers, headteachers and external facilitators are invited to take up the principles of the approach and to adapt practices and supportive structures for their particular contexts to enable teachers, whatever their professional situations and formal roles, to take up their responsibility as leaders of learning.

School-based enquiry and leadership of change require careful and skilled facilitation. This needs to be sensitive to the context of the school, the micro-politics and the macro-politics. It depends on individual people, their environment and their professional situation, their attitudes, aptitudes and personality. The *activities* in this book have been undertaken with groups of teachers on Masters degree courses which support their research and leadership of change, in cluster or network programmes which seek to build cultures of enquiry and shared leadership and also as one-off activities to stimulate discussion and sharing of practice on school development days. We provide many *illustrations* of teachers' leadership of change and of school, cluster and network development, along with *checklists* and *frameworks* to guide and challenge thinking. Individual teachers using these resources may wish to seek support from a trusted colleague or advisor, to talk through dilemmas, gain advice and structure thinking. However, the value of peer support and the power of collaborative learning should not be underestimated, so we would recommend working in groups, teams or across organisations and networks.

We offer these tools and approaches in the hope that users of this book will *adapt* and *customise* these to make them fit for their agreed purposes. Some require people to challenge their current practice and reflect deeply; sometimes this can lead to startling revelations or the uncovering of values and experiences that have been long hidden. Careful judgement is required about when, or indeed whether, to use these ideas and exercises and they need to be sensitively facilitated, with due concern for confidentiality and mutual support. This is discussed in more detail later in the book.

These suggested approaches provide some 'ways in'. They can only be made powerful by teachers and headteachers in the unique context of their individual schools, with internal facilitation (for example, by headteachers, deputy headteachers, professional development co-ordinators) being crucial, but in addition it is helpful to introduce *critical friendship* and *external facilitation* to achieve a balance between contextual knowledge and critical distance. Schools are presented with a bewildering range of support and provision upon which to call and we have found that a deeper connection than the short-term provider–client relationship is important if this complicated work is to be sustained. It needs to be based on values and negotiated to fit the agendas of both partners, as well as the local circumstances (Frost and Durrant, 2003). It is hoped that the 'new relationship' with School Improvement Partners (DfES, 2004a) will help schools in England to make sense of this plethora of options and thus co-ordinate their improvement endeavours.

We have explained in some detail elsewhere how programmes and partnerships for teacher leadership and enquiry can be organised and the different types of support they need (Frost et al., 2000; Frost and Durrant, 2003; Holden, 2002b). In order to be most effective, these require the establishment of clear roles and responsibilities for co-ordinators and facilitators, in the context of trusting long-term relationships where external colleagues are involved (for example, from the university, Local Education Authority or other agencies). As we emphasise throughout the book, teachers need *ongoing support* for their leadership, collaboration, enquiry and learning. A training session may be interesting and helpful on the day, but it is unlikely to have any impact on practice unless it is followed up and the ideas are adapted by individuals in their own professional contexts. This is not simply a question of whether teachers have enough time. The methodologies of school-based enquiry and the dilemmas of leading change are far from straightforward, so teachers require both practical and moral support as questions arise and they continue to learn through the development process.

We stress from experience the importance of *timing* and *environment* for discussion, reflection and planning. It is difficult to engage in this kind of work unless those involved are comfortable, both physically and with each other. Meetings need to be planned so that teachers are not under pressure to choose between several conflicting demands. Meetings at the end of a full teaching day and before a parents' evening may not be productive. If 'twilight' meetings cannot be avoided then drinks and food are essential. Providing refreshments and choosing a pleasant place to meet, either in school or locally off-site, are always worthwhile. They help to build relationships, establish greater levels of trust and 'break the ice' for busy teachers, especially if they have arrived straight from the classroom. Offloading some of the pressures and pleasures of the classroom to one another is part of the work involved.

Schools sometimes find the co-ordination of such activity incredibly difficult amidst the busyness of timetables and schedules. Making sure a room is free, finding a small budget to supply biscuits, checking the caretakers and cleaners will keep the doors unlocked and the heating on at the end of the school day, notifying reception about the arrival of an external facilitator or colleagues from other schools, ensuring the floor is devoid of crisp packets and drink cans, even finding enough milk – all these have been problematic at times in our work with schools. Yet it is surprising how effective this simple attention to detail can be. We have learnt that where schools and headteachers as well as individual teachers prioritise the work, far greater impact is achieved. For teachers just as for pupils, *valuing people* through our ways of working creates the conditions within which they can best learn and support one another, modelling the kind of culture we would want to develop in schools.

Acknowledgements

This book builds on collaborative research and development work initiated, led and still inspired by David Frost, now at the University of Cambridge. It draws on models, frameworks and strategies published in two previous books, *Teacher-Led School Improvement* (Frost et al., 2000) and *Teacher Led Development Work: Guidance and Support* (Frost and Durrant, 2003). It also includes material from a number of recent papers and articles, many of which are co-authored. We feel privileged to have had so many opportunities to build on this work in different contexts and through our different roles in schools, Higher Education and Local Education Authorities and we are grateful to David for his unceasing support and encouragement.

Parts of the book are based on articles previously published in *The Enquirer*, the CANTARNET (Canterbury Action Research Network) journal (CANTARNET, 2005). We have included teachers' stories and examples from this network, based around the Masters in School Development Programme at Canterbury Christ Church University College. We are enormously grateful to this community which has sustained us for nearly ten years, with a high level of critical discourse that has underpinned our work, as people and policies have come and gone. We have developed our ideas further through cluster and network developments in Kent Local Education Authority, in particular NETWORKS, the National College for School Leadership Networked Learning Community in Tunbridge Wells. This has required considerable trust on the part of headteachers and teachers in taking the risks necessary to explore new ways of working.

We are grateful for the support we have enjoyed from colleagues in CELSI (Centre for Education Leadership and School Improvement) and other members of the Faculty of Education at Canterbury Christ Church University College. James Learmonth, CELSI's founder, has provided both of us with an enormous amount of professional and personal encouragement, maintaining an unwavering emphasis on children's learning and experience. Michael Head is a long-time friend, advisor and fellow-enthusiast. In our connections with the University of Cambridge, we particularly value the support of colleagues within the Cambridge Leadership for Learning network. We would also like to thank Alma Harris for her encouragement.

We acknowledge many other colleagues and friends from different parts of the education community, national and international, with whom the approaches and ideas in this book have been developed through enduring partnerships and collaborative working. They are too numerous to name, but this book expresses their enthusiasm and commitment in developing these approaches in practice in different contexts and in challenging us from a variety of perspectives. Each one is both a leader and a learner, and it is with them that we ourselves learn.

Foreword

Almost three decades ago a seminal study by Rosenholtz (1989) found that teacher networks, co-operation among teachers and expanded professional roles served to increase teachers' efficacy and effectiveness. Other influential writers, like Darling-Hammond et al. (1995) also advocated that giving teachers the opportunity to lead change and development was a core component in the building of *professional learning communities* in schools. Recent research has highlighted that a school's means of improving and sustaining improvement largely depend upon its ability to foster and nurture professional learning communities or 'communities of practice' (Morrissey, 2000; Holden, 2002). A recent review of the literature similarly suggests that generating teacher leadership, with its combination of increased collaboration and responsibility, has positive effects on school and student outcomes (Muijs and Harris, 2003). In short, fostering and supporting collaboration between teachers has consistently been identified with enhanced school effectiveness and improvement.

It has been suggested that *'developing a community of practice may be the single best most important way to improve a school'* (Sergiovanni, 2000: 139). A 'community of practice' is one where teachers participate in decision making, have a shared sense of purpose, engage in collaborative work and accept joint responsibility for the outcomes. The term implies a commitment not only to teacher sharing but also the generation of a school-wide culture that makes collaboration expected. Toole and Seashore Louis (2002: 5) note that the idea of a community of practice integrates three robust concepts: a school culture that emphasises *professionalism*, one that emphasises *learning* and one that emphasises *personal connection*. Yet, despite such enthusiastic support, the evolution of professional learning communities within or across schools has not always been straightforward or widespread. Part of the problem resides in the fact that there is no simple checklist or template that will ever adequately guide the formation of professional learning communities. Also it is clear that merely changing the organisational arrangements within schools in isolation will do little to promote pedagogical improvement and that attention must also be paid to building an infrastructure to support collaboration and creating the internal conditions for mutual learning. As Little (2000) argues: *to be most effective, professional learning communities need to exist within a social architecture that helps shape teachers' attitudes and practice.*

Teachers Leading Change is centrally concerned with creating the infrastructure and social architecture within schools to build the capacity for learning. It is a powerful and important book because it addresses the complexity and difficulties associated with building real professional learning communities within schools. While much has been written and espoused about professional learning communities, this book moves us away from the rhetoric to the everyday reality of making it happen. Part of this reality, the authors note, inevitably means 'delving into some dark corners … and acknowledging that there are problems that defy quick slick solutions and there are questions that are open-ended and have no right answers'. In an era of slick standardisation and designer leadership this 'uncertainty' is surely to be welcomed and applauded. The book does not claim to be a blueprint for action but acknowledges that there are different routes to changing practice and that the challenge is to engage teachers in the day-to-day work that makes improvement happen.

The authors bridge theory and practice comprehensively and convincingly. This is not surprising given their experience and expertise in the field. For many years the work of Judy Durrant and Gary Holden, in partnership with David Frost at the University of Cambridge, has built upon and continued the legacy of the 'teacher as researcher' movement established through the influential work of writers such as Lawrence Stenhouse and John Elliot. The work of the Centre for Education Leadership and School Improvement, at Canterbury Christ Church University College, has successively demonstrated the power of professional dialogue and networking. As one of the most successful school improvement centres in the country, it benefited from the wisdom of James Learmonth who established it and whose commitment to teachers leading change is reflected in the pages of this book.

At the heart of *Teachers Leading Change* is a particular set of ideas about school improvement within which teachers play a central role. Part of the reason for the failure of many large-scale improvement initiatives has been their inability to adequately involve or engage teachers in the process of change. Teachers have simply been seen as the recipients of innovation instead of the instigators of innovation. In the model of improvement expounded by Durrant and Holden, teachers' leadership of learning through enquiry is the catalyst for change and development. Central to this model is the idea of teachers as agents of change and the notion of leadership as a distributed or shared phenomenon.

There are a number of important things that the book highlights about teachers leading change. Firstly, it points towards the importance of creating *collegial norms* among teachers and modes of collaboration that evidence has shown contributes to school effectiveness, improvement and development. Secondly, it means giving teachers *opportunities to enquire into practice* which research shows has a positive influence upon the quality of teaching within the school. Thirdly, at its most practical, it allows teachers to *work together* and gives them a legitimate source of authority within the change process. Finally, the idea of teachers leading change *challenges* many current and traditional assumptions about the nature of leadership, the community within which it occurs and the relationship between power, authority and influence.

Throughout the book the authors provide discussion and workshop activities to support teachers leading change. These ideas and activities provide useful illustrations of the approach to teacher enquiry and leadership proposed. Far from providing 'tips for teachers' the activities offer a structured way of engaging with the main concepts and themes explored in the book. They also illustrate quite clearly that the authors understand the processes required to generate collaborative and reflective cultures within schools. In this sense, unlike many other books in the improvement genre, *Teachers Leading Change* is well grounded in the practical realities and complexities of schooling. It 'walks the talk' by providing one of the most comprehensive, insightful and well substantiated accounts of teachers leading learning without becoming, at any point, simply a manual or textbook for teacher research.

The authors argue that we need a new approach to professional development in which 'it can be seen both as an input and an outcome in teachers' leadership of learning'. The tired old models of professional development and training premised upon 'top-down' delivery and prescription have failed to deliver again and again. If sustainable school improvement is to be achieved we undoubtedly need new models and approaches to professional development that place teachers at the heart of organisational learning and change. *Teachers Leading Change* presents the real possibility of generating change and development through a 'new theory of practical action' that puts teachers at the centre of school improvement, where they belong.

Alma Harris
Series Editor

References

Bennett, N., Harvey, J.A., Wise, C. and Woods, P.A. (2003) *Distributed Leadership: A desk study,* www.ncsl.org.uk/literaturereviews.

Darling-Hammond, L., Bullmaster, M. L. and Cobb, V. L. (1995) 'Rethinking teacher leadership through professional development school', *The Elementary School Journal,* 96 (1): 87–106.

Holden, G. (2002) 'Towards a learning community: The role of teacher-led development in school improvement'. Paper presented at the CELSI British Council Leadership in Learning Conference, London, June 2002.

Little, J. W. (2000) 'Assessing the prospects for teacher leadership', in *Jossey-Bass Reader on Educational Leadership.* Chicago: Jossey-Bass. pp. 390–418.

Morrisey, M. (2000) 'Professional learning communities: An ongoing exploration'. Unpublished paper, Southwest Educational Development Laboratory, Austin, Texas.

Muijs, D. and Harris, A. (2003). 'Teacher leadership-improvement through empowerment? An overview of the literature'. *Educational Management & Administration,* 31(4): 437–48.

Rosenholtz, S. (1989). *Teachers Workplace: The social organization of schools.* New York: Longman.

Sergiovanni, T. (2000) *The Lifeworld of Leadership.* London: Jossey-Bass.

Toole, J.C. and Seashore Louis, K.S. (2002) *The Role of Professional Learning Communities in International Education,* education.umn.edu/CAREI/Papers/JULYFINAL.pdf.

1 Teachers as leaders of learning

Teacher leadership, school improvement and professionalism

School leadership is widely agreed to be a, if not the, key factor in determining school effectiveness (Bennett et al., 2003), indeed it can be viewed as something of a panacea (Harris, 2004). The current international discourse embraces shared leadership and the building of leadership capacity and there is increasing emphasis on inclusive leadership models that take into account teachers' leadership and individual agency. Our work is based on the premise that teachers have a central role in the complex processes of school improvement, not only because this is a more effective way of implementing policy, but principally because leadership is a fundamental aspect of humanity and therefore needs to be fostered in everyone (Frost, 2003). This is not simply a matter of sharing or distributing leadership amongst particular individuals by delegating tasks or appointing teachers to specific roles. It requires a new, inclusive concept of teacher professionalism that embraces the leadership dimension. Since school improvement focuses on improving student learning, it follows that all teachers can and should be supported in exercising *leadership of learning*, whatever their professional situation.

In order to build organisational as well as individual capacity for improvement, schools must prioritise so as to achieve sufficient synergy for effective development and to ensure common purpose in their change and growth. Therefore the development of leadership capacity shared amongst all teachers

> ... should not be taken to imply some kind of developmental free-for-all where individuals pursue whatever improvement goals seem important to them. Rather it is argued that teachers need practical support to enable them to deploy whatever energy and ingenuity they have in ways that are strategic and in harmony with overall school priorities. (Frost, 2004: 1–2)

Teachers stress that the headteacher's role is crucial in providing support for their leadership as part of the whole school development process (Frost and Durrant, 2004). In fostering teacher leadership, schools must therefore understand the importance of 'parallel leadership' through which teacher leaders and their headteacher engage in collective action to build the school's capacity for improvement (Crowther et al., 2002). However, there are many conflicts inherent in headteachers' espousal of shared leadership, and many different interpretations by those working in good faith, which result in an inevitable gap between the rhetoric and the reality of shared leadership (Yep and Chrispeels, 2004). In this book we explore the nature of that gap and the ways in which it can be bridged.

School improvement activity spans three areas that in policy terms and in practice are often seen as discrete: professional development, leadership and research/evaluation. Although there are clearly links between each of these perspectives, these relationships are often tentative and weakly expressed rather than each aspect being regarded as integral to the other in the improvement of learning. In this chapter, we explore the limitations of adopting each of these perspectives on school improvement activity and argue that by focusing on teachers' leadership of learning, a more holistic and coherent approach can be achieved.

The professional development perspective

In England currently there is a confusion of emphasis in support for teachers' professional learning. Policy is still significantly characterised by processes and initiatives that are essentially prescriptive and top-down, involving training in delivery and implementation. There is a strong emphasis on narrowly conceived government targets and short-term quantitative measures of standards and progress, too easily disembodied from the learning process and forcing a reliance on external expertise about what to teach and how to teach it. This has resulted in a legacy of professional development in the form of training in curriculum content and pedagogic process. Research by Bottery and Wright (2002, in Bottery, 2004) found that most training was ' … short-term, technical-rational and implementational in nature' while teachers were suffering initative overload accompanied by 'public and punitive' consequences for non-compliance (Bottery, 2004: 187). Bottery points out that this damages teachers, students, education and society as external demands govern pedagogy and professional knowledge.

This prevents the flexible, individual and critical responses that are needed to support learning in local contexts; it therefore places a ceiling of competence on teaching rather than encouraging excellence. How can teachers develop sufficient confidence to superimpose their individual style, imagination and creativity upon what they have learnt from their training, in order to engage themselves and their students enthusiastically in the learning experience?

These more prescriptive approaches are in tension with policy that encourages teachers in collaborative, school-based learning which makes use of their collective experience and expertise (DfES, 2005a). English policy documents describe the features of Continuing Professional Development (CPD) in support of a 'new teacher professionalism' in the following terms:

- Teachers taking more responsibility for their own CPD
- Access to coaching and mentoring

- Sharing expertise through networking and collaboration both internally and externally
- Innovating through engagement in classroom-based research.

(DfES, 2005a: Handout 1)

There is encouraging emphasis here on school-based, collaborative learning, peer support and the generation and use of evidence to improve practice. The intention to give more responsibility to teachers for their professional development is welcome, although its effectiveness depends both on teachers' understanding and ability to respond positively and also on the availability and equity of opportunities for CPD. With limited funding available for professional development and pressure to maintain standards in climates of competition, schools must ensure that teachers are not only trained to implement policy but are also required to provide opportunities for generating and sharing ideas to support development of practice. Teachers are required at the same time to be both unquestioning implementers and creative innovators, in an 'ongoing contestation between state control and professional autonomy' (Helsby, 2000: 93). Recent research guides schools towards a balance: flexibility, collaborative working and use of internal expertise have been found to characterise CPD that has positive outcomes for learning and teaching (Cordingley et al., 2003). The audit in Activity 1.1 below can be used by individuals, groups of teachers or school-wide to determine the extent to which professional development activity matches these characteristics and to discuss the implications.

As Andy Hargreaves (2003) points out, there is a danger of an 'apartheid' between different types of schools. Performance training approaches are used with schools in more challenging circumstances while more 'successful' schools are encouraged to develop 'professional learning communities'. Clearly this raises issues about the nature and scope of professionalism in teachers' work, but the most pressing question is the extent to which teachers' professional development can be linked with sustainable school improvement.

The focus and emphasis of the activity between universities and schools have traditionally been in the realm of enhancing individuals' professional knowledge and learning, starting with initial teacher education and followed by support for continuing professional development through courses and programmes to gain qualifications such as Masters degrees. Providing such activity that has positive student outcomes is a requirement for university accredited courses in England, which are accountable to the Training and Development Agency for Schools (formerly the Teacher Training Agency) and to the government's Office for Standards in Education (OfSTED). All stakeholders have an interest in the effects of professional development activity, but as Cordingley et al. (2003) conclude in their review of collaborative provision, the link between teachers' knowledge or skills, their classroom practice and pupil outcomes is 'complex, dynamic and often not directly observable' (p. 59). Research suggests that most teachers are very cautious in this respect and take a sophisticated view, refusing to underestimate the complexity of their professional situations, classroom activities and the influences of organisational structures and cultures (Frost and Durrant, 2002).

Activity 1.1
An audit of professional development activity

This could be an individual, group or school exercise which could be linked to performance management discussions or appraisals. A recently published research review (Cordingley et al., 2003) broadly concluded that collaborative CPD that links with improvements in teaching and learning has the following features:

- Observation, feedback and peer support
- Use of external expertise linked to school activity
- Scope for teachers to identify their own CPD focus
- Processes to encourage, extend and structure professional dialogue
- Sustaining CPD over time to enable teachers to embed new practice.

Examine your recent CPD activity using the grid in Appendix 1 (www.paulchapman-publishing.co.uk/resource/durrant.pdf) and ask the following:

1 Did your professional development activity fit into these categories (which link with effectiveness in improving learning and teaching)? Did you participate in other forms of professional development that do not fit into these categories but could still be linked with improvements in learning and teaching?

2 Does your analysis have any implications for your professional development next year?

Supporting teachers in taking responsibility for planning, tracking and evaluating the impact of their leadership and professional activities is likely to be more powerful in driving school improvement than the imposition of external criteria to carry out restrospective evaluation of the impact of courses and programmes (Frost and Durrant, 2003). This helps teachers to adopt a critical perspective and to make meaning of the complex change processes in which they are involved, so that they can work strategically for change.

We need a new approach to professional development in which it can be seen as both an input and an outcome in teachers' leadership of learning. McLaughlin (1997) suggests that teachers need to think about their classrooms, cultures and professional roles afresh, rebuilding their professionalism to take account of concepts of teacher leadership and agency. This demands a 'new theory of practical action' (p. 88) around which support can be based. Sachs (2000) places responsibility for reclaiming professionalism with teachers themselves, but recognises the need for 'award restructuring and school reform' so that teachers can reshape their thinking (p. 87). As Stenhouse (1975) has argued, teachers are best supported in developing these new perspectives through their direct involvement in school development processes. It is teachers who are in a position to best understand the communities, cultures and interplay of relationships that constitute a school and to apply this knowledge, to improve not only their practice but also the context in which they are working. This can be better achieved by making leadership of school improvement the main focus of teachers' professional activity and learning, rather than an eventual response or hoped for outcome of that activity.

The leadership perspective

An industry has grown up around leadership as its importance in determining school effectiveness has been increasingly recognised, represented by the current proliferation of publications in the field. In England the National College for School Leadership (NCSL) has well-established programmes for serving head-teachers, aspiring headteachers and middle leaders (NCSL, 2005). These are constructed to relate to roles and status, subscribing to hierarchical leadership patterns and designs that invoke a 'hero paradigm' (Gronn, 2003: 17). At the same time the National College promotes shared leadership for school improvement. While shared and distributed leadership have become increasingly accepted within the discourse and thus pervade the rhetoric, there are many different understandings about school leadership represented within schools, universities, district and national agencies and the wider education community (MacBeath, 2003a). It is helpful to raise awareness, share experiences and generate open discussion within schools as part of the development of shared leadership, as suggested in Activity 1.2 below.

This activity has previously generated fascinating discussion between teachers and headteachers. For example, it led one group of headteachers to agree that school leadership and sharing of that leadership may need to be cyclic depending on the school's culture, circumstances and capacity for improvement. This view has been supported independently, for example by Yep and Chrispeels' research (2004), but it was important that these headteachers also reached their own conclusions, leading them to feel more confident about adjusting their leadership styles as their schools changed, rather than thinking they had to sustain one preferred model.

There is a tendency for the mainstream literature on leadership to bypass fundamental questions about the distinctive nature of educational leadership, concentrating instead on traits or styles of leadership (Frost and Harris, 2003). Yet prescribed leadership models are not easily applied to the unique and changing circumstances of schools, and can be misinterpreted and manipulated. For example, school improvement can be conceived as the implementation of specific tasks dictated by policy (Gunter, 2001), particularly through the authority and action of those with designated leadership roles, while shared leadership can be enacted as delegation. These are mechanistic interpretations that can leave teachers at the mercy of reform, disengaged and untrusting (Bottery, 2004).

Teachers working within programmes supporting their leadership of change in a variety of roles report that their sense of self-efficacy and self-worth increases where they are able to make a difference to children's learning and that they are energised by working and learning collaboratively (Frost et al., 2000; Frost and Durrant, 2002). This increases morale more effectively and sustainably than providing extrinsic rewards, such as financial incentives linked to performance

Activity 1.2
Exploring views of leadership

Activities for exploring different views of leadership can be derived from the literature. MacBeath (2003c), for example, offers a series of definitions of different versions of leadership. These can be used to produce a card-sorting exercise that encourages teachers and headteachers reflecting on their leadership role to discuss approaches and search for meanings. This is equally effective in one school or with people from a number of schools. Cards could be set out as in Appendix 2 (www.paulchapmanpub-lishing.co.uk/resource/durrant.pdf).

The process could be as follows:

● Groups consisting of about five people in each deal out the cards around their table

● Each person in the group takes turns to offer their card and discuss whether this view of leadership is recognisable in their school

● Once all the cards are laid on the table, they can be shaped into a picture of the kinds of leadership that members of the group think are most effective for school improvement

● If this is done with several groups, the exercise can be concluded by each group explaining their preferred model to the others.

Whether using this or other literature the full text can provide background reading and help to clarify definitions, but discussion of meanings and understandings is an important part of the exercise as these aspects are not often clear-cut.

criteria or the teaching of shortage subjects. The challenge is to ensure that school improvement processes take account of the contributions which *all* teachers can and do make as part of their normal professional responsibility. Changing well-established hierarchical cultures, structures and traditions is complex and requires long-term commitment to development within a critical discourse, as discussed further in Chapter 2.

Somewhat paradoxically, it is headteachers who have the greatest influence on the ways in which leadership is interpreted and exercised more widely by members of the school community. Headteachers know that school change involves interactions between different members of the school community, all of whom have different perspectives, agendas and degrees of influence (Gronn, 2003), and it is they who generally set expectations and have the power to orchestrate this activity. Such ideas have gained momentum in the leadership discourse. Sergiovanni (2000) offers the helpful concept of 'leadership density', drawing on Tannenbaum's research which concludes that there is greater power in organisations where leaders surrender authority. He asserts that the total leadership exercised across the organisation is more significant than the amount of strong leadership vested in one individual. Angus (1993) suggests that those in administrative positions may contribute most powerfully to school reform by facilitating the exercise of teachers' agency. This accords with Spillane's notion that leadership is more powerful when 'stretched' over the individuals in an organisation to include both formal and informal leadership roles (Spillane, 2003; see also Frost and Harris, 2003). Crowther et al.'s (2002) concept of parallel leadership is also useful in considering how this can be achieved through collaborative learning, culture building and developing school-wide approaches to pedagogy.

These ideas have been fully explained elsewhere in the literature; here they are used to illustrate the kind of critical discourse in which headteachers and teachers need to be involved and to indicate the complexity of developing more inclusive leadership practices (Yep and Chrispeels, 2004). Clearly, headteachers wishing to facilitate teacher leadership require support for their theoretical understanding and critique as well as their practice, underpinned by commitment to the principles of shared leadership in a radical sense. Meanwhile teachers, supported by policy, need to reconceptualise their day-to-day work to include a leadership dimension.

The research and evaluation perspective

Teachers and headteachers do not engage easily with wider educational research, and there is still mistrust between 'practitioner' and 'academic' research communities despite the importance of recognising the different contributions of both and the need for bridging between the two (Bassey, 2003; Furlong, 2003). This is a conundrum with which policymakers and the educational research community have been wrestling for decades.

Teachers have a significant contribution to make to the body of evidence and knowledge upon which school improvement is based, through their research interpreted through expertise and experience. However, there is a tendency for practitioner research to be expressed in terms of 'research projects', reinforced recently by the frameworks and bidding criteria for government initiatives such as the Best Practice Research Scholarships (DfES, 2003a) where individual teachers were funded for small-scale, sharply focused research. While such projects may have a clear focus on student learning they are often framed to culminate in the dissemination of findings, which has questionable effect, and with improvements to the classroom practice of one person or a small team. The benefits for teachers engaging in research are clear; in particular their research questions often provide the impetus to engage with wider research and to explore and strengthen the links between theory and practice (Keating and Roberts, 2003). However, this depends on the extent to which they are able to engage critically and act appropriately, which often requires a considerable amount of practical and intellectual support. The following exercise (Activity 1.3) enables teachers, with careful facilitation, to explore their aspirations and concerns and to discuss the opportunities and limitations of their current situation.

There is a possibility that research may be seen and expressed as a core purpose for schools, with the assumption that a 'research-engaged school' is

Activity 1.3

Reflecting on your professional role

Use the following to reflect on the questions at the end individually and then discuss as a group. This could be a useful preliminary to the introduction and problematisation of the notion of the teacher as researcher.

Definition of the 'restricted professional'

- High level of classroom competence
- Child-centredness, subject-centredness
- High level of skill in handling and understanding children
- Derives satisfaction from personal relationships with pupils
- Evaluates performance in terms of own perceptions on changes in pupil behaviour and achievement
- Attends short courses of a practical nature.

Definition of the 'extended professional'

- Views work in wider context of school, community and society
- Participates in wide range of professional activities including those beyond the school
- Concern to link theory and practice
- Commitment to some form of curriculum theory and mode of evaluation
- Systematic self-questioning of own teaching as the basis for development
- Commitment and skills to study own teaching
- Concern to question and to test theory in practice by use of those skills.

(drawn from Stenhouse, 1975:143–44)

1 To what extent is it a) desirable and b) realistic to adopt the 'extended' view of a teacher's professional role?

2 What are the implications for schools if this view is *not* adopted?

3 What are the implications if an extended view of professionalism *is* adopted?

4 Can the same kind of role definition be applied to all teachers or does it depend on their experience, personal approach or status?

Note: for teachers at the beginning of their career, under pressure or working in less supportive circumstances, this activity may reinforce an intention to *remain* as a restricted professional. It is best used where teachers are already receptive to participation in enquiry and the linking of theory with practice.

excellent or has more capacity to improve. It may well be the case that schools involved in research and evaluation are more likely to improve, as encouraged through innovative regional policy in England (Handscomb and MacBeath, 2004), but the links to student outcomes and, more importantly, sustained improvement cannot be taken for granted and therefore need to be emphasised consistently in the language used and the support given. Similarly, systematic evaluation processes do not automatically lead to improvement. Under the English inspection regime, self-evaluation is required using particular frameworks and procedures to meet external accountability demands. This may result in limited understandings of the value of a range of self-evaluation approaches to underpin organisational learning and improvement. Different notions and models of teacher research, from involvement in action research to secondment into government research and evaluation projects, have varying degrees of influence on student learning in the classroom and across the school.

Schools must therefore cultivate wisdom and discretion about what constitutes evidence and how teachers and headteachers might use it to improve individual and organisational knowledge and self-knowledge as the basis for improvement. This involves making connections between wider research, practitioner research and evaluation in order to provide complementary information upon which to base school improvement planning and activity. Returning once again to the notion of rebuilding professionalism, engagement through enquiry is a recurring theme (see for example Stenhouse, 1975; McLaughlin, 1997; Sachs, 2000; Crowther et al., 2002; Day, 2004). Enquiry is not simply a source of information from which to make decisions about directions and strategies for change. It is integral to the sustenance of a critical and challenging approach to practice, a focus for collaborative working and a motivating and energising force. Involving teachers in processes of gathering and interpreting evidence is often the first step towards developing their capacity to exercise leadership; it spurs them on to envision and instigate change.

A more holistic approach to school improvement

What happens if we shift the focus away from professional development, designated leadership roles and discrete research and evaluation processes, towards a more coherent emphasis on developing teachers' capacity for leadership, energised by enquiry and focused on learning and school improvement?

Headteachers expect outcomes in any school improvement initiative and they are necessarily accountable for standards of attainment, but many are also willing to embrace complexity, open-endedness and the unexpected, moving towards more organic and inclusive approaches (Durrant et al., 2004; Hadfield, 2003). However, those who encourage collaborative enquiry and a genuine, shared leadership of change (as opposed to simply shared implementation) take risks. It may be dangerous to awaken this 'sleeping giant' of teacher leadership (Katzenmeyer and Moller, 2001); central control is relinquished, hierarchies may be flattened, structures may be changed, 'reculturing' may take place (Stoll, 1999). This involves nothing less than

> ... a challenge of transforming mind-sets, visions, paradigms, images, metaphors, beliefs and shared meanings ... creating a detailed language and code of behaviour ... inventing what amounts to a new way of life. (Morgan, 1997, in Stoll, 1999: 46)

As Stoll (1999) points out, this is not for the faint-hearted. It needs to be an evolutionary rather than revolutionary process, radical but gradual. It requires the development of greater trust between policymakers and schools, greater trust within schools and between stakeholders. Yet the current climate in the English education system erodes trust in the teaching profession and in schools' capacity to prioritise and lead their own development, with a concomitant lack of trust '*of* government *by* teachers' (Bottery, 2004: 102). In many schools, within partnerships working for school improvement and in the realm of policymaking, there is considerable work to be done in developing trustful relationships that transcend the utilitarian and mechanistic. Two-way trust (Bottery, 2004) is necessary if an extended view of professionalism incorporating teachers' engagement in enquiry, leadership and learning is to be taken seriously.

Activity 1.4
Models of school culture

There are some useful models and frameworks in the literature that can help you to begin to discuss and analyse your school's culture, perhaps as a brief prelude to collaborative planning for school improvement or as part of a discussion of the school's values and purposes. The following works give models and ideas for comparison:

Hargreaves, A. (1994) *Changing Teachers, Changing Times: Teachers' work and culture in the postmodern age.* London: Cassell.

Handy, C. and Aitken, R. (1986) *Understanding Schools as Organisations.* London: Penguin Books.

Prosser, J. (ed.) (1999) *School Culture.* London: Paul Chapman Publishing.

● Discuss the extent to which your school displays the characteristics of these different models

or

● Choose one of the following metaphors for your school: 'Our school is like a ... (ship; garden; orchestra; football team; museum; factory; family; zoo; theme park; library ...).' Develop the metaphor through conversation to explore the values, structures and ways of working of your school

then

● Discuss which model or metaphor you would *prefer* for your school.

Peeling back the layers of an organisation to examine what lies at its heart, what makes it tick, its values, languages and behaviour, is both fascinating and challenging. While we explore the notion of school cultures in more depth in the next chapter, some initial thinking can be stimulated through consideration of a range of different models in comparison with experience. Some resources to support this are suggested in Activity 1.4.

Stenhouse (1975) discussed and developed Hoyle's ideas of the 'extended professional' more than thirty years ago and, as discussed earlier, this baton has been taken up by others arguing for a rebuilding or reconceptualisation of teacher professionalism. Most schools are still a long way from embracing the reality, or understanding the potential, of incorporating such a view of professionalism, even in developing classroom practice as Stenhouse envisaged. Reculturing that takes a wider view – in involving teachers in leadership beyond their classrooms, contributions to school improvement and the shaping of agendas for change – is an even greater risk. It demands higher levels of trust in the profession as teachers question existing ways of working, test new approaches and develop confidence in shaping their practice and context. In Chapter 2 we discuss teachers' leadership of learning through enquiry as a key that can unlock school cultures, opening them up to professional and organisational learning that will enhance student learning.

2 *Unlocking school cultures*

School culture: given or gotten?

A key focus of our work over the last ten years has been the facilitation of teacher leadership. What emerges strongly is the importance of school culture as an enabling or inhibiting factor in the success of teachers' attempts to lead change. But how should we define culture, and what is the relationship between individuals and the culture they inhabit? Giddens (1984) persuasively argues that, through the process of *structuration*, culture both shapes and is shaped by social actors. However, it is still legitimate to ask if culture is a 'given', or whether teachers by working collaboratively can change the culture of their schools.

In this chapter, therefore, we examine some current definitions of school culture and go on to explore some of the actors surrounding change in schools, before returning to the topic of teacher leadership and how it can be facilitated.

Defining school culture

Barth (1990) notes that 'what needs to be improved about schools is their culture, the quality of interpersonal relationships, and the nature and quality of learning experiences' (p. 45). It is helpful that Barth highlights the importance of relationships and learning in this analysis. In discussions about culture, it is easy to get side-tracked into talking about structures and systems rather than about relationships between staff, between staff and learners and between the school and the wider community it serves. However, it is no easy matter to define school culture (Prosser, 1999). Deal and Kennedy's well known (1983) definition, 'the way we do things around here', perhaps begs as many questions as it answers. Whose voices are included and whose excluded in this phrase? And is culture a symptom, consequence or a cause of 'the way we do things'?

MacBeath, amplifying Deal and Kennedy's phrase, defines culture as 'a way of seeing and doing things, a set of attitudes to life and accompanying behaviour' (1999: 38). This helpfully extends the concept of culture to include not only norms, but beliefs and values also. However, there remains an ambiguity here – who will succeed in their way of seeing and doing things defining the culture of a school?

These definitions seem to imply that school culture is a given: an inevitable backdrop closely linked to power relations in the school. However, those who

	Social Control	
	High	Low
High	Hothouse	Welfarist
Low	Formal	Survivalist

(Social Cohesion along the vertical axis)

Figure 2.1: A typology of school cultures
Source: Hargreaves, 1999

work in schools know intuitively that culture is not fixed and exists as a shifting set of competing perspectives. Indeed, it is probably more accurate to talk of school *cultures* rather than of a single homogeneous entity. Wrigley points out that 'school cultures are highly contested' (2003: 35), with different voices competing to tell their version of the story of the school. He believes that it is precisely this continuing and competitive dialogue between different perspectives that makes school development possible and interesting. However, Ball (1987) also reminds us that school cultures are often characterised by corrosive rivalries and entrenched positions as individuals and groups attempt to out-manoeuvre one another for scarce resources – be they curriculum time, power or money. In such cultures, school development stalls and conflict reigns.

If school culture is such an elusive and complex concept, what can we do to 'unlock' such cultures and promote open dialogue and collaboration between all members of a school and the wider educational community? Hargreaves (1999) advocates that schools should actively seek to define and shape their own culture. He proposes a set of tools or approaches that they could use to help themselves in this. These tools are based on a set of four 'types' of school culture; the formal, welfarist, hothouse and survivalist. These are in turn linked to axes of social cohesion and social control, as shown in Figure 2.1.

Groups of staff and/or students can be asked to plot their school on this model as a precursor to discussion about the character, direction and ethos of the school (see Activity 2.1 below). This kind of diagnostic approach to culture is, according to Hargreaves (1999), empowering and enabling for a school community.

School culture is shaped by the history, people, metaphors and rituals of a school as well as by external social and political factors. Stoll and Fink (1996) argue that since the pace of change in a post-modern society is so rapid, schools must be either improving or getting worse; it is not possible to stand still. With this in mind, they put forward a model of school cultures which operates on two axes: effective–ineffective and improving–declining, as shown in Figure 2.2.

In this model, *moving* schools are both effective, in terms of measurable output, and improving, in terms of people who work well together, committed to continuous improvement.

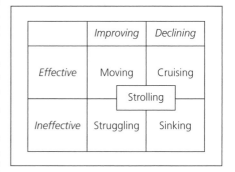

Figure 2.2: A model of school cultures
Source: Stoll and Fink, 1996.

Activity 2.1
Exploring school cultures

The following can be used to stimulate individual or small group reflection but also to give ideas about how the whole school might think about values and purposes. This is something that ought to be essential but for which there is rarely, if ever, any time in the day-to-day life of a school. It could involve students, parents, governors and teaching assistants, as well as teachers.

Building on Activity 1.4 in the last chapter, a useful source of tools and techniques that groups of teachers can use to better understand their school culture can be found in the following works:

Ainscow, M. et al., (1994) *Mapping Change in Schools: The Cambridge Manual of Research Techniques*. Cambridge: Institute of Education.

Hargreaves, D. (1999) 'Helping practitioners explore their school's culture', in J. Prosser, (ed.), *School Culture*. London: Paul Chapman Publishing. pp. 48–65.

Also valuable is a set of school self-evaluation materials published by:

The Scottish Office (1996) *How Good is Our School? Self-evaluation using performance indicators*. Edinburgh: Audit Unit.

A couple of provisos

It is important to use these materials sensitively. Discussions will dig beneath the surface of normal conversation. Uncomfortable issues and tensions may be exposed. Ensure that the discussions or activities are carefully facilitated, which may include setting some agreed ground rules about confidentiality, mutual respect and listening to everyone's point of view. At some points in the life of a school or team, it may not be appropriate to make discussions about school culture the starting point. It may be necessary to concentrate first on the groundwork, for example to improve relationships and build greater mutual trust.

Also make certain that there is an outlet for the discussion or activity that can lead to real change. Although discussion may have an intrinsic value, it is also important that the issues raised are taken seriously and that the school community considers how to address them. Consider the mechanisms and structures that could help a school to capture, prioritise and act upon such outcomes, for example by feeding the results of whole-school discussion into a leadership team meeting. Be realistic and pragmatic about what might be achieved in the short term, as well as shaping visions for the long term, and try to keep the lines of communication open.

Recommended further reading:

MacBeath, J. (1999) *Schools Must Speak for Themselves*. London: Routledge.

MacBeath, J., Schratz, M., Meuret, D. and Jakobsen, L. (2000) *Self-Evaluation in European Schools: A story of change*. London: RoutledgeFalmer.

Cruising schools are characterised by complacency. They are effective in terms of the examination performance of their children, but may be marking time and not anticipating the changes to teaching and learning demanded by a rapidly changing society. They are often located in more affluent areas. *Strolling* schools are neither effective nor ineffective, neither improving nor declining. They are schools in need of external impetus to improve which an inspection or the appointment of a new headteacher could provoke. *Struggling* schools are often to be found in areas of high deprivation. They are ineffective, but are actively putting in place measures to improve, whereas *sinking* schools are both ineffective and show no signs of being able to turn themselves around.

While this is an attractive model in its neatness, it seems to us to be over-simplistic. Schools are much more complex organisations than labels such as 'cruising', 'strolling' or 'sinking' suggest. In any one school, there are likely to be elements of some or all of these features. We know, for example, that subject departments perform differentially (NCSL, 2003) and so it is quite possible to have a 'moving' English department, but a 'strolling' mathematics one.

In our view, the key to unlocking school culture is the encouragement and facilitation of trustful dialogue about the kind of school we are and the kind of school we want to become. This resonates with the valuable work carried out by MacBeath et al. (2000: 92) on school self-evaluation. For them, self-evaluation has two primary functions:

- To stimulate dialogue on objectives, priorities and quality criteria at school and classroom level
- To achieve objectives through the use of appropriate and easily accessible tools.

Not just dialogue, therefore, but action too. Macbeath et al. (2000) have devised a comprehensive set of tools for schools, groups of teachers or individual practitioners to use in order to gather evidence about teaching and learning and to initiate change. We strongly support the use of such tools. Of course, school self-evaluation has become a central plank of the 'new relationship' with schools (DfES, 2004) in which under a revised framework OfSTED inspectors will validate and make judgements on the robustness of a school's ability to evaluate its own progress. MacBeath, as one of the leading thinkers on school self-evaluation, has expressed concern that the process of evaluation which he believes requires time to grow, will become a top-down, box-ticking exercise (Woodward, 2004). However, Wrigley (2003) reminds us that school culture cannot be looked at in isolation from the wider social, political and economic climate that exists beyond the school gates. In the next section we look at some aspects of this wider climate.

Educational change and school culture

Much of the literature on change and innovation regards this as positive, dynamic and leading to improvements in teaching and learning (Beare, 2001;

West-Burnham, 2003; Hargreaves, 2003). Other writers point to the unsettling and distressing effects that change can have on morale, confidence and performance (for example Deal, 1990; A. Hargreaves, 1994). In particular externally mandated, top-down change seems to be most associated with feelings of alienation and a loss of self-esteem. There appears to be a disjunction between rational, planned and centrally controlled change and the emotional impact it has on teachers (Hargreaves, 2004; Hargreaves et al., 2001).

Schools still adopt essentially rationalist approaches to school development planning. The key assumptions of such approaches are that, through a careful audit of school performance, priorities can be established and targets set with success criteria attached. In 1997, the Department for Education and Employment endorsed this view of planning in its advice to schools on target setting, recommending a five-stage school improvement model:

1 How well are we doing?
2 How do we compare with similar schools?
3 What more should we aim to achieve this year?
4 What must we do to make it happen?
5 Taking action and reviewing progress. (DFEE, 1997)

Such a model implies that development priorities can be identified in isolation from one another and that planned interventions can be monitored, measured and evaluated separately. The complex, everyday reality of schools steadfastly refuses to allow itself to be broken up in this logical, systematic way. We would therefore question the degree to which such a model corresponds to reality as it is lived in schools. In practice, schools labour under a multiplicity of confusing, interlinked and sometimes contrasting priorities. Uncertainties about staffing, budgets and pupil rolls mean it is very difficult for school leaders to anticipate the future. This is not a dilemma confined to schools, of course. Uncertainty, diversity, complexity and contradiction are well-established features of advanced post-modern societies. We go on to examine some of these features in more detail, before returning to discuss what schools and teachers can do to unlock their school cultures.

Change in a post-modern world

Most commentators would acknowledge that the education system worldwide is subject to rapid, constant and often unsettling change. Stoll et al. (2003) write of the 'rollercoaster ride' of change, while for Ainscow et al. (1994) schools are 'in the middle of a sea of change' (p. 2) and to Frost et al. (2000) 'change is endemic' (p. 5). These images of vertiginous speed, natural disaster and disease suggest that we are in the midst of a crisis in the world of education. Hargreaves (1994) attributes this sense of disorientation to an inherent irony, in which we employ rational 'modernistic' approaches to schooling in a globalised, post-modern world which is 'fast, compressed, complex, and uncertain'. Thus, those involved in education are caught up in a 'shift from cultures of certainty to cultures of uncertainty' (Hargreaves, 1994: 57).

Some educationalists' response to this uncertainty is to advocate radical change in the way in which children and young people access learning (Beare, 2001). It is argued that schools are essentially modernist in form, structure and purpose and that they retain many features of the industrial age (West-Burnham, 2003). Beare holds that our education systems worldwide are still predicated on a single, uncontested view of reality based on scientific method. In an information-rich society, such models hold back rather than enhance learning, and so many argue that nothing less than a transformation can bring about the necessary change. Beare (2001) draws on understandings of reality emerging from quantum physics to argue that there is a growing 'social realisation' that the 'self' is not a fixed entity which perceives and makes sense of an objective reality, but rather that the 'two are interacting and changing each other in the very act of co-existence' (p. 43). This means that connectedness rather than separation should be our guiding metaphor when thinking about schooling and its transformation. He notes that an extended metaphor of moving forward and upward in small steps and in a single direction permeates the language of education. We follow a *curriculum*, which is divided into age-related segments, through which we progress by being assigned *grades* or *levels* in various distinct and separate subjects, until eventually we *graduate*. He argues that we need to discard this outdated language and replace it with metaphors drawn from networks based on multiple pathways, rather than a single track and the idea of the student as a knowledge worker selecting from a modularised curriculum to personalise the learning experience.

However, finding a new language is one thing, but how do we move to the reality of a transformed, networked education system? West-Burnham identifies three ways in which the concept of transformation is currently discussed:

● Transformation as improved performance
● Transformation as the achievement of optimum effectiveness
● Transformation as profound change.

(West-Burnham, 2003: 1)

The approach favoured by the Department for Education and Skills (DfES) could be characterised as an example of West-Burnham's first type of transformation. With its agenda of 'personalised learning' (DfES, 2005c), the government is requiring schools to raise standards of achievement by paying more attention to how children learn and by tailoring the curriculum towards their learning needs rather than toward the institutional needs of schools. According to West-Burnham (2003), the second type of transformation differs from the first in that the focus moves from the learner to the system as a whole. Approaches to leadership such as those espoused by the National College for School Leadership (NCSL, 2005) could be grouped under this heading. In her remit letter to the NCSL the current and newly appointed Secretary of State for Education underlined the UK government's desire for school leaders to support the drive towards personalisation of the curriculum and, in addition, to promote 'system wide leadership and school improvement' to make 'optimum use of the resources available to the school' (Kelly, 2004). This implies a concern with efficiency and effectiveness, focusing on compliance with a certain policy agenda and on prudent financial management within prescribed limits.

For West-Burnham both of these categories of transformation are unlikely to bring about sustained change, as they rely on incremental rather than deep-rooted change, or as he puts it:

> If a train is going in the wrong direction it doesn't matter how punctual, reliable and comfortable it is – it won't get you where you need to go. (West-Burnham, 2003: 3)

Profound change, on the other hand, ' ... suggests a radical restructuring of the dominant culture and a fundamental rupture with the past' (O'Sullivan, 1999: 5). To achieve this, West-Burnham (2003) argues for a fundamental reconceptualisation of the purpose and nature of school systems. At first glance, this may appear to be an argument for a sudden, disruptive break with current practice and its immediate replacement with an alternative, re-engineered model of learning.

However, Hughes (2002) notes that most teachers do not make dramatic, overnight changes to their practice. Rather than transforming teaching and learning, they improve by tweaking their current practice. We would argue here and elsewhere for a model of transformation based not on a sudden and disruptive overhaul of the educational landscape, but on evolutionary yet nonetheless profound change. Reed and Learmonth (1999) make a useful distinction between shallow and deep approaches to school improvement. Shallow initiatives tend to be short term and related to performance outcomes, while deep school improvement is more long term in scope, concerned with complex issues, eschewing quick and easy answers and relying upon teachers themselves learning how to carry out research into their own practice in order to assess the impact of any strategies they employ. Yet it is not sufficient simply to reflect on these matters. What is important is that the teacher has the skills and support to act on these understandings. The time is right, they argue, for school improvement initiatives to focus on classroom processes so that teachers can begin to develop a language and accompanying practices with which to account for the impact of what they do on student learning.

Deep and shallow change are both important at different times and in different ways. David Hargreaves (2003) approaches this a little differently and places 'radical innovation' and 'incremental innovation' at either end of a continuum, within a quadrant which enables us to map change in relation to its distance from existing practice, as shown in Figure 2.3.

This graphical representation reveals the possibility of progressing from small, evolutionary changes in practice to radical change. Equally a sudden, fundamental change can be followed by a period of incremental innovation as new systems and processes are refined and adapted. In this model, therefore, transformation can be seen to build on small-scale changes to practice, which build confidence and capacity to enable teachers to take greater risks. It is generally helpful for

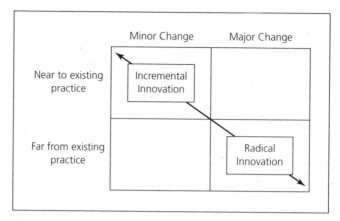

Figure 2.3: The nature of innovation
Source: D.H. Hargreaves, 2003

teachers and headteachers to take the opportunity to stand back and share their different perspectives on school change, as suggested in Activity 2.2 below.

Activity 2.2
Relationships between scope of change and distance from existing practice

Take a range of changes that are taking place in your own practice and/or that of your school, and plot them on Hargreaves's model (Figure 2.3).

1 Does your current experience of school change tend more towards incremental or radical innovation?

2 Can an innovation bring about major change and yet be close to existing practice?

If the only way to meet the challenges of the twenty-first century is through a transformed educational system, what form should this transformation take? Is it, as West-Burnham (2003) suggests, a complete reconceptualisation of schooling and learning, or is it more like Hughes's (2002) tweaking?

Stoll and Fink (1996), while observing that many of our schools would be 'good ... if this were 1965', believe the answers to the challenges facing education lie not in sweeping structural reform, nor in policy mandates, but in a new way of thinking about schooling. Like Beare (2001), they argue that we need to see the education system as an organic whole, rather than a set of discrete units, and that we should seek to make connections between the various parts of the education 'ecosystem'. Senge (1993) advises leaders in organisations to cultivate the 'art of seeing the forest *and* the trees' through the development of *systems thinking, personal mastery, mental models, shared vision* and *team learning* amongst all stakeholders. The model that underlies these arguments is one in which all parts of an organisation are connected not in a linear fashion where any one part only talks to those parts above and below it, but in an ongoing cycle of dialogue, feedback and continuous improvement.

Rational, linear approaches to school improvement have led to a superficial concern with observable, easily measurable change rather than a willingness to grapple with complex issues of learning in institutional settings (Clarke, 2000). Clarke believes that in espousing these linear models of school improvement, we risk losing the opportunity to tap into the wisdom and experience of teachers and learners and to embrace the ever evolving, contingent and complex nature of learning and educational change.

Developing a sense of community and facilitating dialogue are fundamental to sustainable change. Indeed, social interaction is the process by which mere information becomes knowledge (Fullan, 2003). The idea of self-sustaining networks of educators sharing good practice and taking ownership of curriculum development across school, national and international boundaries is both beguiling and popular. Through reflection, enquiry and collaboration, learning communities provide the challenge and support individuals need to improve teaching and learning.

Towards communities of learning

Hargreaves (1998), in developing a notion of the 'knowledge creating school', borrows from the medical profession and some of the newer high technology industries in order to articulate a vision of school improvement in which the boundaries between research and practice are deliberately blurred. Schools need to encourage and facilitate a climate of enquiry, evidence gathering and collaboration. Co-workers subject the resulting knowledge to critical scrutiny in a process of validation, before this is disseminated within and beyond the school. Hargreaves does not underestimate the difficulty and complexity of achieving this, but goes on to argue that while the skills necessary to undertake the process of knowledge creation already exist in schools, they may need to be nurtured. He identifies those seeds which can help nurture the process. First, in a phrase echoing Hughes's (2002) tweaking, a knowledge-creating school begins when teachers 'tinker' in their classrooms, refining and making small, incremental changes to their practice. However, for tinkering to move from an individualised, essentially insular activity to one which is shared and public and which genuinely contributes to knowledge creation, this process has to be explicitly managed and the strategies put in place that encourage collaboration between teachers and the dissemination of ideas.

In a later publication, David Hargreaves (2003) further argues that teachers working together in networks are the key to the transformation of teaching and learning. They do this by engaging in classroom innovation, nourished by what he calls 'lateral networks' of colleagues debating, sharing and revising practice both in their own settings and, via the Internet, across regional, national and international boundaries, in effect by creating communities of practice. The challenge for schools, he argues, is to identify, deploy and increase the capacity for innovation – capacity contained in the material, intellectual, social and organisational capital of a school.

McLaughlin (1997) submits that school-based and extended communities of practice foster critical friendship and sharing of good practice across departmental, school and district boundaries. Costa and Kallick define the 'critical friend' as

> ... a trusted person who asks provocative questions, provides data to be analysed through another lens and offers critique of a person's work as a friend. The friend is an advocate for the success of that work. (Costa and Kallick, 1993: 50)

This critical friend, therefore, offers both challenge and support. According to McLaughlin, critical friendship can be stimulated by teachers networking within and between schools. These are 'powerful learning tools because they engage people in collective work on authentic problems that emerge from their own efforts' (McLaughlin, 1997: 87). Fullan (2003) further underlines the vital role that external facilitation, whether from higher education or LEAs, plays in such communities, providing the challenge and support necessary to ensure that there is a continuing focus on change and improvement. McLaughlin sees such partnerships as being at the heart of a 'new professionalism', founded on the following principles:

- Increasing opportunities for professional dialogue
- Reducing teachers' professional isolation
- Providing a rich menu of 'nested' opportunities for learning and discourse
- Connecting professional development opportunities to meaningful content and change efforts
- Creating an environment of professional safety and trust
- Restructuring time, space and scale within schools.

(McLaughlin, 1997: 89)

While few teachers would disagree about the potency of these principles, many would also point out that the ever-increasing volume of externally mandated change has militated against the growth of the kind of reflective community McLaughlin envisages. Teachers we work with specifically lament the lack of time to engage in collaborative work. However, there are encouraging signs that policy-makers are beginning to recognise this fact. In England and Wales, a process of workforce remodelling is under way which aims to reduce the number of administrative tasks teachers carry out to enable them to engage in activities related to teaching and learning. In addition, a recent DfES publication opens with the statement that ' ... becoming a professional learning community, where CPD is central to the life of the school and to raising pupil achievement takes time' (DfES, 2005a: iii). The rest of the publication gives schools advice on the kinds of CPD arrangements that are most supportive of the creation of professional learning communities. Key strategies recommended include the development of peer coaching and mentoring and the encouragement of classroom-based research. The ideas contained in this publication are grounded in credible research into the positive role teachers can play in initiating and sustaining change. Day describes communities of reflective practice, in which teachers are recognised as schools' 'greatest intellectual and emotional assets' by giving them the time to reflect on their practice and contribute to school-wide change (Day, 1999: 228).

Teaching and learning are best served by creating the circumstances in which teachers can realise their educational values in practice, to become professionally fulfilled by acting collaboratively as leaders of learning. These collaborative networks can themselves help create the cultural conditions necessary for the transformation of teaching and learning. The professional learning community is not a commodity to be introduced into a school and bought into with varying degrees of enthusiasm by staff. Rather, a process arises from the growing trust and understanding that develops between colleagues as they are given time, space and resources to engage in critical debate.

Fielding (1999), however, warns that much of what currently takes place under the banner of communities of learning is in fact 'corrosive' of community. He argues that teaching is 'primarily a personal, not a functional activity', yet all our efforts at improving schools seem to be focused on technical, outcome-driven measures, rather than on the quality of learning relationships and the development of genuine dialogue between teachers and students. Fielding also goes on to suggest that discourses concerned with both school effectiveness and school improvement have run their respective course, and that what we need now is a commitment to transformative education. Such a transformation would begin with moving away from the language of the market towards a language which recognises 'the contested complexities of negotiation, dialogue and discussion', and which 'captures delight as well as definition; nuance as well as number'. He further argues that in order to achieve this we need a version of leadership which replaces the commercial metaphor of 'ownership' with the more creative notion of 'authorship'. Finally, and crucially, students must become partners in learning, co-researchers rather than mere sources of data so that we can move towards a community based on open dialogue and genuine collaboration.

Notwithstanding Fielding's reservations, Fullan (2003) argues forcibly that just as successful commercial enterprises now place a high premium on knowledge creation and transfer, so we in education must do the same. It is through social interaction that mere information is transformed into knowledge, and it is through sustained interaction, he argues, that knowledge becomes wisdom and 'deep change' becomes a possibility.

However, interaction in itself is not sufficient. Fullan highlights the danger of so-called 'communities of learning' simply reinforcing underperformance, and argues that the way to avoid this is to unlock and engage the passion and commitment of all members of a community. We would agree that a prerequisite for schools to meet the challenges of the twenty-first century is for them to cease acting as isolated units and begin working as professional learning communities, fuelled by dialogue, collaboration and enquiry.

Fullan's fears notwithstanding, schools in England will be expected to play a more proactive role in their own school improvement as underlined by several recent policy initiatives. For example, in the document *A New Relationship with Schools* (DfES, 2004a), the government proposes radical changes to the ways in which schools are led, changes which will affect school inspection, schools' relationships with central and local government, school self-evaluation and planning, data collection from and communication with schools. The innovations described are no longer couched in the form of prescriptions, but rather as invitations to schools to become partners with policymakers in driving the agenda forward.

New directions in school improvement

What can we draw from the literature on school improvement and school effectiveness to support this transformation agenda? Influential in the UK has been the Improving the Quality of Education for All (IQEA) project based at the University of Cambridge (Hopkins et al., 1994). Hopkins notes that there are three major components to the generic 'framework for school improvement' devised by the IQEA group: the 'givens', the 'strategic dimension' and the 'capacity building dimension' (1996: 41). *Givens* are factors that cannot be changed very easily by the school itself. These might include externally driven innovations or the existing 'background, organisation and values' of the school. The *strategic dimension* concerns the process of identifying, selecting and prioritising foci for school improvement. Most schools, Hopkins states, have now become adept at identifying a number of desired outcomes ranging from improved teacher performance to increases in student learning capacity or self-esteem. However, he also notes that those schools who begin the process of school improvement by identifying student learning goals and working back from there appear to progress more rapidly. Hopkins's (1996) *capacity building dimension* relates to the attempts of school improvers to address not only the development priorities identified, but also requires a focus on the internal, cultural conditions of the school. In this vision, school improvement is not a simple technical matter of getting the job done, but an organic process that has as much to do with changing the culture of the school as with any specific pedagogical practices. The work of the IQEA project is underscored by five principles:

- All members of the school have the opportunity to contribute to the school's vision
- External pressures for change provide opportunities for schools to secure internal priorities
- The school seeks to create opportunities for all members of the school community to learn
- The school seeks to put in place structures which encourage collaboration and lead to the empowerment of individuals and groups
- Monitoring and evaluation are shared by all members of staff.

(Based on Ainscow et al., 1994: 5)

These principles are designed as 'an overall approach rather than prescribing a course of action' (Ainscow et al., 1994: 5). The team found that cultures which were collaborative, had high expectations of students and staff and held shared values were more likely to benefit from involvement with the project (Ainscow et al., 1994). Hopkins calls this 'authentic' school improvement as it causes schools to develop collaborative, enquiry-based approaches to improvement which focus on the learning, progress and achievement of pupils. He identifies the following characteristics of authentic school improvement:

● Achievement focused
● Empowering in aspiration
● Research based and theory rich
● Context specific
● Capacity building in nature
● Enquiry driven
● Implementation oriented
● Interventionist and strategic
● Externally supported
● Systemic.

(based on Hopkins, 2001: 16–17)

All this seems daunting, but he does not intend that we understand this as a list of discrete projects schools might undertake, but as an overall approach to putting in place the 'enabling conditions' which schools need to action to improve pupil learning.

Hopkins (2001) is also critical of the tendency in effectiveness studies to 'backward map' from outcomes to school and teacher characteristics. He argues that these correlations do not help teachers to understand the relationship between an effect and a cause. However, for Sammons et al. school effectiveness research 'seeks to investigate empirically through longitudinal research the ways in which schools can promote student progress' (1997: 8). Although the list of 11 characteristics of school effectiveness given in Table 2.1 may seem arbitrary at first glance, Stoll (1996) points out that the large number of studies that have been carried out across the world consistently come up with similar lists, suggesting that these are findings that should be taken seriously. What is noteworthy for our purposes is that all 11 characteristics are concerned, directly or indirectly, with aspects of school culture.

An objection to models such as that produced by Sammons et al. (1997) could be that they rely too heavily on outcomes and do not give schools enough support in deciding on what inputs might lead to those outcomes. Equally, it is difficult to see how the various indicators of effectiveness relate to one another. Elliott, in arguing for a model of curriculum predicated on process rather than predefined outcomes, makes the point that successful school improvement hinges on 'the restructuring of (teachers') practical consciousness through the reconstruction of their store of mutual knowledge' (Elliott, 1998: 188). He goes on to say that 'discursive consciousness implies a capacity for discourse with

Table 2.1: *Eleven features of effective schools*

Characteristic	Examples
Professional leadership	Firm and purposeful A participative approach The leading professional
Shared vision and goals	Unity of purpose Consistency of practice Collegiality and collaboration
A learning environment	An orderly atmosphere An attractive working environment
Concentration on teaching and learning	Maximisation of learning time Academic emphasis Focus on achievement
Purposeful teaching	Efficient organisation Clarity of purpose Structured lessons Adaptive practice
High expectations	High expectations all around Communicating expectations Providing intellectual challenge
Positive reinforcement	Clear and fair discipline Feedback
Monitoring progress	Monitoring pupil performance Evaluating school performance
Pupil rights and responsibilities	Raising pupil self-esteem Positions of responsibility Control of work
Home/school partnership	Parental involvement in their children's learning
A learning organisation	School-based staff development

Source: Sammons et al., 1997

others about one's practice and effects' (p. 188). By this he means that school improvement is essentially a discursive rather than a rational process. In addition, he argues that undertaking collaborative action research is a key way in which teachers can develop their capacity to engage in these discursive practices.

While such a table as the one above enables us to identify indicators of effectiveness, as Hopkins (2001) notes, there is little clue as to how a school could achieve these qualities. Joyce et al. (1999) address this dilemma by emphasising the role of teacher leadership in school culture. They support the notion of the school as 'a centre of enquiry', in which the focus is less on specific, highly targeted innovations and more on

> a fluid, continuous enquiry to make education better on a day to day basis. The aspiration is to make all schools into learning communities for teachers as well as students, making use of the best models of learning for both. (Joyce et al., 1999: 11)

In order to put this vision into practice, Joyce et al. developed seven hypotheses, based on their previous knowledge and research, that they believed would lead to 'evolutionary school improvement'. Their hypotheses differ from the lists of indicators of effectiveness (for example, Sammons et al., 1997) in that they do not describe 'ideal' or steady states (for example 'professional leadership'), rather they look forward to ideal *processes*. They present their list as an invitation to enquiry rather than as a blueprint for change. In summary, the seven hypotheses are:

- Schools who give teachers time to carry out enquiry will benefit from increased school improvement activity
- Schools that are democratically managed with high community involvement will create the right structural conditions for enquiry to flourish
- Schools who make constant use of information and data about performance will increase enquiry into how to help students improve their learning
- Schools who make use of current research findings about teaching and learning in their day-to-day work will develop more successful school improvement initiatives
- School-based staff development increases enquiry into new practices
- Staff development conceived as an ongoing process of enquiry rather than a series of one-off events leads to initiatives that have more effect
- Small work teams, based on peer coaching and with pastoral oversight of a specific group of pupils, create a more caring atmosphere for both adults and children.

(based on Joyce et al., 1999: 10–14)

There is a clear sense from this list of what a professional learning community might look like and an indication of how one might go about building one. In addition, we are attracted to the notion of fluidity, and to the emphasis placed on the open-ended processes of continuous enquiry rather than on a restricted list of specific projects, which might be implied by, for example, Sammons et al's (1997) list.

Moving on

Harris (2000) suggests that there are six future directions that school improvement should take if there is to be a greater impact on student learning:

● Using policy directives to foster school improvement
● Ensuring systematic programme evaluation
● Rigorous monitoring of the implementation phase to ensure compliance
● Using school effectiveness research to inform practice
● Refocusing on the classroom rather than the wider organisation of the school
● Providing differentiated improvement strategies.

(Harris, 2000: 10)

The language Harris uses is rather different to that chosen by Joyce et al. (1999). Phrases such as 'policy directive', 'rigorous monitoring' and 'ensure compliance', sit a little uneasily with the appeal to shared values and enquiry-based development found in the earlier models. However, such an emphasis on the positive leadership of school improvement initiatives is perhaps a symptom of the failure of past efforts to bring about sustained improvement (Barber, 1996). It is also consonant with Fullan's (1999) advocacy of district-wide involvement in, and leadership of, school reform. What Harris seems to be implying here is that if schools are to improve, then the strategies employed need to be vigorously driven and evaluated. Harris is taking the reasonable view that if an LEA, school or subject department has invested time and resources into a school improvement initiative, then there have to be measures in place to ensure that the plans are followed through. This is an important and sometimes uncomfortable point: collaboration, networking and sharing will not in themselves guarantee improvements in teaching and learning. Indeed, it is possible that unchallenging and unchallenged collaboration might simply reinforce unhelpful practices that hold back rather than enable progress. The key is to exert the right level of challenge in the right place.

Education leadership and school culture

If school culture is an important determinant in how staff and students experience organisational life, then an important determinant of school culture is leadership. The importance of leadership in school improvement has been recognised in recent years by government in a number of policy initiatives. These include the creation of a professional qualification, the National Professional Qualification for Headship (NPQH) for aspiring headteachers and the establishment of the National College for School Leadership (NCSL, 2005). According to the NCSL Prospectus (DfEE, 1999: 7), the college's mission is to ' ... set the pace and direction of national debate on school leadership' and 'act as a powerhouse for high quality research feeding into school-level improvement'.

For Harris and Lambert, the key to this is that leaders should be skilled in building capacity in their schools; that is building relationships, trust and community. This in turn involves people, teams and networks working together to form professional learning communities committed to the development of leadership capacity throughout the school, not just the headteacher or the senior management team, implying:

> a form of leadership that is distributed and shared, that belongs to the many rather than the few. (Harris and Lambert, 2003: 7)

They go on to note that many top-down initiatives run out of steam once the initial push for implementation is over. This is because policymakers have invested in systems rather than people/classrooms and in the outcomes of change rather than in the processes of change. It is important, therefore, to build the culture as well as the systems by focusing on the school's shared norms, values and beliefs. In order to develop the kind of leadership capacity schools must confront the challenges of a fast changing post-modern world, schools need to encourage collaborative practices, based on the needs of learners rather than out-moded hierarchies. Such practices might include the formation of task- rather than role-focused teams charged with using action research approaches in order to gather, analyse and act on evidence related to pupil achievement, and the facilitation by those in leadership positions of teacher-led change.

Top-down support for bottom-up change

'Top-down support for bottom-up change' is a phrase which gained currency in the United States (for example, see Darling-Hammond and McLaughlin, 1995) and arises from the realisation that traditional top-down approaches to educational reform are not effective in an educational climate that demands that teachers do not simply learn new techniques for the transmission of curriculum content, but that they also develop the ability to teach for pupil understanding. In order to meet this challenge, Darling-Hammond and McLaughlin (1995) argue that professional development should focus on building school and teacher capacity to construct knowledge for use in their own contexts. Key elements of such a capacity-building strategy are the promotion of teacher enquiry, the encouragement of teacher networks and the creation of partnerships between schools, districts and universities.

Fullan and Hargreaves (1992) point out that the key success indicator of any innovatory programme is the extent to which teachers' classroom practice is changed. They draw a distinction between large-scale, top-down innovations that demand rapid, radical changes in practice and small-scale, school-initiated, collaborative attempts to work on specific areas of practice. The former have a poor record of success, while the long-term effects of the latter approach appear to be more lasting over time and establish deeper roots within the culture of the school.

The idea that school improvement can be best served by a combination of 'bottom-up' and 'top-down' approaches is echoed by Stoll and Fink's (1996) notion of 'invitational leadership'. Stoll and Fink point out that organisational change is not so much about structural or bureaucratic innovation, but is concerned with changes in people's thoughts, actions and beliefs. Therefore, since successful change (Fullan, 1993) is rooted in an individual perception of reality and sense of self, it is at the level of the individual that those who wish to implement change need to concentrate their efforts. For Stoll and Fink, invitational leadership shows concern for individuals and is based on four basic premises: optimism, respect, trust and support. *Optimism* in this sense refers to the degree to which the leader affirms colleagues' worth and encourages them to reach their potential. *Respect* is shown through qualities such as courtesy and civility, but also through the encouragement of critical debate. *Trust* is to be understood as the leader's ability to have confidence in the ability of others to act with integrity; invitational leaders, in turn, 'through their relationships, policies and practices behave with integrity' (1996: 109). *Support* is not a passive quality in this formulation, but a conscious and deliberate orientation towards support, care and encouragement.

Invitational leadership, therefore, is 'about communicating invitational messages to individuals and groups with whom leaders interact in order to build and act on a shared and evolving vision of enhanced educational experiences for pupils' (Stoll and Fink, 1996: 109), providing 'top-down' support for 'bottom-up' innovation. Embedded in this vision is the necessity for ongoing critical debate. However, we would argue that the idea of invitational leadership is not confined to those who inhabit senior management positions.

Leithwood et al. believe that transformational leadership, which focuses on the 'commitments and capacities of organisational members', is the most appropriate model for the third millennium. The role of a leader is to capture the imagination of workers so that they do not simply fulfil their contractual obligations, but become engaged in the collective purpose of the organisation. A transformational leader does not hoard power and decision making:

> Power is attributed by organisation members to whomever is able to inspire their commitments to collective aspirations and the desire for personal and collective mastery of the capacities needed to accomplish such aspirations. (Leithwood et al., 1999: 9)

In order to build the school's capacity, those in formal leadership positions need to give attention to fostering teacher leadership, building teachers' commitment to change and creating a culture in which teachers can develop their professional knowledge and skills.

Teacher leadership

Harris and Lambert define teacher leadership as follows:

> ... teacher leadership is not a formal role ... it is more a form of agency where teachers are empowered to lead development work that impacts directly on the quality of teaching and learning. (Harris and Lambert, 2003: 43)

They go on to identify three main types of teacher leadership activity:

- The leadership of other teachers through coaching, mentoring, and leading working groups
- The leadership of new approaches to teaching and learning
- Leadership of specific tasks that help improve practice.

(Harris and Lambert, 2003: 43)

All three types rely on dialogue and the development of collaborative cultures and focus on what teacher leaders do, but in order to realise the full potential of teacher leadership we must look further than tasks and roles. Teacher leadership need not be tied to particular roles, tasks or status; it is a dimension of all teachers' professionalism. Frost and Durrant (2003) emphasise the importance of values, vision and strategy for all teachers. Teacher leadership arises as a result of a process of reconciling shared educational values with a vision of how these values could look in practice, allayed to a strategy for achieving the vision. Teachers need practical support to develop and exercise their leadership in their own professional situations, in a climate where individual agency is understood and fostered. Rooting teachers' leadership in their own values, visions and strategies, rather than in designated tasks or roles, is fundamental to our understanding of the unlocking of school cultures.

In the next two chapters we discuss how involvement in research, with an emphasis on approaching the change process through enquiry, enables teachers to develop their own and one another's leadership capacity and also to contribute to organisational capacity for improvement. In Chapter 3, we offer frameworks and examples that focus beyond teacher research, showing how enquiry can become integral to leadership of learning and ultimately to school transformation, while Chapter 4 offers guidance on different aspects of enquiry, discussing strategies that teachers can use to work towards their visions for improving learning in all its dimensions.

3 Teacher research – and beyond

We are still a long way from understanding the dimensions of teacher professionalism and school improvement processes that link professional learning, leadership and student learning. Frost and Harris (2003) have argued that we need to develop a research agenda that explores different forms of teacher leadership in different contexts, including leadership conceived as a normal part of teachers' work rather than linked to particular roles and tasks. This chapter contributes to this agenda by examining and illustrating ways in which teachers' leadership of learning can be supported and scaffolded, drawing on previous research and development work (Frost et al., 2000; Frost and Durrant, 2002; 2003; Holden, 2002a; 2002b). The most highly developed examples involve the exploratory development of learning communities based on principles of enquiry and shared leadership, in schools and across networks of schools.

Teacher research to support leadership of learning

Engagement in research and its evidence enables teachers to link their own learning with student learning. Through this they develop their own and others' capacity as leaders of change. We explore the importance of engaging in enquiry both for individual teachers and their schools and consider the contribution teachers can make to educational knowledge and understanding as members of the wider research community. There are many conflicts of understanding and interest in this field. Even the terms used may distinguish subtly between the more rigorous sounding 'teacher research', the perhaps more accessible but less definitive 'enquiry' and the term 'action research' which seems to move in and out of common currency. We have found ourselves using terms interchangeably to report on the overlapping debates reflecting our normal discourse with schools and different parts of the educational community. We argue that more important than semantics is teachers' inclusion and participation in those debates and their critique of the language of policy and practice. There are useful discussions elsewhere in the literature about the nature of research, teacher research, action research and school-based enquiry and these also chart the ebb and flow of the discourse (for example Bassey, 2003; Day, 1999; Elliott, 1991; Frost et al., 2003; Furlong, 2003; Hammersley, 1993; Hitchcock and Hughes, 1989; Hopkins, 2001; McKernan, 1996;

Somekh, 1995, amongst many others). We believe that school-based enquiry can be much more powerful if we can think beyond the limits of teacher research, focusing instead on teachers' leadership of learning and the building of individual and collective capacity for school improvement.

While it is widely recognised that an enquiry approach is considered important in building capacity for change within schools, deep and sustainable school change focused on improving pupil learning depends on teachers as agents of that change. Teachers are working in a climate where rhetoric about shared or distributed leadership abounds. Yet, as we have argued in Chapter 1, teacher research, leadership and continuing professional development are often considered separately in relation to school improvement by academics, policymakers and practitioners. At best, the links between them are made crudely, for example through courses to train teachers in leadership skills, by using simplistic tools to measure the impact of CPD and by assuming that teacher action research leads to sustained changes of practice. Evaluations of current policy initiatives, carried out separately for each discrete project or programme, are often expected, indeed required, to identify cause and effect and to chart short-term improvements where the complex reality of schools defies such classification and compartmentalisation, as we have noted earlier. This leads to frustration and disengagement on the part of teachers and headteachers, who see reality distorted and over-simplified in the statistics and findings of educational research. They are beset with conflicting advice as such findings are presented through the media, in digests and by the introduction of the latest ideas into schools through suites of training courses. The teacher's task is to interpret and synthesise this advice and information in order to determine that which is worthwhile in contributing to their professional knowledge, then to go about the complex task of changing practice. We would argue that teachers and their schools are more likely to be able to assimilate this information if they are involved in enquiry and critical discourse around practice and organisational development.

In order to ground our discussion in the real circumstances and issues surrounding schools and classrooms, we describe and discuss a number of examples from our own experience. Here teachers are engaged in school-based enquiry that departs from the more traditional notion of 'research projects'; instead the focus is overtly and primarily on leading change. Most of these projects have been initiated by schools working in collaboration with a university, sometimes in partnership with the LEA. They include both award-bearing and non-accredited programmes, all based in schools or localities, often designed individually to meet schools' needs and purposes. This work has a number of common themes:

- The drawing together of different kinds of evidence including professional experience
- The encouragement of dialogue about learning
- The involvement of external critical friends
- Collaborative working and learning within equitable partnerships
- Reflective, critical, challenging but supportive approaches

- Representation of a range of different voices and perspectives
- A clear aim to improve student, professional and organisational learning.

Drawn from a number of schools in different phases and circumstances, these examples demonstrate what can actually be achieved by teachers, schools and external agencies working together in complex school environments subject to changing macro- and micro-political contexts. From more than ten years of research and development of such approaches, we suggest how individual teachers and their schools can think beyond their own discrete projects, towards developing cultures in which leadership of learning based on enquiry is considered to be integral to teachers' professionalism. This work is based on the premise that there is a role for all members of the school community, not only as *implementers* of change but as *agents* of change.

Strategies and frameworks for supporting teacher leadership

Our initial experience of frameworks of support for teacher leadership was in the context of partnerships between Canterbury Christ Church University College and many schools, groups of schools, LEAs (districts) and other agencies. Through a Masters programme established in the early 1990s, frameworks and strategies were developed to support teachers leading change in their own professional situations, whatever their role or status. While a summary is included here, an account of the development of the programme and more detailed explanations and guidance have been published previously (Frost et al., 2000; Frost and Durrant, 2003).

The framework shown in the diagram below (Figure 3.1) concentrates on the notion of leading 'development work', which encourages teachers to focus, for clarity, on one aspect of improvement that they are leading within the school or between a group of schools. While it is recognised that the process of leading development work is necessarily complex and emphatically non-linear, the elements are shown in this way to ensure that the process is rigorous and systematic and that teachers engage in all the key elements of reflection, planning, enquiry and action in relation to their chosen focus. This clearly has roots in well-

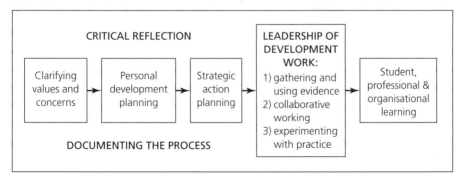

Figure 3.1: A framework for teacher-led development work

established action research approaches (for example Elliott, 1991; Altrighter et al., 1993; McNiff, 1988; McKernan, 1996). In this instance there is greater emphasis on teachers' strategic leadership of learning for school improvement, introducing a fresh dimension beyond changing classroom practice and focusing on building capacity for change. The elements and processes of this framework are now being used in a range of contexts to support teacher-led school improvement.

Teachers begin with a rare opportunity for reflection in order to clarify their own values and concerns in their current professional situations. This helps them to identify a focus for development and negotiate a development plan within the school (for example with their line manager, headteacher or subject team). The scope of the planned work could be anything from improvement of one aspect of student learning to collaborative development across a group of schools. While teachers are inevitably involved in many different developments simultaneously, it is helpful to choose one aspect for particular attention in order to develop their understanding and leadership through enquiry. Having identified their development priorities, teachers then plan strategically for enquiry to support their leadership of change. Ideally for this reflection and planning they need considerable time to develop and discuss their ideas, supported by peers and senior colleagues and by external critical friendship.

The professional and strategic action in which teacher leaders engage has three essential components:

- Gathering and using evidence
- Experimenting with practice
- Collaborating to lead change.

As teachers plan and lead development in their schools, it is important for them to engage critically with both the nature and the process of change and to document the development to provide a basis for reflection, analysis and evaluation. Critical reflection and documentation are therefore shown in the diagram as continuing throughout the process. Within a Masters programme, a flexible assessment structure can be based on portfolios of evidence and linked critical writing (Frost and Durrant, 2003). In programmes without awards, documentation can be linked with school processes such as appraisal and performance management and can support career development. All this has to be carefully managed to ensure that the purpose is clear and that the process is supportive of teachers' leadership rather than becoming an end in itself. It is helpful to think of such documentation as a resource that can be used for a variety of audiences and purposes, as discussed in more detail in Chapter 4.

One cycle within this process from planning through to evaluating outcomes might take a whole academic year, but the model can be used flexibly to fit with school schedules and individual teacher requirements. Where originally this model was developed within a part-time Masters programme, schools and networks are now working over different timescales, with a variety of arrangements for internal and external support including coaching and mentoring by trained and experienced teacher leaders.

The outcomes of this process include the professional learning of the individual teacher leader, but this is seen as an additional outcome, with the primary focus being improved student, professional and organisational learning. Outcomes may also involve learning between schools, including larger-scale knowledge transfer through networks, districts and beyond using wider collaborative working, publication and dissemination. Teachers benefit from skilled facilitation in the initial use of the framework, after which they become adept at integrating it flexibly and critically with their practice. This model has proved to be robust, embracing various policy and funding arrangements, changing priorities and approaches in higher education and fluctuating emphases in the academic research community.

While this is the model with which we have been working predominantly and which best expresses the elements we have found to be important in supporting teachers' leadership of development work, other frameworks can be used, adapted or built into this overarching framework. As we have argued in Chapter 2, this approach has the potential to drive cultural change in schools. As such approaches gain wider credence, for example through interpretations of the introduction of new policies for Continuing Professional Development (DfES, 2005a) and network development (NCSL, 2005) that emphasise teacher leadership through enquiry, the aim should be systemic change. If interpretations are still restricted to an individual 'research project' or 'professional development' approach which will engage small numbers of enthusiasts within the profession, with less emphasis on leading learning for school improvement, the outcomes remain limited.

Teachers need to develop access to wider research in order to relate theory and practice in the thematic field of their development work and to support their leadership of change. They therefore need to engage in critical reflection and documentation, discussion and writing for a range of different audiences, professional as well as academic. Connections with the wider discourse are further encouraged through networks and activities that bring locally-based groups of teachers together. These 'communities of practice' (Wenger, 1998) experiment in valuing all voices and perspectives, engender a sense of belonging and encourage participants to feel that their experiences and ideas are worth sharing. Thus such collaborative activity increases a sense of personal efficacy and confidence as teacher leaders and widens the impact of their work. Emphasis on processes and networks enables teachers and their schools to aim for sustainable school change (Lieberman, 1996) rather than individual professional development related to piecemeal improvements in classroom practice.

Accountability and impact

A university is held accountable for the impact of its award-bearing programmes and challenged both by inspectors and by school and LEA (district) stakeholders to demonstrate the effectiveness of its programmes. Student, professional and organisational learning outcomes are difficult to quantify since they reflect student needs and teacher priorities in the unique and changing situations of individual classrooms and schools. Teachers' and schools' thinking on this aspect of teacher-led development work needs careful structuring to ensure clarity of focus (while taking account of unexpected outcomes) and to support systematic planning and evaluation. Research has previously identified a wide range of possible impacts of teacher-led development work, which are sum-marised in Figure 3.2. (see also Frost and Durrant, 2002; 2004.)

Impact on teachers
a) Classroom practice
b) Personal capacity
c) Interpersonal capacity.

Impact on the school as an organisation
a) Structures and processes
b) Culture and capacity.

Impact beyond the school
a) Critique and debate
b) Creation and transfer of professional knowledge
c) Improvements in social capital in the community.

Impact on pupils' learning
a) Attainment
b) Disposition
c) Metacognition.

Figure 3.2: The impact of teacher-led development work: a conceptual framework
Source: Frost and Durrant, 2002

The full framework for impact (see Appendix 3: www.paulchapmanpublishing.co.uk/resource/durrant.pdf), which includes sections on 'factors that influence impact' and 'evidence for impact', can be used as a basis of support for teachers in planning, tracking and assessing the outcomes of their leadership. This enables them to engage in sophisticated thinking about the effects of their professional actions and to explore the relationships between different dimensions and levels of learning, rather than forcing them into simplistic analysis and summative evaluation.

Teachers have identified the headteacher's support as one of the main factors influencing the effectiveness of their activity in leading school change (Frost and Durrant, 2004). Headteachers manage the interplay of activity within schools that leads to change towards common purposes (Gronn, 2003). A climate that encourages individual teachers to exercise leadership requires complementary or parallel leadership by headteachers (Crowther et al., 2002) to support and co-ordinate teachers' endeavours, including the fostering of critical dialogue, enquiry and collaborative activity, and the recognition and celebration of teachers' development activities. This includes balancing appropriate internal and external support for the extension of their professionalism as leaders of learning (Frost and Durrant, 2004). Teacher leaders' views on ways in which headteachers can support their leadership are summarised in Appendix 4 (www.paulchapmanpublishing.co.uk/resource/durrant.pdf).

Teachers learning collaboratively as leaders of change

As teachers engage with the frameworks depicted in Figures 3.1 and 3.2, they begin to reconceptualise their roles in relation to school development (Frost and Durrant, 2002; Frost et al., 2000). Teachers following this process not only progress in their professional learning, but more importantly they develop greater professional confidence and adopt new approaches taking account of their individual and collective agency (Durrant, 2003; CANTARNET, 2005). Since there is a focus here on school development rather than professional development or research, teachers begin to see themselves as change agents, exercising leadership of learning beyond their classrooms and gaining control of their own professional activities. They draw colleagues into collaboration, develop peer support, gain confidence and earn the authority to shape the structures and cultures within which they work.

David Hargreaves (2003) recommends that individual teacher 'champions' be supported and rewarded as they share their knowledge through contacts and networks. How then is the balance to be achieved between identification of a selected group of experts who focus on priority areas for change and the issues of ownership, passion and involvement, as well as the need for time and resources, that need to be addressed in order to motivate *all* teachers within these learning communities to adapt, change and learn? These issues can be addressed by embracing the notion of enhancing teacher agency whilst emphasising the importance of collaborative working within the context of school, local and national priorities. Teachers' leadership and engagement in school change has to be an organisational rather than an individual enterprise.

Stories of teacher leadership and school change

The approaches supported by the frameworks described earlier in this chapter are not restricted to what would normally be called 'research'. Teachers' leadership of school development involves them in strategic planning and action for change, of which enquiry is a key element. In the next section, we illustrate the power and potential of enabling teachers to take a central role in leading student learning and contributing to genuine learning communities. All the scenarios described involve a university and other external agencies in 'critical friendship' (Swaffield, 2003b; Costa and Kallick, 1993) and facilitation, with a view to developing sustainable models in which schools can take responsibility internally for supporting learning and growth. These examples show the building of individual and organisational capacity for school improvement, enhancing schools' responsiveness and creativity in leading and managing change. Each scenario relates to the process framework in Figure 3.1 and outcomes can be linked to the impact framework in Figure 3.2.

Rebekah's story (Example 3.1) shows how she linked with the school's development priorities and cluster arrangements and used her allocated responsibility to involve colleagues from a consortium of schools in improving student learning across the curriculum, effecting change even with limited funding and resources.

Example 3.1: Rebekah's story

Developing secondary school students' independent learning skills

Rebekah is head of her school's Learning Resource Centre. Alongside the school's building programme and application for specialist school status in science, she wanted to develop the centre as a key facility to support and develop students' independent and lifelong learning skills.

Rebekah's initial data gathering showed that most students saw the centre simply as a place to complete homework and undertake internet research. They did not have the skills to use the resources effectively and found the environment daunting, while teachers had unrealistically high expectations of pupils' abilities in this respect. The centre had no full-time librarian, outdated books and resources and limited space.

After reading about independent learning and study skills, Rebekah audited the National Curriculum at Key Stage 3 to determine how these skills were introduced in different subjects. She listed strategies to build confidence in learning skills development, drew up an action plan which included targets for both students and teachers, and introduced a scheme of work to help students to learn how to find resources independently and use them critically. Her reading on pedagogic styles helped her to combine instruction with practical and interactive elements to enable maximum pupil development and involvement.

Rebekah had to find creative solutions to the lack of both allocated time and dedicated staff. She enlisted full-time librarians from two schools already in partnership with her own to teach this series of lessons. She put her case to the heads of faculty and the departments of English, Social Science and Science each released one lesson for Year 7 students, while the school also allowed her one lesson previously allocated for personal and social education. During these lessons, students learnt to use the Learning Resources Centre, reinforced subsequently by a form designed by Rebekah, entitled '*Learning to be an Information Detective*', copies of which were made available in the centre to frame each investigation. Evaluations showed that use of the centre had increased, teachers were supportive and pupils had grown in confidence. Funding will now be sought so that resources can be improved and Rebekah will develop a system of reinforcement to build upon the induction in Year 7.

Rebekah has published an account of this work in a network journal (CANTAR-NET, 2005). She has also offered up her initial 'dilemma' to stimulate discussion and sharing between colleagues at a network conference.

(South, 2004)

Rebekah has found considerable influence within her school, winning support by planning strategically, building collaborative links and using evidence carefully in support of her leadership. She has found creative ways to overcome a lack of resources and time by employing existing links with other schools. It is significant that while Rebekah has drawn on the expertise of colleagues, she has also contributed practically in designing materials that support and sustain the initiative, which characterises the approach of teacher leaders as shown in Appendix 5 (www.paulchapmanpublishing.co.uk/resource/durrant.pdf). Her approach suggests that this is a development that will be built upon in the future. It has become embedded to the extent that it is owned by colleagues and Rebekah has planned for progression and sustainability. School-based research combined with evidence from a wider spectrum have been used as a foundation for change, to evaluate current practice, involve stakeholders, direct innovation and shape process. Rebekah has now undertaken enquiry to support wider improvements in the school learning environment.

Example 3.2: Janette's story

Collaboration to improve primary–secondary transition

Janette, as Director of Studies in a large rural comprehensive school, had responsibility for transition from the many feeder primary schools, an issue identified as a school development priority. She secured DfES funding from the Best Practice Research Scholarship programme and had access to a wide range of existing data.

Janette noted issues from her experience and reading and as they emerged from the data. One of the most pressing was to ensure that information transfer from primary to secondary school was efficient and effective: did the teachers feel the right information was being made available to the right people? From additional data gathering she uncovered some unexpected perceptions, for example a drama and workshop for Year 6 students designed to allay fears about secondary school was causing concern by suggesting problems they had not considered.

She began by funding a series of development meetings to investigate different options and approaches with the Year 7 team from her own school and interested groups of Year 6 teachers from the primary school. She devised a range of data gathering activities that would determine teacher, parent and student perceptions, experiences, opinions and ideas to complement the existing, mostly quantitative data around transition. She documented particular issues and incidents, for example a case study of one pupil who found it particularly difficult to settle into Year 7. Teachers' focus groups were used to analyse data and discuss ways forward based on the data collected. Year 6 and Year 7 teachers also observed one another's classrooms, establishing greater trust, knowledge and empathy as a basis for developing new strategies across the transition boundary. In the first year, evaluations showed that information transfer processes have been improved, induction of pupils and their parents is more effective and there is increased support for teachers preparing Year 6 pupils and receiving Year 7 pupils.

Janette is now building on her transition work to draw other feeder schools into collaborative developments and is strengthening links with parents during transition, sharing this development work with other local schools through the LEA, including presenting at an LEA conference on transition.

(Hall, 2004)

In Example, 3.2, Janette, with a post of wider responsibility and with extra resources at her disposal through government funding for her individual research through a Best Practice Research Scholarship (DfES, 2003a).

Both Janette and Rebekah were working from positions of responsibility that required them to lead change across the curriculum and enabled them to involve colleagues. They gained support from peers and an external tutor through a part-time Masters programme which supported them in their

---

Example 3.3: Debbie's story
Inclusion in the secondary music classroom

Debbie entered her current school through a Graduate Registered Teachers pro-gramme, building on previous experience in the private sector. She was interested in the effects of inclusion policy on the progression of pupils of average ability, wanting to develop strategies to help pupils of *all* abilities to achieve a higher standard. She began her enquiry with the firm belief that it must be more effective to group students according to ability, but through her reading discovered much research to the contrary, and thus was challenged to investigate this in her own situation, focusing on Key Stage 3 music.

As part of her data gathering she devised a lesson for several Year 9 classes grouped according to ability and a Year 8 mixed ability class. While she realised that a direct comparison could not be made and there were different issues for each class, she felt that it would still be valuable to compare students' reactions as they tackled the same lesson. She discovered that where pupils were set differentiated tasks in the form of melody lines of varying difficulty within a set piece, the resulting perfor-mance from the younger, mixed ability class was comparable with the upper two sets of the older class, while the lower ability classes became demoralised and produced a poorer performance. Pupils in the mixed class worked with one another to accom-modate each other's abilities and all experienced raised self-esteem as they contributed to a satisfying outcome.

Debbie surveyed and interviewed pupils about their views, and found that they overwhelmingly preferred mixed classes which raised self-esteem for all abilities, removing the stigma of being in bottom sets or the pressure of being in the top set.

Debbie also realised that she had concentrated harder on differentiation and creative pedagogy in a mixed class and had worked harder to address different learning styles. This knowledge has encouraged her to address these aspects in all her teaching. During the course of this year she has been promoted to Head of Music so is now challenged to apply her knowledge and experience in leading colleagues in her department. She has recognised that she is working within a school where setting is the norm, and is consid-ering widening her enquiry to investigate whether the approaches that she has found most effective in music are valuable in other curriculum areas.

(Edmonds, 2004)

planning of strategic action and in developing their leadership capacity in their particular school situations, as well as offering methodological guidance for their research. Alongside external support, these examples show that the internal support schools can give is crucial but this cannot be taken for granted. Where this support is only nominal or, for example, schools are lacking a key protagonist such as a senior teacher who acts as contact and co-ordinator, teachers can find that their leadership is stifled and their efforts are frustrated or marginalised (Frost and Durrant, 2002).

This breadth of support and leadership emphasis can be applied even where teachers have an explicit classroom focus and when there is no designated post of responsibility. Debbie, in Example 3.3, adopted this approach in her early career. She demonstrates that engaging with wider research to inform experiments with practice has resulted in fundamental changes in her attitude to classroom teaching and she has been left with challenges about how she might develop this further in her school.

Debbie's story illustrates the power of research to change not only behaviour but also attitude. She has found through her research and reading that she has to challenge the current structures embedded in the school system. She has developed and evaluated new pedagogic approaches and now needs to find ways of developing greater influence through supporting colleagues and working collaboratively both in her subject area and across the curriculum, so it is her leadership skills and her understanding of colleagues' professional learning that need development. Change will not happen easily or rapidly, but at the end of this research she has been left with the conviction that she will need to exercise leadership to address these issues as part of the school improvement agenda and that she has some evidence to support her argument for change.

Activity 3.1
What makes change happen?

This activity can be used to move teacher thinking beyond a focus on research towards leadership supported by enquiry.

- Distribute the previous examples within groups of three, a different example for each person. Working individually, classify the activities in which Rebekah, Janette and Debbie became involved during the course of leading development work (examples could be planning; evaluating; collaborating; leading; learning; consulting; documenting; reading; researching; decision making and so on)

- Using the framework in Figure 3.2 or the more detailed one in Appendix 3 (www.paulchapmanpublishing.co.uk/resource/durrant.pdf), discuss the effects of Rebekah, Janette and Debbie's leadership on pupil, professional and organisational learning and on learning beyond their schools

- Compare ideas within the group. What is it that actually makes change happen? What can increase the impact of teachers' leadership?

These three examples show that research on its own does not necessarily lead to changes that improve pupil learning. It is the exercise of individual leadership that makes the difference between the gathering of evidence for a research project and the use of evidence to inform change. It is individual leadership again that progresses the developments beyond a single classroom, curriculum area or aspect of school life. Where teachers gather evidence not only to solve practical problems but explicitly to support their leadership, through the process of investigation as well as the findings, this has great potential to enhance their own and others' professionalism and agency. However, in most schools research is still viewed as an optional extra for enthusiasts and those with the ambition to improve their personal qualifications, while leadership is still tied to designated posts of responsibility. If leadership based on enquiry is to become integral to *all* teachers' professionalism, how can this be achieved in practical terms, even within a political context over which schools have no control?

From the few to the many: enquiry and leadership for all

Ruth, a headteacher of a large urban primary school in South-East England, has encouraged her whole staff and pupils throughout the school to lead learning by involving them in collaborative enquiry. Example 3.4 tells her story.

Ruth's example demonstrates the power of parallel leadership (Crowther et al., 2002). While her own leadership was supported by the process framework shown in Figure 3.1, she also embedded these elements into the school's way of working. Within a system of high external accountability, she chose a focus that matched her personal values and priorities with school and district priorities through the unifying theme of pupil voice. Her planning was highly strategic, making use of existing initiatives, projects, funding and policy support wherever possible. In leading the development work she enabled teachers to engage in the three elements shown in Figure 3.1, allowing them time to work collaboratively, guiding their enquiry by providing frameworks and tools to adapt (having prepared thoroughly herself through methodological reading and planning) and giving them the encouragement and confidence to experiment with practice. Meanwhile she surrounded this with her own critical reflection and the reflective dialogue she encouraged amongst all staff, including support staff, and students. Administrative staff were also involved in helping to collate evidence and document progress.

The impact of this development work has been wide ranging and complex. In relation to the framework summarised in Figure 3.2, it is clear that the personal and interpersonal capacity of teachers and other members of staff has increased. This is multi-layered, with teachers exercising leadership to involve and encourage colleagues. Significant changes in practice including a more creative curriculum are being implemented, in which students can see some of their own views acted upon. The collaboration in year teams and across the school has gathered momentum, indicating that the school is building social capital, changing its structures and culture to create a more effective learning environment. This in turn has led to increased self-confidence and motivation in

Example 3.4: Ruth's story

Encouraging teacher leadership through collaborative enquiry

As headteacher, Ruth wanted to develop 'pupil voice' in her school, a focus identified through her previous school-based research and development work, her reading and inspection evidence. This focus linked the OfSTED action plan, the school improvement plan and the development priorities of the Education Action Zone in which her school is situated, with a strong emphasis on raising standards of pupil performance.

Ruth designed a questionnaire to explore pupils' ideas and experiences about their learning, but she was worried about being swamped in increasing mountains of data and about how to instigate whole school change. She therefore decided to involve all the staff in the enquiry. At a staff meeting, teams were invited to customise the language and content of the instrument for their own year groups, taking the risk of producing less comparable data for the sake of involvement and spreading the workload. The questionnaires were refined collaboratively and by this time the teachers were becoming very interested in what they might discover. All staff agreed to administer the survey themselves and the year group leaders undertook to collate responses.

Teachers felt a high degree of ownership of this 'messy' data and began to identify emerging issues, some authenticating their own experience and some presenting new questions and challenges, for example the serious issue of decreasing confidence in learners between the ages of 4 and 11. Year teams discussed the issues raised for their respective groups, while Ruth constructed an overview of school-wide issues. The teachers began to take the initiative to experiment with practice. Ruth revitalised the School Council to deal with immediate practical issues; for example children had said they found their pens difficult to use, so students of all ages experimented to find the best writing implements and the preferred tools (ballpoint pens) were adopted straight away.

The value and power of the process has taken teachers by surprise; pupils have found a new vocabulary and new identities as learners and the dialogue has '... created a real buzz around the school ... .' Ruth has celebrated the personal achievement of completing her Masters degree and where the budget and logistics allow, she is encouraging as many staff as possible to work towards further professional and academic qualifications, which supports more enquiry-based development work. She has also presented at a network conference at the partner university and the school is receiving many visitors as news of its success has spread within the Education Action Zone and LEA.

Now committed to involving pupils, the school has been challenged about the extent to which pupils can genuinely exercise influence over curriculum and pedagogy. An exciting new creative curriculum initiative, in which the foundation subjects are to be delivered through the arts, can be traced back to the comments of one child in discussion with his teacher, prompted by the initial questionnaire. Early evidence indicates that this initiative is proving valuable in motivating students and is giving them great enjoyment and pride in their learning.

(Waller, 2004)

students, greater awareness and involvement of themselves as learners and improved achievement. Ruth has gathered and presented evidence of children's enjoyment and confidence in learning, including photographs of groups making music within the arts curriculum project, children's articulate statements of what helps and hinders their learning and assessments demonstrating improvements in speaking and listening in the early years.

Ruth would not claim to have planned these precise outcomes. She is a shrewd leader of an unpredictable process. While long-term evaluation is not yet possible, it seems that the excitement, motivation and commitment generated by the work around pupil voice have provided an excellent foundation for innovation and sustenance of change through shared leadership of learning.

Ruth emphasises collaborative approaches and the development of collective responsibility for learning, rather than coercing and directing staff in relation to performance targets. She rarely uses the word 'I' – always 'we' – and places value on simple strategies such as always saying 'please' and 'thank you'. She has reaped the benefits of 'letting go', allowing her staff to exercise leadership, but has ensured that there is common purpose and that their work is based upon sound evidence, effectively interrelating the three elements of research, leadership and professional learning around children's learning. In this example, Ruth encourages flexibility, choice and risk taking, showing that 'change is a journey, not a blueprint' (Fullan, 1993: 24). Working within a system of high external accountability and prescription, she makes use of projects, funding and support where appropriate in order to energise staff and students in moving the school forwards.

The activity below can be used to structure strategic planning for teacher-led change, whatever the context.

Activity 3.2
Drawing up an action plan

- Use the framework in Figure 3.1 to inform discussion at a meeting of a school development group, working party or team charged with a given school development task. Push the conversation further than 'what we need to do by when' towards more detailed discussion of purposes and processes that will best enable change to happen and involve the people concerned. Use Examples 3.1, 3.2, 3.3 and 3.4 for ideas.

- From this, draw up an action plan for the development in hand that takes account of the aspects listed in Figure 3.1, *as far as possible within your current school context*. Set out intended actions, timescales and criteria for review.

An action plan needs to be specific. It should detail who is going to be involved at different stages, when and where meetings are going to happen, how dialogue is going to be supported. It might cover a few months, or even weeks if the change is fast, after which it can be reviewed and revised.

For further reflection:

- Are there any of the aspects that require deeper consideration within your school? For example, is the school prone to establishing committees and working parties to address issues that never get beyond the talking stage? Is more emphasis needed on planning or evidence gathering for evaluation? Is it difficult for teachers to collaborate and engage in dialogue because they have no appropriate places to meet? How will you begin to prioritise and address such issues?

Frost and Durrant (2003) provide more tools, proformas and workshop outlines to support action planning for teacher leaders.

The framework and principles described above were initially used only within this and similar school-based Masters programmes. If teachers' leadership is an integral part of their professionalism, we need to explore other applications. How can the knowledge, skill and personal and interpersonal capacity of teachers to lead change (Mitchell and Sackney, 2000) be more powerfully developed and collectively applied, as Ruth has started to do in her school? The next section explores what we have learnt so far through developing similar approaches where a university brings its theoretical and methodological expertise, connections to the wider discourse and external critical perspective into school-based consultancy.

New roles for external agencies

The role of higher education in providing accreditation and support for teachers' initial education, professional development and research is well established, but universities have recently been challenged to adjust their activities in a number of ways. In England there has been a shift of location away from the academy towards schools and local centres, a greater emphasis on practitioner research and research partnerships with schools, and an increase in what are known as 'knowledge transfer' activities. This has involved university staff concerned with school improvement in reconceptualising their role, while higher education institutions have had to reshape their structures and activities in order to accommodate new, more flexible ways of working that pay closer attention to the relationships between theory and practice.

In 1998, Canterbury Christ Church University College launched the Centre for Education Leadership and School Improvement (CELSI), a department concerned not only with accredited programmes and research but also with the development of school-based consultancy. Over the last six years, CELSI has been piloting and evaluating projects and the following examples are indicative of pilot work that is subject to ongoing evaluation in order to develop transferable principles and processes for supporting effective and sustainable school improvement. Many of these consultancy projects are bespoke, tailored to the needs and agendas of schools, and all involve the university in providing critical friendship. They draw upon the principles and ways of working outlined at the beginning of this chapter and rep-resented in Figure 3.1. Examples 3.5 and 3.6 are early experiments in supporting school self-evaluation, responding to the need for a critical but supportive and involving process to help schools 'know themselves', as a complement, or perhaps antidote, to a judgemental and punitive inspection regime. Example 3.5 involved every member of staff in a large secondary school in departmental review.

Example 3.5

Whole school improvement planning through departmental review

Sixteen university staff, including associates with inspection and/or teaching experi-ence, were paired with heads of subject departments for reviews covering every department in a large secondary school including 16–19 provision, focusing on aspects of learning and teaching. The intention was not to deliver hard messages but to offer critical friendship for heads of department and gather evidence through dis-cussion, observation of lessons and meetings. Up to three visits were made to each department over a few months, many involving formative feedback and practical suggestions for improvement. Reports were negotiated and agreed with heads of department before internal publication.

Heads of department working with their teams set the agendas for review and co-wrote the reports and resulting action plans. Teachers and middle leaders with designated roles were supported in looking at evidence in their own professional sit-uations and practices. The headteacher was aware of many of the issues that would be uncovered, using the reviews as part of the strategy for improvement. Action plans were included in the school improvement plan, given legitimacy by external support and critical feedback, and generally the staff felt ownership of the process and planning.

In a school that had some challenging issues to confront, this supported self-review provided a stronger foundation for improvement. The headteacher allowed for teachers' agency and voice and took their planning seriously. Soon after this the school was subject to a government inspection; this uncovered the same issues, but the headteacher and her staff could demonstrate that they were already aware and that staff had begun to move towards improvement.

(Durrant et al., 2004)

Example 3.6 illustrates how the university provided intense support for   one teacher's leadership of a department team through a week of one-to-one critical friendship.

Example 3.7 shows how the same principles and approaches were transferred into a new situation where there was no previous relationship between the university and schools. This involved the university in a project to support Sicilian schools in drawing teachers and other members of a school network

---

Example 3.6
Supporting an individual teacher's team leadership

A critical friend from the university worked intensively alongside a head of mathematics in a grammar school (higher ability students aged 11–18) to develop a week-long 'conversation' in order to move thinking and professional knowledge forward. He conducted observations, talked to teachers and pupils, was invited to meetings and stimulated and participated in discussions. The review was documented through handwritten summaries completed each evening and presented the following day – significant in expressing the open-endedness of the work and lessening the bureaucracy of a formal report. An informal meeting took place each day between the visitor, deputy head and head of department to ensure that the project was running smoothly and to discuss any issues arising.

For the teacher, this process of departmental review yielded outcomes more powerful than any summative report. She said it ' … freed me to think, instead of to see if x,y and z are happening', and asserted that ' … you don't know where you are until you articulate it.' She was emphatic and enthusiastic about the direct effect that the project had had on her practice. At the evaluation meeting, which was held several months after the review had taken place, she reflected that it was

> … the best [professional development] I've ever had in my life. Loads of things have been implemented. Everything was really, really positive. I spent a day this week talking to students as a direct result of what [the reviewer] said. It's become what we do on a regular basis.

She welcomed the fact that the critical friend was not passive in observation but was making 'practical and useful' suggestions resulting in immediate changes in practice. The reviewer's collaboration in the enquiry, sharpness and criticality of the external viewpoint and mutual enthusiasm for learning helped to move her forwards. Both the head of department and deputy head continued to return to this intense experience for inspiration and to fuel further reflection and action. The school was left considering whether they could sustain similar activity internally, since external support of this intensity was not financially viable for the whole school. The deputy head has since successfully instigated pairing of teachers within the school, non-hierarchically, to support one another in improving practice through mutual observation, dialogue and critical friendship.

(Durrant et al., 2004)

---

into dialogue around the considerable amount of data they had already gathered for self-evaluation, using well-established processes and formats (MacBeath et al., 2000).

Cultural contrasts here serve to highlight issues and offer challenges underpinned by trust, support and friendship. It is important that the learning is seen as two-way, both between schools and higher education and between countries. Discussion has focused sharply on pedagogic practices and on improving stu-

Example 3.7

From self-evaluation to school improvement in a Sicilian school network

A colleague working for the Italian Ministry of Education and the headteacher of a large secondary school in southern Sicily organised an intensive four day visit by two critical friends from Canterbury Christ Church University College with the aim of mutual learning about supporting school improvement based on self-evaluation.

Focus groups involving teachers, ancillary workers, parents, pupils and local community representatives enabled exploration of school improvement issues, collective reflection, the building of collaborative relationships and support for strategic discussion, facilitated by the external critical friends. Sessions had to be carefully organised using a circle of chairs, agreement of an ethical code, sensitive listening and chairing and detailed documentation. Teachers gradually revealed to one another that after much meticulous and systematic self-evaluation, schools were often unsure as to how to move forward. Valuable evidence was often in the hands of one or two teachers or a working party. Although the teachers concerned had presented to groups with political influence including Teachers' Assemblies (the decision-making bodies in schools), headteachers and school improvement groups, the link with action for improvement was often tenuous because processes were not in place to make this happen.

Focus groups were also generating further evidence, as people explored one another's perceptions and delved deeper through questioning to make meaning of each other's comments. It was notable that while a small number of teachers carried the burden of the self-evaluation work, the other teachers said that they wanted more involvement and opportunities for innovation.

The critical friends helped these school communities in beginning to discover ways in which they could help one another to move forwards within and between schools. A recurring theme was students' concern that their curriculum lacked relevance, so a number of groups explored ways in which the local community and environment might support learning. There were other discussions about involving students and staff in review, development of rewards and sanctions and other school decision-making to improve mutual respect, and about how to work collaboratively to clarify intended learning outcomes linked to effective classroom practices. A summative report simply reflected the discussion back to schools, drawing out clear, initial steps forward for each school.

This has been followed up with further collaborative work. It is significant that Giuseppe, the headteacher who had convened the Sicilian network of schools, had involved himself and contributed to the wider discourse of school improvement, as with Ruth in Example 3.4, including presentation of a paper on pupil voice at an international conference (Micciche, 2005). The following year, a small group of English headteachers visited colleagues in Sicily to build on school self-evaluation and learn together, conferencing, visiting, observing and staying in each other's homes. English headteachers intend to reciprocate this hospitality within the year.

(Durrant, 2004; Micciche, 2005)

dent learning, highlighted through school self-evaluation. Such activity may result in the introduction of some training for teachers, arising directly from their dialogue around the evidence gathered through classroom observation.

The school improvement processes illustrated in these examples are explicitly context specific, achieved by supporting critical dialogue around evidence, making practice visible, authorising contributions from different voices and framing plans for change. In evaluation of these projects in England and Sicily as described in Examples 3.5, 3.6 and 3.7, the critical dialogue was described as 'liberating' both by participants in school and also by the external visitors. This was because it was both *authentic*, focusing on real concerns rather than the abstract and theoretical, and also *critical* in that these everyday concerns were subjected to scrutiny through enquiry, reflection and discussion (Frost and Durrant, 2003). Teachers' expertise and knowledge of their subjects and their professional settings were valued and built upon.

Importantly, this supportive process was not thought to be a 'soft option' by schools or by university staff, who were keenly aware of the need for a rigorous yet flexible process and for developing criticality to offer challenge for individuals, departments and schools. It was motivated and driven by passionate concern for improving student learning. As the external 'visitors' withdrew at the end of these projects, teachers and headteachers were left engaged with rich evidence, motivated not only with focused plans for change but also with the responsibility to make that change happen. Through this work, we can demonstrate some ways in which initial engagement can take place and pave the way for teachers' leadership of school improvement, employing some of the processes that have been modelled. After this, the extent to which teachers can carry the work through depends on the quality of support within the school and an ability to draw upon additional external support where appropriate (Durrant et al., 2004).

Schools are now beginning to develop further ideas about how to sustain such approaches without losing the benefits of external involvement, given that concentrated support as shown in the examples above is too expensive and intense in the long term. By making use of existing cluster arrangements and building capacity for internal support, schools can still benefit from overarching partnerships to develop the theory and practice of more coherent approaches to school improvement focusing on shared leadership of learning. Experienced teacher leaders play a crucial part in sustaining such developments over time. They can support colleagues through formal and informal mentoring, contribute expertise in enquiry methodology and the development of leadership skills as well as in specific themes and aspects of the curriculum, provide encouragement and practical help and also continue to influence school structures and cultures to create a supportive climate for the development of more dispersed leadership practices. The importance of this internal support has been stressed by teacher leaders themselves (Frost and Durrant, 2004).

Multi-faceted development of leadership of learning at all levels, between as well as within schools, is illustrated in Example 3.8 below.

Example 3.8

A network approach to leadership of learning

The Tunbridge Wells (NCSL)Networked Learning Community is part of a National College for School Leadership initiative with funding matched by schools. It originated from a Beacon School cluster around one junior school and involves 20 primary schools, five secondary and two special schools across the town. Higher education has been involved from the outset, supported by an officer from the LEA. It is significant that the Networked Learning Community is virtually synonymous with the local cluster of schools formed by reorganisation within the LEA.

Canterbury Christ Church University College (CCCUC) led launch conferences to engage all teachers in focusing on pupil learning, in particular the implications of recent research about learning styles, development of reflective practice and cultures of enquiry. Since then, a sophisticated range of roles for higher education has developed, many of which overlap within projects and programmes. These include:

● Continuing professional development and leadership development programmes for every career stage

● Consultancy: facilitation, evaluation, guidance and dissemination

● Award-bearing programmes for academic qualifications and credit

● Mentoring of school-based research.

Surrounding these individual projects, the schools/LEA/higher education partnership has planned strategically for leadership development.

Newly Qualified Teachers (NQTs) have been supported by a bespoke programme for a number of years, pre-dating the NCSL funding. The programme emphasises observation, reflection, discussion, peer support and enquiry (Alcock, 2003). The focus for group sessions and individual support is negotiated following an audit of individual professional needs with Induction Tutors and the higher education tutor. NQTs observe classroom practice across the network to access expertise offered by network schools.

Those in their second and third year of teaching choose a classroom focus for enquiry and development linked directly to school and network improvement plans. Seminar sessions provide support for enquiry and address other relevant issues, for example being effective subject leaders; time and stress management; initiating change.

Entering the first year of NCSL funding, headteachers wanted to make their own meetings more developmental. They initiated a Collaborative Leadership Learning (CLL) programme (NCSL, 2005) which broadly follows the process shown in Figure 3.1. Headteachers initially used contemporary articles and 'think pieces' to share understandings about their roles and values in relation to school and network priorities. They have a collective development plan and have engaged in enquiry and supported one another in experimenting and taking risks to develop more flexible and creative approaches in their schools. This has included 'learning visits' based on the NCSL guidance for Learning Walks (NCSL, 2005). Focusing on interesting developments rather than successes or problems encouraged equitable 'learning from each other'. Far from disappearing down a cul-de-sac of leadership theory or methodological paradigm, they relished this rare opportunity to discuss children's learning –. their core concern – for example one headteacher chose a group reading focus, returning with her Special Needs and Literacy Co-ordinators to prompt wider discussion, leading to improved practice.

Headteachers then constructed a self-evaluation tool modelled on an established format (MacBeath, 2003a; 2003b) to explore shared leadership practices in their schools. Trustful dialogue and critical sharing of ideas around visits and survey instruments generated wider discussion in schools around evidence, learning and leadership. Tools such as the protocol for visits and a self-evaluation instrument have been circulated by email so that they can be adapted to school purposes. As there is already such emphasis on accountability, the group's function is to empower and support their wider use rather than exerting pressure. This includes generosity towards headteachers who have not engaged with the group or are unable to attend particular meetings; the group is committed to working on behalf of all network schools.

The partnership (university, schools network and LEA) has now designed a coherent framework of support to include middle managers and deputy headteachers so that the development of leadership of learning is supported across the network. The intention is to move from *leadership structures* to *leadership cultures* where leadership of learning is a shared responsibility.

Headteachers have been struck by the quality and depth of this work, realising the implications for the network and sometimes for the whole LEA. There is powerful evidence here that development of leadership capacity does not have to be linked to role, status or length of experience. Teachers lead a wide range of development work, developing professional knowledge and skills in processes of enquiry, reflective practice, leadership and collaborative working. There is a focus beyond skills and competencies (although these are important too). Headteachers want to increase the professional confidence, agency and voice of teachers and work collaboratively to articulate values and purposes and put them into practice. Higher education facilitation has assisted strategic planning and provided inputs, programmes and frameworks, helping teachers to link practice and contemporary theory, and preventing the 'myopia' that might stifle or misdirect improvement efforts through a lack of critical distance (Lieberman and McLaughlin, 1996).

Funding is finite and most schools are not involved in the Networked Learning Community programme so it is important to discuss less intensive models for groups of schools without NCSL funding, but just as important is capturing the imagination of teachers and headteachers and demonstrating the real value of these ways of working. Collaborative leadership learning becomes more powerful and sustainable for all teachers through mentoring of school-based enquiry and facilitation of collaborative activity by experienced teachers who can be supported externally. An important issue is how to extend involvement to all schools, since participation is necessarily voluntary, resulting in a high level of involvement in network activities by some schools where others have hardly engaged at all. The consensus seems to be that momentum is built by working with those who *are* engaged, building capacity on behalf of the cluster or network and drawing others in.

None of these examples provides a 'solution' to school improvement through teacher leadership, but each offers insights about effective processes for teacher-led school improvement. Teachers are invited to reconceptualise themselves as leaders of learning and their role in school improvement is taken seriously, which means that schools are aiming for cultural change. Where these models are developing, we are therefore starting to see not only the parallel leadership of headteachers working with their staff to common purpose (Crowther et al., 2002), but also multiple parallel lines of leadership with experienced teacher leaders developing capacity for leadership across schools and networks by supporting their colleagues in leading change. This principally and typically involves a whole repertoire of subtle and small scale approaches, encouraging, nurturing, modelling and coaching, as shown in Appendix 5 (www.paul chapmanpublishing.co.uk/resource/durrant.pdf) (see also Frost, 2005).

As experience broadens, what can we learn from these pilot projects?

Key ingredients for improvement

Evaluations with stakeholders (Durrant et al., 2004) suggest a set of key ingredients (Figure 3.3) that are needed for school improvement based on the premise that teachers have a central role in leading change.

---

1 CLARITY OF FOCUS: Unless the purpose of the activity is clear, the process has no value or foundation. This includes moral as well as practical purpose.

2 EVIDENCE: Gathering and use of evidence from classrooms and school contexts involves and energises teachers, challenges practice and directs leadership of change.

3 COLLABORATION: Teachers develop confidence in leadership by sharing professional knowledge and dilemmas and planning coherent improvement strategies.

4 TRUST: Individual and organisational self-confidence and mutual support are the foundation for shared leadership, which requires trust within and between schools.

5 DIALOGUE: Members of the school community need opportunities for their voices to be heard, raising the level of dialogue so that it is both critical and supportive.

6 PLANNING: Unless decisions are made, targets set, responsibilities agreed and structures put in place, improvement will not happen.

7 LEADERSHIP: Change requires professional action from teachers and headteachers working in parallel according to a common purpose.

Figure 3.3: Suggested key ingredients for sustaining school improvement
Source: Durrant, 2005

These work in conjunction with the elements of the framework shown in Figure 3.1 and explained in the first part of this chapter, namely, clarifying values and concerns, development planning, action planning, leading change through enquiry, collaboration and experimentation, critical reflection, and communication and documentation of evidence and process. However, rather than forming stages in a process of leading change, the characteristics in Figure 3.3 provide the kind of climate within which improvements in learning, as framed in Figure 3.2, can take place. This list shows where attention needs to be directed in order to move schools forward. There are no surprises here; for example, the list resonates with research by Harris (2004) in her examination of leadership for school improvement in those schools in challenging circumstances.

This is not a checklist or a progression of items but an encapsulation of elements that need to be included in working for school improvement, patiently and passionately, over the long term. Eliminating responsibility for any one of these ingredients unbalances the processes and makes them less effective – without collaboration the scope of the work is limited, without focus and planning there is incoherence, without leadership there is no change. All teachers can contribute to the development of these characteristics in their schools based upon the shared values and common purposes of members of school communities. Teachers and schools benefit from using the process frameworks such as those presented in Figure 3.1 and Figure 3.2, not only to ensure that all these ingredients are included, but also to scaffold further development of the characteristics.

Schools are realising that such approaches bridge between professional development, leadership and research as suggested in Chapter 1. They may require external agents such as universities to develop new ways of working that meet the complex world of schools rather than compartmentalising, and they may also require LEA advisors and independent consultants to adjust their approaches. All this demands flexibility and mutual learning which are more effective through partnership or collaborative models than through strictly delineated business models and provider–client relationships. It is important nevertheless to structure the work carefully through a memorandum of agreement setting out financial arrangements, roles and responsibilities (Frost and Durrant, 2003; Durrant et al., 2004).

External agents, while still bringing their thematic expertise into schools, provide facilitation, critical friendship and methodological expertise. They also need sensitivity and understanding and a working knowledge of schools and their policy context. The credibility of classroom experience is significant for schools and enables external colleagues to participate in authentic discussion about practice. A number of stakeholders, agencies and partners may need to work strategically alongside one another through complex local and regional relationships and structures. They need to respond to individual and school agendas while maintaining some critical distance. There may be considerable change in their working conditions as they travel long distances to meet the needs of schools, attend meetings with various groups and partners, relocate teaching and consultancy into localities and employ distance learning, e-learning and e-communication methods with students and colleagues.

However, it is what happens *within* schools that is most important, since they themselves are ultimately responsible for drawing together the support they need in order to initiate and sustain improvement. By focusing on leadership of learning schools can over time build up expertise and individual confidence, internal capacity and capacity across networks, enabling them to improve from the inside (Stoll, 1999). Where the mixture of people, processes and circumstances is right, it is not just the examination results or structures, but the cultures of schools that can change (Holden, 2002a; 2002b; Frost, 2005; Harris, 2004), moving towards powerful and inclusive learning communities, even in the most challenging circumstances.

4 Enquiry to support teachers leading change

In this chapter, we demonstrate how enquiry and leadership of change can be integrated, through enquiry taking on a fresh focus to support the change process and the development of leadership capacity. Research enables teachers to see the everyday in classrooms and schools in new ways, making the tacit explicit and enabling them to learn from what they experience. We move beyond the straitjacket of teacher research projects which, while they have been liberating for many, are in danger of constraining us to a problem-solving model.

The following section focuses on how teachers can integrate a range of enquiry strategies with their everyday practice to support leadership of change and engage colleagues, students and others in the process. It is important to point out that this section is not intended to replace the many excellent methodological texts available, but to offer new ways of thinking to make tried and tested techniques and strategies work more powerfully for school change. This section is not intended to be a comprehensive research manual; we have not, for example, included explanation and discussion of methodological techniques and issues that have been explored comprehensively elsewhere. The intention is to offer ideas for embedding creative enquiry into the professional lives of teachers and into school development processes. Sound methodological approaches are an essential foundation and while this chapter gives an overview of how they might be approached and used most effectively, it is not meant to substitute for more detailed methodological planning and analysis supported by a full range of literature.

Central to an enquiry approach for teachers is children's learning, supported by professional learning and, if change is to be sustainable, organisational learning. Improvements in learning are achieved as teachers shape practice according to their own developing understandings, concerns and priorities. This often requires cultural change within which teachers can gain the confidence, the tools and the strategies to 'make a difference' which, as Fullan (1993) reminds us, is the reason that the vast majority of teachers came into the profession in the first place. If we are to break the cycle of professional development 'apartheid' and deprofessionalisation identified by Andy Hargreaves (Hargreaves and Evans, 1997; A. Hargreaves, 2003), teachers have to be *critical activists*; there is a need to engage 'intellectually, emotionally and politically' with school improvement processes (Bascia and Hargreaves, 2000: 20). This increases their ability to think and act strategically as they confront the complexity of real-life situations, enabling them to collaborate in leading learning and managing change more effectively. Teachers' experiences and perceptions of their own agency, activity and ability to influence structures, systems, interrelationships and layers of learning are crucial factors in the equation (Giddens, 1984; Gronn, 2003; Frost and Durrant, 2003; Frost et al., 2000).

We would argue that while these approaches could be confined within the mechanistic investigation, implementation and evaluation of 'what works' in the classroom or school scenario, they can be used more powerfully by teachers not only to increase 'situational understanding' and the transferable practical wisdom used to make professional judgements but also in an emancipatory way. Teachers can use evidence derived from their enquiry to *inform leadership* of change, providing indications as to how to shape the systems and cultures within which they are working, but more than this teachers can use the enquiry processes themselves as *part of their strategic action* for change. Thus their leadership consists of the three elements already discussed in Chapter 3: gathering and using evidence, experimenting with practice and collaboration to lead and manage change (Frost and Durrant, 2003). Our experience is that through these processes supported by critical reflection, teachers come to a new understanding of their own professionalism.

These approaches cannot be adopted lightly. Complex ethical and professional dilemmas often arise as teachers manage the blurred boundaries of the overlapping roles of teacher, researcher and leader. This makes it all the more important to adopt a critical approach with rigorous attention to methodology and linked professional action. A reflexive approach, in which teachers interrogate purposes and processes as part of the enquiry, is essential in order that the full implications of their activity are properly understood and are governed by principles of equity, justice and respect amongst those who are involved or affected. Clearly an organisational view is needed if these ideas are to have real and sustained effect. This is not only about creating a culture to support enquiry-based leadership of change, but also about enabling individuals' leadership to continue to shape the school culture, in a reciprocal process as discussed in Chapter 2. In this section of the book we show what this approach looks like in practice and how it can be supported.

Enquiry Section 1
Finding a Focus

Teachers wishing to exercise leadership through school-based enquiry face the initial dilemma of identifying a focus for their work. Most teachers, even in their early careers, have multiple roles and responsibilities and all teachers can be leaders of learning. Where there are many conflicting demands, it is tempting to try to encompass everything at once. More effective is to identify clearly some main professional priorities and concerns and then to choose one particular aspect upon which to focus enquiry and thus develop leadership of change.

Eventually, through focused application, teachers begin to conceptualise themselves as leaders of learning and build enquiry habitually into their everyday practice, as these experienced teacher leaders explain:

> I think if we can try and create a culture of learning which includes recording, researching ... evaluating, identifying good bits of work, then it's got to have an effect. (Frost and Durrant, 2002: 154)

> To think that you can make a change, you can even initiate it, you can take charge, take responsibility – that's great. For me, it revived the fact that you can take one step back and look at teaching again ... rather than simply being in a classroom and doing a job ... .

> ... I became much more focused on teaching as a whole, on strategies and school approaches to things, simply because I'd revived my interest again – started to reflect. I find myself doing it all the time, whether it's the new AS levels or Key Stage Three literacy. You don't lose it. I'm someone who can actually have an input to education ... . (unpublished teacher interview)

This is the start of a journey that involves teachers in reflection, learning, enquiry/research, strategy, agency, leadership and school change. The teachers above have become comfortable with this as their normal way of working. They are taking responsibility for change, can understand the cultural dimension and are enthusiastic about making a difference beyond, as well as within, their classrooms.

Juggling priorities and agendas for development

Over many years we have used and developed the model discussed in Chapter 3 (see Figure 3.1) which ensures that emphasis is placed on clarifying and negotiating individual concerns and priorities within the context of the school agenda and the wider development priorities. Teachers and headteachers usually make reference to a number of plans: it is possible for a teacher in an English school to be working simultaneously on the school improvement plan, a cluster or network development plan, the Local Education Authority strategic plan, the OfSTED action plan, the subject or year group plan and individual targets for performance management. Some of these are explicit in the teacher's mind and some are managed by senior staff. Most are imposed, possibly with a degree of consultation and negotiation with the individual teacher concerned.

Usually teachers can say immediately which initiative or development is currently consuming most of their time and energy. This is likely to be the aspect that would be most valuable for deeper investigation, but this may not necessarily be so. Leadership and enquiry begin with passion and commitment that stem from individuals' values and professional agendas and these may be somewhat in tension with institutional priorities. Teachers must therefore reflect and explore not only their roles, responsibilities and the issues arising in their practice, but also their purposes, beliefs and passions. This is, in fact, the first important step in enquiry.

Getting in touch with values and purposes

Teachers need structure and facilitation for considering their current roles and responsibilities, values and concerns, strengths and needs, experiences and aspirations (Frost et al., 2000; Frost and Durrant, 2003). This can be done through individual reflection supported by discussion with a colleague or a critical friend, someone who is able to offer both support and challenge in confidential discussion. In groups it can be organised through paired discussion. This kind of conversation is already taking place in some schools through performance management discussions, mentoring and coaching or external tutoring. Sometimes it happens informally where teachers find a trusted colleague or friend to whom they turn for guidance, support and critical conversation. Teachers are often thirsty for space to explore these deeper questions, space which has disappeared since they finished their initial training, where they were probably coached to be 'reflective practitioners'. Revisiting questions such as 'Why did I decide to become a teacher?' usually has an immediate refreshing and invigorating effect. Comments like those in Figure 4.1 are common. These principles that drive commitment, unremarkable in themselves, are vital in a challenging profession. They can become lost in the busyness and pressure of school life and it is never indulgent to revisit such themes from time to time.

It's about caring for children and wanting them to have the best in life.

If I can make one difference to one person's life one day then it's been worthwhile.

I have always enjoyed learning and being a teacher meant I could carry on learning and convey that to the children.

I want to raise their aspirations; I want then to have the chances I had.

I really love my subject and I wanted other people to catch my enthusiasm.

It is just really rewarding to see them achieve things and see the smiles on their faces.

It's the most important job there is.

Figure 4.1: Teachers' comments about their values and purposes

By articulating this in a group, teachers find strength in common purposes and ideals and discover that everyone confronts the barriers to achieving these. Following an exercise to revisit these more fundamental questions, teachers can take a wider and slightly more dispassionate view of their roles and responsibilities. These are worth mapping, through activities such as one of those suggested below.

Activity 4.1
Considering professional roles and responsibilities

Teachers can map their current professional roles and responsibilities (both formal and informal) in one of the following ways:

- Draw a 'mind map' representing your different areas and lines of responsibility and identifying the groups and individuals with whom you work
- Sketch in words or pictures the different roles you have to assume in your day-to-day work. It may be helpful to think about the different 'hats' or 'badges' you wear
- Put yourself at the centre and draw concentric circles representing your classroom, your team or department, your faculty, your school, your cluster, consortium or group of schools, your national subject affiliation, your region and so on, as appropriate. In each circle note your relevant role and responsibility.

It may be appropriate to include roles and activities that are relevant but not directly concerned with school, such as community youth worker, parent, hockey coach – these may figure importantly in people's lives and influence their approaches to professional roles.

It is worth noting that the outcomes of this exercise obviously depend to a large extent on degree of experience, status and also opportunity, taking into account personal as well as professional circumstances. Discussion often highlights teachers' views that their direct responsibility for children's learning – their classroom practice – is the most important of their roles.

Group discussion might explore these questions:

1 Where do conflicts of role and priority occur?
2 Which kinds of role and responsibility take up the most time and energy?
3 Which roles are formal and which have been acquired or assumed? Is there a difference in attitudes towards these?
4 Where do the greatest challenges lie?

This provides time and space for teachers to hear one another's perspectives on their own roles and responsibilities and it may generate ideas about how they might work better together. It can also uncover powerful insights within cross-hierarchical groups (Frost et al., 2000); it is sometimes surprising, for example, that many formal roles have been distributed to teachers with little explanation or definition and scant training or support.

In working towards a focus for enquiry and leadership, teachers need to consider the extent to which there are opportunities for development that they may wish to pursue in their own professional situations. Following an exercise such as the one above, individuals should be able to identify which aspects of their work are concerned with administrative tasks, line management and maintaining quality of classroom practice. This could include, for example, running the school pantomime, being examinations secretary, co-ordinating trips and visits or managing information technology resources. The division is not clear-cut, but there are likely to be other aspects of a teacher's work that are more developmental, such as literacy co-ordinator implementing the Key Stage Three Strategy, induction mentor for newly qualified teachers, study support co-ordinator or director of assessment for learning. The important question is which aspects involve the teacher in managing change. Exercises such as Activity 4.2 below, widely used in leadership programmes, are relevant for all teachers.

Activity 4.2

Maintenance or development?

Consider ten tasks you have carried out in the last week in school. Write them on to cards or sticky notelets. Classify them under the headings of *maintenance* and *development*. It may be helpful to ask the question, 'Did this involve me in leading change?'

1 What insights does this give you into your current role and day-to-day work?

2 Does every teacher have a responsibility for both maintenance and development?

3 To what extent do these tasks contribute to leading improvements in learning?

Individual and shared priorities for development

Reflection such as this, both individually and in groups, should enable teachers to identify their own personal development priorities. Where considering these in relation to school priorities, it is worth checking whether teachers are familiar with objectives and action points in the existing plans to which they are working. Cross referencing has a two-way purpose. It ensures that teachers are contributing to the shared purposes of the school in choosing a focus that fits with the direction of school change already identified. It also provides an opportunity for them to raise issues and concerns that may have been overlooked or are perceived to have too low a priority. Working through steps such as those above with groups of staff, perhaps involving parents, students and support staff, can be a means to the development of a shared vision and development priorities for the school that can be expressed in the school improvement plan.

Seeking coherence: parallel leadership and plate spinning

Headteachers need to look at this from a different perspective. They are responsible for the coherence and synergy of school improvement activity and for the priority that is given to different activities. Interviews with teacher leaders (Frost and Durrant, 2002; 2004) showed that their headteacher's support has a significant effect on the effectiveness and impact of their leadership (see Appendix 4 (www.paulchapmanpublishing.co.uk/resource/durrant.pdf)). Teachers therefore need to be working in parallel (Crowther et al., 2002) with the headteacher and other senior staff. This may require negotiation where there are conflicts between individual and institutional agendas.

When headteachers talk about their responsibility for drawing together different strands of development work within a coherent vision, they invent analogies that are to do with juggling or spinning plates. Can they go ever faster and spin more and more plates? Can they trust members of staff to keep certain plates spinning? Can they risk members of staff spinning new plates? Can they afford to let any plates drop? It is helpful sometimes to think analytically, using frameworks and concepts such as those offered by Hargreaves (2001). He suggests that headteachers should consider the extent to which school improvement activity has high *leverage,* that is maximum potential effect for the amount of energy input. It may be appropriate to encourage teachers to lead change that is likely to have greater leverage. Teachers need to be involved in sharing responsibility by choosing a focus for enquiry and development that will enable them to make a significant difference to students' learning in the context of school priorities.

The grounds for negotiation are not straightforward; the current emphasis on testing in England has forced schools to focus on short-term improvement in student attainment which has led to conclusions that measured improvements are the result of teachers drilling for the tests rather than sustainable improvement in learning. The Chief Inspector of Schools has expressed concern that while some schools are beginning to explore greater flexibility within the curriculum, some are not sufficiently confident to stray from the numeracy and literacy strategies to offer a richer curriculum that meets students' needs. This is eventually counter-productive in that test results plateau short of government targets, while children's 'Excellence and Enjoyment' (DfES, 2004) is overridden by booster classes and mock tests, even in the primary classroom (Slater, 2005). Schools need to develop the confidence to use strategies that have long-term leverage for more profound and sustained impact, such as embedding assessment for learning (Assessment Reform Group, 1999), in the knowledge that these raise standards by improving deeper learning and understanding.

Having negotiated development priorities and consulted the headteacher, teachers wishing to use an enquiry approach to support their leadership of change should be absolutely clear about their focus. It is useful to express this in two ways:

- What are you aiming to change or improve?
- What is your research question?

Some examples of themes are shown in Figure 4.2 below. These include areas of focus for enquiry and development chosen first by a group of newly qualified teachers and then by a group of more experienced teachers.

Each of these points is expressed as a priority for change but could also be expressed as a research question, which can usually be broken down into a series of more specific questions. For example:

Development focus:	Encouraging boys to write creatively
Overall research question:	How can boys' creative writing be encouraged?
Subsidiary questions:	What does creative writing look like?
	What encourages boys to write creatively?
	What hinders their creative writing?
	How does creative writing benefit boys' learning and literacy?
	What teaching strategies can be used to motivate boys to write creatively?

Newly qualified teachers

● Using the outdoor environment as an effective teaching resource
● Using analysis of pupils' learning styles to inform practice
● Encouraging boys to write creatively
● Teaching specific aspects of literacy, in particular reading, in the Foundation Stage
● Developing self-esteem to reach the less-motivated, through a multiple intelligence approach
● Evaluating a more play-centred approach to the curriculum in a Year 1 class
● Developing speech and language for pupils in the Reception class with difficulty in this area.

More experienced teachers

● Implementing the Key Stage Three literacy strategy
● Professional development to embed assessment for learning across the school
● Developing leadership of the history department
● Improving the learning environment in the science classroom
● Improving pastoral support for students as a Head of Year
● Introducing an induction programme for newly qualified teachers
● Improving creativity through learning out of school hours
● Making the best use of circle time in a primary school
● Addressing the spiritual needs of students across the curriculum in a church school
● Improving support for students with special educational needs through design and technology.

Figure 4.2: Examples of focus for enquiry and development

All the areas of focus in Figure 4.2 were derived from teachers' immediate concerns and agendas and all can be negotiated to fit with school development priorities. Most of the above themes are refined to concentrate on one year group, one class or even a few selected students. Teachers need flexibility and guidance as they follow up particular lines of enquiry or if there are unexpected developments or circumstances.

It is teacher leaders' responsibility, guided by mentors, managers, external tutors or critical friends, to ensure that they have chosen an appropriate focus for change and to gain endorsement and active support for their leadership. As they develop their individual agency, they can plan deliberate strategies to raise the profile of their work, seeking support and collaboration from colleagues to move the work forward. While this book concentrates on individual teachers leading change, it is of course possible for teachers to collaborate in leadership and enquiry from the planning stage, through forming a working party or working in an existing team. Even so, this usually needs to be co-ordinated by one person who may act as administrator, chair, overall leader or facilitator for the group.

The following sections explore how to go about leading change through enquiry and how teachers may learn powerfully as researchers and leaders to build greater collective capacity for school change.

Enquiry Section 2
The Art of Case Study

Classrooms and schools are already subjected to scrutiny by observers and inspectors to meet the demands of external and internal accountability. This has value in giving particular points of reference, but if teachers are to be genuinely engaged in processes of improvement, it is essential that they develop a detailed and analytical understanding of their own multi-faceted professional situations. In the long-established traditions of 'reflection in and on action' (Schon, 1983) and the 'teacher as researcher' (Stenhouse, 1975), classrooms and schools need to be investigated systematically by those who know them best. Teachers, head-teachers and others working in schools, through an enquiry approach involving observation, gathering of evidence, reflection and analysis, can open up new ways of seeing, learning to make the familiar strange. This requires discipline, planning and structuring, but the rewards are great, as has been demonstrated through 'learning walks' and 'research lessons' as ways of looking directly at schools and classrooms (NCSL, 2005). Teachers, through identifying and sharing practice, can develop new confidence, while taken-for-granted practice and long-held assumptions are questioned and challenged. Causes for both celebration and concern are brought into the open which provides strong impetus for change.

Practice under scrutiny

Elmore (2004) suggests that while teachers may engage in practice and know it at an intuitive level, their practice is rarely explicitly known and articulated. This is true on an individual level but there may also be 'institutional wallpaper' that needs tearing down (Elmore, 2002). The enormous knowledge that teachers possess is difficult to reflect upon, analyse and share because most of it is tacit (Hargreaves, 1998). However, it is important that practice is made explicit as the basis for the reflection, analysis and collaborative working that provide the foundations for improvement. It often requires considerable encouragement to convince teachers that their everyday work is worthy of analysis and to reassure them that this can be affirming rather than threatening. Through structured support, teachers can not only make their classroom practice explicit but also examine the institutional context. In this section we consider how detailed investigation of practice may open up new understandings for teachers as the basis for improvement.

Case study is the technique of focusing enquiry on an instance and revealing how events come together to create particular outcomes. It is not a method of collecting data but a means of organising and presenting information: it can involve many different forms of data collection, both quantitative and qualitative, as considered in later sections. Themes, topics or key variables may be isolated and discussed but the individual or local situation – the 'case' – is the focus of attention. This situation provides the raw materials for change and is also the context for teachers' development and examination of their leadership of change.

New ways of seeing

Alain de Botton, in his book *The Art of Travel* (de Botton, 2002), takes the reader on an exploration of travel, visiting different parts of the world under the guidance of philosophers, explorers and artists. He encounters the exoticism of Amsterdam with Flaubert and the promised paradise of Barbados with Huysmans, contrasts the city with the countryside in the Lake District with Wordsworth and contemplates the sublime expanses of the Sinai desert through the eyes of Job. The 'travelling spaces' in between are illuminated through the paintings of Hopper. He returns at the end of the book to his London home, where initially he feels despair and indifference to his familiar surroundings, until he begins to apply the new perspectives he has gained:

> … I tried to reverse the process of habituation, to disassociate my surroundings from the uses I had found for them until then. I forced myself to obey a particular mental command: to look around me as though I had never been in this place before. And slowly, my travels began to bear fruit. Under the command to consider everything as of potential interest, objects released latent layers of value. (de Botton, 2002: 251)

Alain de Botton's travelling companions, through their writing, encouraged him to engage in a deeper and richer experience by looking at the world from different perspectives. Thus Ruskin suggests that we learn to see better what is there by observing properly in order to draw. We cannot record something accurately without asking a series of questions. We move from merely noticing something to gaining deeper understanding about its constituent parts. Far from happening automatically, de Botton found that he had to learn new skills and motivation in order to do this:

> Ruskin discussed, with reference to his own illustrations, the difference between the way we usually imagine the branches of trees before we draw them and the way they reveal themselves once we have looked more closely with the help of a pad and pencil: 'The stem does not merely send off a wild branch here and there to take its own way, but all the branches share in one great fountain-like impulse. That is to say … the boughs all carry their minor divisions right out to the bounding curve. And the type of each separate bough is approximating … to the shape of a plant of broccoli'. (de Botton, 2002: 227)

Along with new skills this approach to the accurate examination of detail requires a sense of adventure, a willingness to challenge the status quo and to look for real rather than assumed information. For example, where artists had previously used pastel shades to depict the landscape of Provence, van Gogh accurately used the juxtaposition of opposing colours such as cobalt blue and vibrant yellow, colours that de Botton saw in the real landscape as his eyes were opened by the paintings along with the artist's writing. As a result of careful observation and representation of reality, both Van Gough and his audience came to new understandings.

For groups of teachers, these messages are best conveyed through a practical exercise, as suggested in Activity 4.3 below.

Activity 4.3

Exploring new ways of seeing

These two alternative exercises enable teachers to think about the possibilities of examining their classrooms and professional contexts in new ways.

● Spend ten minutes making a sketch, as accurately as possible, of a branch, flower or leaf that has been brought into the room. Spend the following five minutes writing down what you learnt about the object that you didn't know before. Compare results within a group.

   1 Discuss the implications of examining, recording and analysing what happens from day to day in your classroom.
   2 What are the barriers to such detailed investigation and what might be the benefits?

or:

● Gather a series of pictures of trees, both paintings and photographs. Post them around the room. Move from picture to picture in silence and make notes about the interpretations. When everyone has looked at all the pictures, compare notes.

   1 To what extent do the pictures depend on the subject (the tree), the person (the artist), the interpretation (the painting or photography) and the audience (you)?
   2 How would these pictures look if each artist had depicted the same tree from the same angle at the same time?
   3 What implications does this have for teachers' study of their own schools and classrooms?

It is essential to identify what 'the case' actually is. It may be one class or one school but the reality is often more complex, for example the investigation may incorporate studies of three individual students within one class. Defining the scope of the study sets the necessary parameters that will help to clarify thinking and provide a measure of control, since any investigation within the school setting will uncover infinite connections and links and threaten to make any study unmanageable.

Teachers examining their classroom and organisational practice should consider both elucidation for their own purposes, in order to make individual improvements, and implications for their organisations. Who are the audiences for this investigation, who needs to be involved and who could benefit from what is being learnt?

From description to study

It is important to distinguish at this point between plain description and something that is worthy to be called a 'study'. Although any report or presentation requires selection and interpretation in its construction, it can remain as a narrative at a relatively superficial level unless there is a deliberate attempt to analyse, question and draw out issues and implications. However, a plain narrative is a good place to start and this can be deepened though questioning and discussion around the evidence. The use of analytical frameworks gives structure, for example critical incident analysis or 'change frames' (see Enquiry Section 4). Analysis can be supported by a group of colleagues, through the use of an external critical friend to provide some critical distance and/or with reference to the literature. In planning a case study it is helpful to consider the process by which deeper understandings will be reached and the eventual form the study will take, in order to raise the sights of the investigation from a story to a genuine study.

Hitchcock and Hughes (1989) suggest three main elements that should be included in a case study to ensure that it is analytical:

Discussion
The case study is put into social and political context, including ideas and information from background reading on relevant theories and topics and a consideration of events leading up to the period of detailed study.

Narrative
This gives the actions and viewpoints of the people involved as a rich, vivid and detailed description of events drawing on detailed evidence. It is important that the narrator uses the personal voice rather than trying to achieve a false sense of objectivity in the writing.

Analysis and critical writing
This is written in the light of personal experience as a teacher looks for meanings in a situation. The narrative is accompanied by an interpretation, constructing a debate between events and analysis.

(drawn from Hitchcock and Hughes, 1989)

Improving practice through case study

Starting with narrative, teachers can delve further beneath the surface and into the issues and factors that have influenced particular situations, with ever finer-grained questioning (Elmore, 2004). In contrast with external evaluations, it is important for teachers to work to their own agendas and use their own language to describe their classrooms, schools and activities (Smyth and Shacklock, 1998). The more they are disenfranchised by alien language and imposed agendas, the less likely it is that they will be motivated to change their practice.

Case study can be used at different stages in the change process or can encompass a whole process of change. In the first instance, study of a teacher's professional situation can be used to gather information from which issues and concerns can be identified in order to clarify what needs to be improved. If a focus has already been identified, a case study can be made to investigate current practice and examine the influencing factors and relationships. As changes are made to practice, case study enables the teacher to evaluate various effects upon a complex set of variables. In approaching a case study, it is helpful to distinguish the 'study' from the 'case record' (Stenhouse, 1978), which is the body of evidence from which interpretations will be derived. This enables others to return to the evidence so that the case study can be approached critically by other people and verified.

After a focus has been determined, Activity 4.4 gives guidance that can be used in defining the scope clearly.

Activity 4.4
Planning a case study

Plan the scope of your case study under these headings, then discuss and refine with a colleague, mentor, your headteacher or an external advisor.

1 What is the focus and purpose for your case study?
2 Who should be involved in the planning?
3 Who is directly involved during the gathering of evidence?
4 What is your own role in the situation to be studied?
5 What is the timescale for the study?
6 Who should be consulted or informed?
7 What background reading and investigation of theory would you like to do?
8 How will the details of the study be interpreted and analysed?
9 What is the intended audience for the case study?
10 How will it be reported and presented?

Case study as paradox

The case study approach has achieved respectability more recently, but it is still criticised for its concentration on the particular. How can the ideas and conclusions from one situation be applied more generally? Simons (1996) suggests that the weakness of case study, its uniqueness, is also its strength – 'the paradox of case study'. Both Stenhouse (1985) and Simons (1996) agree that in complex educational situations it is essential to generate in-depth understanding which can only be done through focusing on particular instances.

Simons, like de Botton (2002), finds inspiration in artists' interpretations of nature. She uses Rollo May's description of Cezanne's paintings of trees to illustrate how one person's interpretation of reality can lead us to view related examples in a different way and with greater understanding. By looking at the paintings we are led to a deeper comprehension of the phenomena in question, *through the artist's perspective*. In the same way a teacher's individual perspective through the presentation of a case study can reveal insights and offer interpretations which might otherwise not be evident. More objective research covering a range of instances and seeking comparison has a different role – it aims for a wider perspective through sampling, but the detail and meaning of individual contexts may be sacrificed.

Stenhouse (1985) argues that practitioners are not generally responsible for formulating policy across cases, although he recognises that this element is present in their work. He suggests that they are generally responsible for making sense of their own cases, applying their knowledge and understanding to individual situations. There are generalisations, predictions and tendencies which apply to all cases, but he argues for the need for teachers to develop perceptiveness and gain the ability to read new situations, to revise their interpretations in the light of experience and thus make judgements. The usefulness of a case study depends on its further application. Its greater power may be in prompting teachers to 'ask hard questions about practice' (Elmore, 2002) and providing insights about 'our students', 'our class' and 'our school' as a basis for individual and organisational improvement.

Reporting a case study

Case study research has previously been criticised for its lack of definition and its methodological inadequacy, with a tendency for ethical concerns to override important theoretical and methodological issues (Atkinson and Delamont, 1985). The plethora of 'case study' reports on educational websites bears this out, since they can be limited to short descriptions concluding with a few 'learning points' or 'emerging issues' rather than analysis. Obviously it is important with any form of research to encourage a high level of reflexivity and critical awareness, so that the nature of the work, its limitations and the extent of its applicability are understood. Stenhouse (1975) argued that research should be reported so that it can be subjected to criticism and also made useful to others. This does not necessarily involve formal publication; a group of teacher researchers sharing their experiences and ideas, or the circulation of a discussion brief to colleagues, might give interpretations of particular situations which have been the focus of research. Somekh argues that it is inappropriate to attempt to validate action research findings through scientific or statistical methods; rather we should concentrate first on evaluation through the continuous enquiry process, followed by further validation through

> ... the process of communicating a range of outcomes to other practitioners ... who will make implicit comparisons with their own repertoire of experience and judge the work to be worthwhile or not on this basis. (Somekh, 1995: 341)

Case studies are a key element of the cumulative body of educational knowledge that can and should be used to inform the profession more widely. Atkinson and Delamont (1985) argue that studies need to be developed into more general frameworks, in order to produce cumulative knowledge and give theoretical insight. While it is important for individual teachers to make meaning within their own professional situations through enquiry, reflection and action, Hargreaves (1998) suggests that teachers have a vital role to play in professional knowledge creation. This involves 'tinkering' with ideas and practices, experimenting and refining and then communicating the outcomes so that this kind of knowledge can be applied in other contexts where appropriate. The process can be facilitated through networks and clusters with external agents acting as 'brokers' in the development, adaptation and dissemination of professional knowledge (Frost et al., 2000).

Whitehead (1989) believes that there should be a dialogue between teacher researchers as they live out their own cases. We can study the gradual emergence of our own values and perceptions over time, by describing and explaining the improvement of practice through individual case studies. The dialogue surrounding this process can create what Whitehead calls a 'living theory'. He sets this within the community of practitioner researchers, but such dialogue focused on improving learning might more usefully be considered as the heart of the school improvement process. This can be made explicit through professional debate, correspondence with critical friends, formal and informal publication, groups and networks (Durrant, 2003). Within professional communities, teachers can know their own practice and development and subject it to public scrutiny as the basis for leading change.

Enquiry Section 3
Ethical Enquiry

The guiding principle for all educational research is that it should be conducted with a respect for people, knowledge, democratic values and quality of research (BERA, 2004). For teachers wishing to use evidence and enquiry approaches habitually to support leadership of change, it is important to cultivate an approach in which ethical issues are considered as a matter of course and as part of the ongoing development process.

Raising ethical awareness where research meets practice

While the need for ethical principles is not in the least contestable, for teachers combining research with leadership of change and integrating enquiry with day-to-day practice, the ethical dimension can be complex and can also be overlooked all too easily, for a number of reasons. First, in planning enquiry within a busy professional life there is a tendency to concentrate on the practical details of evidence gathering, at the expense of attending to underlying principles that seem more theoretical. Second, teachers can perceive their research as separate from other forms of educational research and therefore not subject to the same rules and principles. Third, they may simply be unaware of the necessary considerations, perhaps because they do not have sufficient support, training and mentoring in methodology. Finally, it is often difficult to distinguish 'research' and 'teaching' from one another. When is a discussion with students about their learning part of good classroom practice and when does it become research? The boundaries may be impossible to define. Nevertheless, just as there is a strong ethical code of practice for teaching, this needs to be complemented by research ethics where teachers are engaging in any kind of enquiry. It is therefore important to consider this dimension of research carefully at the *planning* stage, since ethical groundwork cannot be done retrospectively.

Each situation and each piece of research is unique and must be considered on their own merits. For this reason it is possible to give guidance but difficult to set rigid rules for establishing an ethical code. It is therefore strongly advisable to work on these issues with an external mentor or advisor who can give support from a more distant and critical perspective and also to check any plans with the headteacher or another senior colleague who has an overview of implications within the school. In practice, deciding the issues that need to be addressed, agreeing an ethical code and negotiating permission should not be too onerous and all this avoids complications later on; it also becomes less daunting with experience. Where awareness has been raised during the planning stage, ethical issues that arise subsequently are more likely to be noticed and dealt with promptly and effectively.

There are five main areas that need attention:

- Consultation and involvement
- Confidentiality and authorisation
- Quality and rigour

- Interpretation and voice
- Authorship and ownership.

The guidance given in this section under each of these headings draws on the British Educational Research Association guidelines (BERA, 2004) with accompanying interpretations for the purposes of school-based research by teachers leading change. A full checklist of questions is to be found in Appendix 6 (www.paulchapmanpublishing.co.uk/resource/durrant.pdf), while specific issues can be followed up in more depth through the methodological literature.

Consultation and involvement

Consultation in its simplest form involves seeking consent from those participating in the research. It is advisable to formalise this even where it involves colleagues and students routinely encountered as part of a teacher's everyday work, because it indicates that a different process and a different relationship are being established. An initial conversation seeking permission where a teacher wishes to interview colleagues can be reinforced with a letter or memo to set out intentions and clarify what is going to happen. With students, similarly, an initial conversation with a class, group or individual might be followed up with something in writing, but this is less straightforward because of the teacher's authority over the students. It is important to consider whether the research is inviting voluntary participation or whether it is considered to be development of practice as part of the normal interactions in teaching and learning, in which case it may offer no choice to students. Involving parents and a wider circle of people in research is perhaps more clear-cut because any data gathering is likely to require establishing processes and encounters that would not normally occur, rather than building on normal relationships and interactions.

It is important to seek permission from carers or parents as well as from young people involved in research. Particular care needs to be taken with investigations that involve young children or people who are especially vulnerable – those who are less able to articulate their concerns, less confident in asking questions and less aware of implications. Parents and colleagues can also be vulnerable and lacking in confidence. It is always advisable to document any agreements or correspondence. Agreements should attend to the points set out in Figure 4.3 and are best set out in writing.

---

1 The purpose of the investigation: what are you trying to find out?
2 The process of the investigation: what will it involve, when will it take place, what are the timescales?
3 What will happen to the information gathered?
4 To what extent do participants have choice and control over the investigation?
5 Is a permission slip appropriate to assure consent from, or on behalf of, participants?

Figure 4.3: Framework for permission agreement

This does sound stringent, especially where it applies to people with whom a teacher researcher may be working every day, but documents can be worded creatively and invitationally, particularly for students. A letter can be presented as an attractive handout, introducing the idea of the 'teacher as learner', 'our investigation' and so on. Wording is crucial with colleagues, for example, 'I am conducting research into assessment … ' may sound more intimidating and less relevant than, 'We are gathering information to develop our assessment policy and practice.' It is helpful to make explicit the links with school development priorities and to invite rather than command participation, for example, 'As part of our school aim to improve the learning environment this year, I am investigating the opinions and ideas of different groups. Please tell me what you think so that your views are taken into account.'

Beyond seeking permission and clarifying purpose, it is helpful to consider the extent to which people will be active participants rather than simply respondents in the investigation. Will they contribute to the research design? Will their agendas be taken into account? To what extent will the process be reciprocal? Such questions should be considered from the outset and built into any initial negotiations and documentation (see also Enquiry Section 5).

Confidentiality and authorisation

When gathering information from members of a school community, it is most important to preserve confidentiality, since colleagues and students may be discussing situations and relationships involving one another. Clear information about what the information will be used for, who will read it, where it will be stored and how it will be analysed and reported should be provided for all participants. Usually, anonymising by changing names and a few details is not sufficient since people know one another and can easily trace the origins of comments and opinions, so reporting may have to be in the form of generalised statements if complete openness is inappropriate.

In some cases there may be reasons for more open sharing of information but this must be voluntary and governed by its own ethical code. Focus groups can be a valuable forum for expressing ideas and developing trustful dialogue, which can then be recorded. In order to ensure that people are comfortable, ground rules should be decided as the group is convened. Agreeing that the discussion remains confidential is a good starting point (and may in itself be sufficient). It may also be appropriate to agree not to name individuals, to concentrate on positive comments rather than critical ones, and to establish that no-one is going to be challenged or criticised for their opinion, the purpose being to understand a range of viewpoints, not to win an argument. It may be helpful to break the ice at a first meeting by facilitating an activity based on Figure 4.4, enabling the group to decide whether rules may be appropriate to govern their own discussion. This is often a sobering activity as participants realise the care that is being taken, reflecting the seriousness of their forthcoming discussion.

In reporting accounts of research and development work, the same issues apply but even greater sensitivity may be needed. It is tempting to tell success stories that

1 Everything we say stays in the room.

2 Name no names.

3 Say only positive things.

4 Do not argue against anyone; ask questions to understand their viewpoint.

5 Everyone must have the opportunity to speak at every meeting.

6 When one person speaks, everyone listens.

7 Everyone is entitled to their opinion.

8 Our common purpose is to …

Figure 4.4: Some possible 'ground rules' for a focus group

show the school and colleagues' work in a good light. More critical analysis of the problematic aspects of situations and stories of struggle are both more authentic and more interesting and valuable for the audience, but present greater difficulties in terms of negotiating permission. Various kinds of writing can be used (active or passive voices, storytelling or more analytical accounts) to convey different messages to a number of audiences and it may well be appropriate to eliminate detail to preserve confidentiality. Any draft publications should be checked with participants, the headteacher and any other interested parties. Debriefing meetings, letters or conversations should be planned so that participants are fully aware of the progress and outcomes of any research process. It is important to ensure that everyone's interests are treated with equal care, including those of students, colleagues and parents. Where research has genuinely been planned to involve participants in change as opposed to simply data collection, this kind of reporting should integrate more easily with the development process (see Enquiry Sections 7 and 8).

In addition, it is worth considering the use of fictional narratives to present typical scenarios, encourage debate and raise sensitive issues. This technique has been used successfully in previous research, for example to stimulate discussion with headteachers about the barriers faced by teachers in leading change (Frost et al., 2000). Discussion was stimulated by presenting several illustrations with an amalgamation of evidence from individual teachers' stories, so that no-one felt threatened or criticised and all could consider how these fictitious teachers could be better supported. A similar strategy could be used to pose teachers' dilemmas in classroom management, convey students' experiences of excellent lessons and so on, so that evidence is presented and issues are discussed without singling out individual people. Participants in this kind of discussion readily use such opportunities to reflect very critically on their own practice, and with care, touches such as eccentric character names can be used to lighten the mood (see Frost and Durrant, 2003).

Quality and rigour

It is important to recognise that within the educational research community there are a variety of research paradigms, preferred methodologies and approaches. Problematic concepts such as data and evidence, reliability and validity, subjectivity and objectivity can be discussed from these different perspectives. All researchers have a responsibility to engage in debate, discussion and critical analysis of ideas and understandings, both from their own particular field and in the context of a broad spectrum of research approaches. This is healthy for the educational research community, enhancing intellectual capital. It also ensures that those who are involved in research, whether as active or passive subjects of the research or part of the context (for example, a class of pupils being taught by a teacher who is the 'subject' of the research), are giving their time and their contributions to something worthwhile that has been subjected to critical scrutiny and has demonstrated a certain degree of rigour in process and interpretation.

This should not be taken to mean that teacher research has to attain a false objectivity – to become something that it is not – more that it needs to be seen for what it *is* and to be as valuable as it can be. Figure 4.5 below suggests some ways of ensuring that quality and criticality are maintained, taking into account the nature and limitations of the school setting.

- Discuss the research process and strategies with external critical friends (university tutor, LEA advisor, colleague who is conducting other research and so on)
- Offer your research plan for discussion within a group of colleagues, showing interest from a professional and/or methodological point of view
- Work on your ideas with a group of students (the syllabus for many school subjects includes issues involved in gathering data)
- Use checklists from the literature to guide planning and design of tools such as surveys and interview schedules
- Pilot strategies and amend accordingly
- Adopt a reflexive approach, which can be aided by writing specifically about methodology.

Figure 4.5: Some strategies for improving the quality and rigour of research

Somekh (1995) suggests that peer scrutiny, far from being a 'soft option', can often be most powerful and exacting. Colleagues can bring their professional understandings and empathies to the discussion and have a vested interest in the quality of the research. Designing a high quality research strategy is not simply an academic exercise, it is about planning rigorous practical processes producing high quality data that accurately represent the situation or phenomena being investigated. Colleagues are often best placed to notice the limitations and loopholes in proposed approaches, since they can envisage the practicalities. They may even have a natural suspicion that requires the teacher researcher to justify fully her chosen approach. Finally, involving colleagues helps to raise awareness of the research and issues that are the subject of the investigation, which paves the way for change.

Interpretation and voice

Every stage of a research process involves a degree of selection and interpretation, providing opportunities for misinterpretation and inaccurate representation of the evidence. This is true for quantitative data as much as for qualitative data; ambiguities, inaccuracies and inappropriate methods can remain hidden within numerical and graphical as well as textual summaries, while all data can lend itself to a range of meanings. Accuracy depends initially on the design and methodology of the data collection. Following this, the processing of data also needs careful planning to ensure that accuracy is retained.

In school-based research, it is important to confront the question of validity, or the accuracy and truth of interpretation. Hammersley helpfully suggests that different types of enquiry require different orientations to the criteria of relevance and validity. He suggests that

> In the case of validity, practitioners should accept what seems beyond reasonable doubt on the basis of their experience, and judge the results of any inquiry on that basis. Often that experience will be personal, and even where it is collective the collectivity will usually be relatively local in character. (Hammersley, 1993: 251)

Hammersley contrasts the practical orientations of practitioner researchers with the aims of researchers concerned with satisfying the scrutiny of the wider, more cosmopolitan educational research community. He concludes that 'researchers and practitioners may well come to different but equally justifiable judgements about what assumptions are and are not beyond reasonable doubt' (p. 251). There is fuel for much debate where the boundaries between research and practice are crossed. It must not be assumed that this is one-sided; although some practitioner research may not stand up to increased methodological scrutiny, there is also a range of quality in wider educational research where teachers would be quick to identify flaws in methodology and argument.

The most effective way of ensuring that the data represents views and situations accurately is to build in checks of validity and interpretation with participants and peers. The use of triangulation, the comparison of sets of data representing different perspectives, should be considered in all research designs. This can reinforce interpretations or highlight differences in viewpoints. There is much to be gained from checking interpretations with respondents, for example by sending them a list of key points from an interview and asking them whether a) it represents what they said or b) they wish to add anything further or change the emphasis. While checking the validity of the research, this can also provide another loop of data gathering, although care must be taken that it does not reinforce bias.

Fielding (2004) has challenged researchers to consider the problems and pitfalls in researching other people's viewpoints. This is discussed in more detail in Enquiry Section 5. In ethical terms, he asserts that it is important to consider whether methodologies enable us to move towards a more engaging, more imaginative, more just, more democratic, different society. Do some approaches too easily reinforce subjugation, placing new interpretations on what has been said through making a series of re-descriptions? Does research aim to control or empower? Is the discussion partial – does it allow people to say what they want to say? To what extent does it rest on assumptions over which respondents have no control? To what extent can people's voices be accurately understood by those working from a different viewpoint, and what are the implications of 'spoilt' or non-responses? Whose voices have been chosen and is this at the expense of others (especially if participation is voluntary)? What would happen if different groups interpreted the data in their own language?

Children, young people and vulnerable adults who are capable of forming their own views should be free to express them in all matters affecting them, commensurate with age and maturity (UN, 1989). This presents an enormous challenge to schools even without an overt research dimension, involving not only protecting children's rights but also taking account of their wishes. It may yet be important to make a start, whilst knowing there is a great deal more that could be achieved in different circumstances (with more time, with a climate of less surveillance or with more enthusiastic support).

Teacher researchers, as actors in the situations they are researching and often in positions of power over respondents, need to be aware of the implications of such questions for their research. If using enquiry to support a managed change process, as we have advocated, the dilemma for the researcher is the extent to which the complex relationship between research and development can be made explicit so that participants in the research understand that they are also involved in change. This leads us to suggest that co-constructive and collaborative approaches that are to do with developing or understanding something together might be more ethically acceptable and strategically powerful than approaching people as respondents in someone else's research.

Authorship, ownership and accountability

One of the most important questions to ask of any research is 'Whose research is it?' Teachers undertaking enquiry as part of their leadership of change should seek to involve and engage other members of the school community, particularly colleagues and students. Teachers may feel that they are working on behalf of their school, focusing their enquiry and leadership on aspects of development that are school priorities. Alternatively, they may be involved in projects or programmes where they are working in partnership with academics or other external researchers and advisors including government and professional agencies. Issues of ownership and accountability are therefore likely to surface.

It is essential to set out an ethical code of practice for any research but particularly important to do this jointly and formally where stakeholders other than the individual teacher might be said to have ownership or sponsorship. This could apply for example where the teacher is part of an LEA sponsored project across a number of schools, is working on doctoral research that links with that of a university supervisor or is supported by a network project co-funded by the school. In order to avoid conflict in such situations, it is helpful to set out roles and responsibilities for the different partners or collaborators right at the start, to clarify any financial arrangements and to decide about how the work is going to be reported. It is also advisable to review this regularly (perhaps annually) since understandings may shift and circumstances alter, particularly where there are individual changes of responsibility.

In most cases this is unproblematic but where issues do arise they can be complex and difficult to resolve. Activity 4.5 below gives two fictional but possible scenarios for discussion.

Activity 4.5
Avoiding ethical problems

The following scenarios could occur where research is taking place in the context of external projects or programmes. Discuss how the situations may have arisen, the extent to which they are problematic and how difficulties could have been avoided by careful planning and negotiation beforehand.

A Some Physical Education teachers worked with the Local Education Authority advisor to develop and evaluate some lesson materials and resources for a new syllabus. This was funded by the LEA to allow them some time out of school for collaborative writing and analysis. They discovered the following year that some of these same materials had been distributed in courses run by the LEA with no reference to their school or individual involvement.

B The headteacher of a primary school was surprised to find that an article critical of the school's assessment policy and practice was published in a local education newsletter, by a teacher on a research-based Masters programme funded by the school. Although it had been anonymised, enough details had been included to enable the school to be identified. This caused embarrassment to the head and angered staff, especially as the teacher concerned had been given responsibility in the previous year for improving assessment.

In reporting research, enquiry and development work, publication on its own is unlikely to make very much impact. Interactive and collaborative dissemination are likely to be much more powerful where teacher researchers draw colleagues into investigating, challenging and changing practice. That said, there are many circumstances where written publication of the outcomes of teachers' enquiry and leadership of change is valuable. This includes compiling portfolios and writing assignments for professional or academic accreditation, sharing ideas and outcomes through a network or school bulletin for colleagues' interest and information, gaining personal satisfaction, confidence and enjoyment from publication beyond the school and contributing knowledge, experience and analysis to the wider discourse. Occasionally there may be a financial incentive; as well as writing books and articles, teachers are sometimes funded to write case studies or reports about their research and development work.

Where writing and publication are appropriate, a careful consideration of *audience* and *purpose* helps to address ethical issues. It may be appropriate to preserve anonymity but this may involve changing details as well as names, since it is usually straightforward to trace an article back to its author. Trying to avoid this by generalising across a number of examples may still allow identification of key messages. However, if the teacher author is serious about effecting change, it should be possible to consider styles and genres of writing that support that process for their own school and for others. Writing that shows the school, colleagues and students in a positive light, working to improve learning and teaching and addressing real issues, can be a great boost to the confidence of the school concerned, while colleagues from other schools may find stories of struggle, small steps in improvement and analysis of issues much more helpful than glittering success stories. Publication, as long as it is handled with care, can be a form of recognition for teachers and their schools, a way of connecting with the wider discourse and acknowledging that what they are doing is worthy of notice and comment.

The uniqueness of ethical dilemmas

While ethical issues can be considered systematically, for example by using Appendix 6 (www.paulchapmanpublishing.co.uk/resource/durrant.pdf), Activity 4.6 below also offers some dilemmas based on real examples that can be used with groups to raise awareness and anticipate the kinds of issues that may arise.

Activity 4.6
Ethical dilemmas

What advice would you give to these teachers who have ethical dilemmas in their school-based research? (Small groups could each consider a different scenario and report back.)

Teacher A

I am the new head of mathematics and am concerned about standards of teaching and assessment in the department. We need to raise attainment and I think staff need to focus more clearly on the quality of learning that goes on in their classrooms and improve formative assessment. I want to conduct interviews with Year 7 pupils about their experiences of teaching and learning in maths.

Teacher B

As a form tutor with pastoral responsibility for a class of 28 Year 10 students (age 15), I am interested in improving the support for one boy who has Asperger's syndrome. I am a history teacher – I have very little time allocated for pastoral matters and I am finding that most is taken up with supporting this one student. I would like to do an in-depth case study to see if I can develop ideas that could help colleagues in similar situations.

Teacher C

I have some strong criticisms of the leadership team in my school, arising from my research into the school's implementation of the National Numeracy Strategy. I have found it helpful to write about it and feel that my research provides insights that should be shared. I have started to write about this in my Masters dissertation but I know that this is a public document that will go into the local university library. How can I write an honest account?

Teacher D

I am going to try a new scheme of work with some of my Year 8 classes and compare their experience and standards of work with the other half of the year group who will continue with the old course. Colleagues have asked me why I am not using the new scheme with all my classes but I am worried that this will invalidate my research as I won't have a control group.

Teacher E

I have been doing some interviews to investigate the ways in which my school sustains continuity of learning during teachers' absence for courses, trips and illness. During one of these interviews, a colleague confessed that for some time he has been bullied by the Head and that this is the reason for his frequent sick leave. What shall I do with this information?

Teachers who consider the ethical issues and implications of their research hold a mirror up to their practice. This can result in profound changes in their professional approach as they examine participation, consultation, the nature of relationships and the motivations and agendas of students, colleagues and others in learning processes. As teachers infuse such thinking into their day-to-day practice, they offer challenges for more respectful relationships and greater justice and equity in their schools.

Enquiry Section 4
Reflecting on Practice

Although reflection seems at face value to be an entirely positive approach to cultivate in teachers, reflective approaches to practice have not always been warmly welcomed. England's former Chief Inspector of Schools was unequivocal in his view.

> Put bluntly, do we want reflective practitioners, or do we want teachers who can teach children to read? (Woodhead, 1998)

The glib answer is, of course, that reflection improves practice, but teachers have to ensure that the process does not become self-indulgent and inward looking, creating a cocoon within which they can make themselves feel more comfortable by manipulating their own thoughts, either consciously or subconsciously. In fact, reflection can be extremely challenging. It might unearth hidden feelings, questions, values and agendas and it usually increases understanding both as a professional and a private individual, in relation to the wider political, social and institutional context within which professional action takes place. This leads McKernan to see reflection and enquiry as essential in supporting the development of teachers' capacity for self-evaluation and self-improvement, a capacity which he sees as ' ... perhaps the most outstanding feature of the professional' (1996: 46). He goes on to discuss the characteristics of the 'extended professional' as previously raised by Stenhouse (1975) (see Chapter 1) which include connecting with the wider discourse, linking theory and practice and adopting an evaluative, enquiry-based approach in the classroom.

Reflective practice to support teacher leadership

If teachers are to develop a leadership dimension to their practice as well as an enquiry approach, the reflective stance becomes even more important. In engaging in research to support their leadership, they have to examine their own roles, behaviour and relationships in their particular social situations (Somekh, 1995). This involves a sophisticated and analytical kind of reflection, where evidence is gathered and used to inform an ever-deepening understanding not only of practice but also of purpose and strategy. Somekh believes that participation in the situation under study makes interpretations, judgements and decisions more complex than they would be for an 'outsider researcher', because feelings, values and subjectivities are involved. Teachers usually have a subconscious awareness of this complexity but it needs to be articulated in order to be fully understood and brought to bear in developing their leadership capacity.

Smyth (1991) contrasts the passive connotations of reflection as deliberation or contemplation with notions of an active and even militant approach leading to changes in practice. While he acknowledges the importance of Schon's ideas (Schon, 1983), he urges that we need to recognise that we operate in a politicised world and should place our reflections within that context rather than turning inwards. He cites Fay who sketches the characteristics of support groups that might offer a collaborative framework for this kind of reflection, characteristics which echo our own experience (Frost et al., 2000; Frost and Durrant, 2003):

> ... groups that are relatively small, relatively egalitarian ... relatively free of recrimination between members, relatively committed to rationally discussing ... members' situations and experiences, and relatively insistent that ... members take responsibility for whatever claims, decisions or actions they undertake to make. (Smyth, 1991: 108)

Smyth draws attention to the potentially subversive nature of such activities, which can bring about 'authentic, liberating change' (Smyth, 1991: 108) as people are supported in breaking out of their current situations through discussion based on rational reflection.

While we might acknowledge that reflection can be a powerful tool in enhancing understanding of our actions within professional situations, it is difficult sometimes on an individual level to know where to begin and how to proceed. All teachers think about their practice, whether in the form of general musings on the way home from school or for the purpose of seeking to influence their future actions (Schon, 1983), but focusing reflections, injecting criticality and challenging oneself in order to effect change requires a disciplined approach and conscious attention to the process itself. Also it is worth noting that teachers and headteachers committed to improving student learning are notoriously self-critical, so support for reflection needs to be carefully structured and thought through, and it has to lead somewhere – it must be linked positively to planning and action.

Reflection as part of systematic enquiry

Many teachers assume that the appropriate starting point for school-based enquiry is a survey by questionnaire or audit to gain an overview from which to generalise about the case in question. Teaching, however, is about relationships and these may not be best examined through the restricted and somewhat artificial structures of a survey sheet. Surveys are also extraneous to practice, being removed from the action and usually requiring respondents to comment on their perceptions of their own experiences in a generalised way. On the other hand, supporting reflection by writing on the blank pages of a 'learning journal' can seem nebulous and ill-defined, quickly becoming superfluous. What is needed is a focus for reflection that is rooted in real situations and has immediacy and relevance. Example 4.1 shows how a structured exercise was used to stimulate reflection within a group through peer support, prior to collaborative enquiry. The example used here involved a group of headteachers but similar activities could be facilitated for teachers or teaching assistants.

Tripp has developed an approach to the investigation of practice and the enhancement of professional judgement through identification and analysis of significant episodes or 'critical incidents'. He writes:

People often ask what a critical incident is and how to recognise one. The answer is, of course, that critical incidents are not 'things' which exist independently of an observer and are awaiting discovery like gold nuggets or desert islands, but like all data, critical incidents are created. Incidents happen but critical incidents are produced by the way we look at a situation: a critical incident is an interpretation of the significance of an event. To take something as a critical incident is a value judgement we make, and the basis of the judgement is the significance we attach to the meaning of the incident. (Tripp, 1993: 8)

Example 4.1

Paired reflection to find shared purposes and priorities

Headteachers were asked to work in pairs to begin reflecting on their leadership roles. They were asked to identify one leadership experience they felt positive about and one that they felt negative about (regardless of the difficulty of the situation or the outward 'success' of their actions). They were then asked to talk to their partners about the leadership issues emerging from the discussion.

This experienced group of school leaders became completely engrossed in the paired discussion for the best part of an hour. Chosen incidents included counselling parents about relationships and social circumstances, working with local councils and businesses, inspiring children in the classroom, finding a missing child, spending frustrating afternoons being diverted from what they saw as their core task, working with staff on planning and professional development, mediating with the church over complex political arrangements for Harvest Festival, managing successful community projects, unblocking drains and overseeing building work.

When they returned to the room, someone asked for the tissues, only half jokingly. Many of the headteachers had not had the opportunity to focus on their own practice like this for a long time. They could have continued with their paired discussions but they were interrupted deliberately so that we could analyse this experience of intense sharing. They concluded that providing space for reflection and sharing had dual roles that at first appeared contradictory. It initially enabled them to acknowledge to one another that everyone was in the same situation in dealing with the relentless ephemera of school life and further allowed them to offer each other some mutual support. Secondly they were able to stand back a little and take stock of what they were doing, to prioritise and question. They concluded that what felt like distractions were often vitally important, for example the hours spent in meetings and on the telephone dealing with child protection issues. They needed to acknowledge this while at the same time keeping their minds set on a clear vision and working strategically towards their schools' shared goals.

By drawing together onto flipcharts the issues emerging from their paired discussion, the group clarified shared purposes and priorities and wrote a group development plan to guide their collaborative enquiry and leadership learning.

Tripp suggests that by focusing their attentions on such incidents in a structured and analytical way, teachers can develop their own 'grounded theory' about aspects of their practice rather than trying to apply academic theory to their experience. This approach could be used to gain awareness of a particular aspect of practice by consciously focusing on it so as to identify and record relevant critical incidents. Alternatively a series of incidents (perhaps written in a journal) could be collected and analysed together to see if patterns emerge, in order to find a focus for action research. This approach relies heavily on individual commitment and could prove very insular, although Tripp does suggest that it can be used collaboratively. It is a powerful technique particularly if reinforced by the processes of action research (data gathering, wider reflection, action and evaluation), in order to develop increased understanding and control over professional judgements. (Pollard (2002a) offers more activities, exercises and frameworks.)

The same idea can be used with groups of teachers as a practice in preparation for further systematic enquiry, with each person choosing a significant incident from classroom practice and using the following summary of Tripp's guidelines (see Activity 4.7 below) in order to analyse in detail and consider the implications. As with the example of the headteachers above this can be done as a paired exercise, but it is equally valuable when used individually. It can be undertaken without preparation if members of the group are given time there and then to write a 'story' about something that has happened in their classroom that day, as the basis for reflection and analysis. Note that ethical issues are extremely important in such work, both in order to protect those who may be the subjects of teachers' stories and because people need a safe and trusting environment in which to put their own practice under scrutiny (see Enquiry Section 3).

Activity 4.7
Critical Incident Analysis

1 Describe an incident from your recent professional experience. It could be something which happened in your classroom, an interchange between yourself and a student or colleague, one moment at a meeting. Choose something interesting, annoying, inspiring, thought-provoking or typical.

2 Suggest an explanation within the immediate context.

3 Ask questions which delve deeper into the meanings behind the incident; for example try different ways of thinking about it; keep asking why; explore your dilemma; consider personal theories and values that would influence judgement.

4 What implications does this have for your future practice?

(from Tripp, 1993)

The power of channelled reflection and analysis is always evident when teachers engage in such direct discussion of their everyday practice. The process is helpful not only in influencing the thinking and actions of the individuals concerned through using their own stories but also, where used in a group, it may raise issues for the schools to consider.

Having built confidence in the technique, critical incident analysis may be introduced as part of a teacher's systematic enquiry, as illustrated in Example 4.2 (see also Skoyles et al., 1998).

Example 4.2

Using critical incident analysis to support improvement

Richard wanted to develop more of a collective commitment to a learning ethos and culture but found himself dealing with a stream of behaviour management issues and having to mediate in incidents between pupils and teachers. He decided to analyse some both typical and remarkable incidents from a single week so that he could look for causes, patterns and common issues in these incidents in order to work out strategies for diverting greater attention to learning.

Gail established a nurture group for a small number of Year 6 (age ll) students likely to be excluded. While she had data on reported behaviour, attendance and achievement, she also wanted to gain greater insight into the experience of the students she was supporting and of the ways that colleagues in her team were dealing with difficult situations and relationships. She used stories of particular incidents to illustrate for colleagues a range of scenarios and how they might be handled in the best interests of students.

While this technique focuses in on incidents that may be very short-lived and disconnected, other analytical frameworks can be used to reflect on the wider picture and upon the processes and purposes of change. Teachers leading change need to be in touch with what is happening in the classrooms and corridors of their schools but they may also need a reflective overview. Fink's (1998) idea of 'Change Frames', provides an excellent strategy whereby teachers can analyse changes in which they are involved. The seven frames offer 'multiple lenses' through which those involved in change and leading change can better ask questions about the challenges they are confronting, as a kind of diagnostic tool. They provide the following dimensions for viewing change:

Purpose: What meanings are given to the change, what is its source, what are its intended outcomes?

Passion: How does the change affect the emotions of the people involved?

Political: How can power be used positively for change?

Structural: Does the use of time, space, roles and responsibilities make sense or does it need to change?

Cultural: How does the change affect the school's 'way of life'?

Learning: What learning will result from the change, for pupils, teachers and others and for the organisation?

Leadership: How does formal and informal leadership promote organisational learning and development?

(from Fink, 1998: 56)

These frames can be used to consider different perspectives on developments that teachers may be involved in or may wish to instigate. These can help them in seeing change from all angles so that they can highlight aspects that may need attention and plan strategically in order to lead change effectively. Use of these frames also aids headteachers in considering every dimension in their overviews of school development and looking at patterns across a range of different initiatives.

Space and time for reflection

Finally, it is worth considering creative ways of providing space for reflection. As long as this is carefully prepared, with a clear purpose, motivated and sympathetic teachers, structure and follow-up, it can be extremely valuable. Activities such as those suggested in Figure 4.6 may be appropriate as part of a programme of support for professional development or as part of a development day. It is important to use these in a spirit of experimentation and when teachers are most likely to be receptive; no-one should be made to feel uncomfortable and care should be taken not to introduce these approaches at inappropriate times. Attempting to contrive a calm and reflective atmosphere during busy and stressful times may be disastrous (for example, reading poetry is probably inappropriate after a pre-inspection planning meeting).

- Play some music as background to a structured activity
- Post pictures, photographs or quotations from children around the walls and walk the group around the room in silence, allowing them to note their thoughts
- Read a poem and follow it by silent reflection and individual writing
- Invite people to go for a walk around the school or around the grounds of an off-site conference
- Ask teachers to draw their own learning journey
- Use thinking games such as 'what would we put in a time capsule to represent this school?'; 'what are your three essential teaching resources?'
- Ask everyone to look at the same piece of writing by a student and note down their thoughts, then compare these.

Figure 4.6: Ideas for stimulating individual and collaborative reflection

McKernan uses some interesting language in his discussion on reflective practice. He includes the terms listed in Activity 4.8 below which can be used by teachers to look back on their own reflective activity and to evaluate its effects on their professional capacity and on the development of their practice.

Activity 4.8
Reflecting on reflective practice

The following benefits have been suggested for teachers engaging in reflective practice. These words and phrases can be distributed on cards or as a list to a group of teachers who have engaged in some reflection as a one-off activity or over an extended period of time. Individuals should rank them in order of importance, rejecting any which do not apply, as an evaluative exercise. Sharing the results of this reflection will help to explore the potential of reflective practice.

- Intellectual health and pleasure
- Joy
- Emancipation
- Changing the world of the school by understanding it
- Enlightenment
- Creative and imaginative potential for enquiry
- Professional autonomy
- Freedom
- Empowerment
- Interest
- Teaching as an 'enquiry-discovery' occupation
- Greater capacity for self-evaluation
- Greater capacity for self-improvement.

(from McKernan, 1996)

The ensuing discussion could focus on a) how more opportunities for reflection and a more reflective culture could be encouraged in school and b) whether there are any disadvantages or threats where teachers adopt a more reflective approach.

Change can only start from where teachers are. Many reforms and externally imposed initiatives ignore this fact. Teachers, by reflecting on the details that they are concerned with from day to day and reviewing processes and perspectives, can both articulate practice and increase their understanding of their own situations and roles. This enables them to expand their current professional practice by using it as a starting point for leadership of change. Subsequently, teachers' experience of development work is enriched through layers of systematic reflection focusing on practice, professional learning, the change process and leadership development.

Enquiry Section 5
Voices for Change

Voice is the key to the involvement of different groups in school improvement. Providing information as a sound basis for change is one justification for building people's ideas and opinions into discussion and decision making. In addition, it raises awareness, demonstrates that people have a stake in change and encourages ownership. Giving voice generates energy and enthusiasm, develops self-confidence and self-efficacy and improves relationships. It values people and helps to transform school cultures. As MacBeath found in his research on self-evaluation

> … 'stakeholders' in schools welcome discussion and clarification of priorities as challenging, empowering and important in the context of their own school's development. [The discussion] was experienced by adults and young people as empowering and words like 'uplifting', 'challenging', 'fun' and 'exciting' were frequently used to describe the process. (MacBeath, 1999: 23)

This is not, then, a sterile exercise in finding out what people think about things but a process of engagement, learning and connection.

A 'pedagogy of voice'

The inclusion agenda in schools and in society is founded upon relational principles of social participation, social integration and power that build human and social capital amongst communities (Ranson, 2000). An inclusive society supports the development of human agency which, as we have argued earlier, involves people having control over their own lives and the ability to help shape the contexts within which they live and work. Voice is not simply about the opportunity to communicate ideas and opinions, it is about having the power to influence change.

Ranson argues that in order to foster learning between a multitude of voices engaged in multi-layered activity, as in schools, there is a need for 'procedures and traditions of conversation and dialogue, translation and negotiation' in order to meet the challenge of reaching '… shared understanding and agreement – a common voice – about the learning process, its purposes, beliefs and activities' (2000: 266). Following Engestrom, he defines the creation of a learning community to include reflexive questioning of the existing community of practice, leading to dialogue so as to transform current practice and *design the future together*. Therefore a 'pedagogy of voice' is needed that enables learners to explore self and identity, develop self-understanding and self-respect and improve agency, capability and potential.

Agency and active participation are crucial in shaping both communities and the processes in which people are engaged. An important attribute is the openness that enables people to develop their understanding of one another, both to challenge and be challenged. They acquire judgement and sensitivity through conversation, leading towards mutual accountability and responsibility for one another's development. Schools need to take account of this argument in supporting teacher leadership, while teachers can use these ideas powerfully in their leadership of change.

Direction and dissonance

Hargreaves and Fullan (1992) point out that there is an important tension between vision and voice in school improvement. Their argument is made in relation to teachers' voice, but resonates more widely. They would argue that while vision is widely agreed to be essential in developing consistency and confidence amongst a community, there are some who would say that the key to teachers' construction and reconstruction of professional purposes and priorities, making the connections between individual and collective growth, is their articulation of voice. Obviously a balance is needed, since

> A world of voice without vision is a world reduced to chaotic babble, where all voices are valid and there is no means to arbitrate between them, reconcile them or draw them together. This is … a world from which community and authority have disappeared. It is a world where the authority of voice has supplanted the voice of authority to an excessive degree. (Hargreaves and Fullan, 1992: 5)

Yet schools are still, by and large, hierarchical institutions where powerful, high status voices prevail and the balance is set to favour vision. There is limited time for meetings and conversations, which tends to push the agenda towards task-orientated activities and maintenance rather than discussion and development. Both these tendencies encourage contrived collegiality and purpose (Hargreaves, 1994). Given the amount of business that has to be covered it may be tempting to allow ideas and proposals only a brief airing amongst staff before going ahead with pre-determined plans or making minor adjustments. There is also the danger that contradictory voices will be unhelpful and divert schools from the path determined by the headteacher, senior staff or governors. However, it has been argued that the critique afforded by dissenting voices is essential in shaping plans and testing the validity of ideas for change. While a sense of direction and cohesion is essential, this can result in a warm congeniality which can be expressed in over-optimism, blandness, lack of incisive leadership and unreasonable risk-taking. Criticism, argument and disagreement, when positively focused, generate new ideas, challenge cultures and test rationales and strategies for change.

It is clear that if dialogue is avoided then this is a missed opportunity. It robs teachers of the chance to participate in decision-making processes and therefore they cannot contribute their ideas, experiences and critical perspectives – their 'practical judgement and wisdom' (Hargreaves and Fullan, 1993: 6). It also prevents pupils from contributing their views as 'expert witnesses' (Rudduck and Flutter, 2000) in learning and teaching. Without the contribution from different voices it is impossible to aspire to any kind of shared vision. Without shared vision, it is more difficult to engage members of the school community in improvement processes and they are unlikely to assume ownership of change.

For teachers leading change, there are two main aspects to consider. Firstly, how can teacher leaders use an enquiry approach to their leadership of change in order to balance their vision against the voices of those involved in, or affected by, the change? Secondly, how can teacher leaders make their own voices heard in school improvement processes, participating in the development of a community of practice that enables everyone to contribute and learn together.

Student voice: purpose and potential

The case for student involvement in school-based enquiry and school improvement has been made powerfully elsewhere (Rudduck and Flutter, 2004; Fielding, 2004). A particularly accessible set of resources has been developed through the 'Consulting Pupils about Teaching and Learning' project funded by the Economic and Social Research Council's Teaching and Learning Research Programme (MacBeath et al., 2003; Fielding and Bragg, 2003; Arnot et al., 2004; ESRC, 2005). These provide not only a rationale but ideas, illustrations and formats that can be used with students and to build teachers' confidence in the value of student participation. Fielding and Bragg (2003) point out that it is children's right to participate in activities and decision making in matters affecting them and to have their views heard (UN, 1989).

In schools, this can involve

- Active learning methods involving enquiry
- Involvement in adult-led research to provide a distinctive youth perspective, for example by designing language and formats to reach young people whose views might otherwise be hidden
- Research directed by young people themselves encouraging democratic participation and personal growth.

(Fielding and Bragg, 2003)

This reflects policy development in England that encourages young people's perspectives through the OfSTED framework and DfES guidelines (DfES, 2005c). As Fielding and Bragg note, this has its roots in the long-established traditions of reflective practice and 'teacher-as-researcher' (Elliott, 1991; Schon, 1983; Stenhouse, 1975). They conclude from their research that through active participation, students acquire skills, become engaged as active and lifelong learners and contribute valuably to school improvement processes. All this has positive effects on relationships, changes personal and professional identities and can bridge between childhood and adulthood (Fielding and Bragg, 2003).

A 'ladder of participation' has been used by teachers involved in the Consulting Pupils project (ESRC, 2001) to analyse and challenge the extent to which pupils are involved in research and development work. According to this framework, handing out pre-prepared questionnaires to students in order to gain their views or experiences of learning is only the first rung on the ladder, since students are merely respondents to an imposed agenda, their voices are structured into a given format and they may have no control over the analysis and interpretation.

Questionnaires like this can be enormously valuable in providing information upon which teachers might act and are a useful first step, but they are used with disturbing frequency – the default option for school-based enquiry – and their impact in generating dialogue and informing change is questionable if used uncritically and with minimal planning. Ascending the ladder involves pupils participating actively in decision making initiated and interpreted by teachers at stage 2, while at stage 3 they have an active role in enquiry and decision making as researchers themselves. At the final stage, pupils are co-researchers with teachers, setting agendas, planning interventions and evaluating impact (ESRC, 2001).

Why should students carry out research?

Traditionally students have been portrayed as lacking in sufficient maturity, insight or experience to have anything useful to say about school improvement. Rudduck and Flutter (2000) point out that children are not learning to become members of society, they are *already* members of society, and as such we should put in place structures that enable their legitimate voices to be heard. As well as looking at where these voices may be heard, and thinking critically about them, we need to find new opportunities for 'dialogic encounters'. This is educative for both researchers and the researched; it includes 'double description' and 'double consciousness' as each embraces understanding of the other and those people involved may change in ways unconnected with the research. Some commentators go further (for example, Fielding, 2001; 2004) and suggest that pupils' sense of agency and commitment to learning can be improved if they are not only encouraged to give their views about schooling, but also encouraged to gather, analyse and present evidence to support those views, entering into a dialogue with the school about future directions. The National College for School Leadership has encouraged this across all their networks, leading in some networks of schools to vibrant discussion underpinning improvement in learning and teaching relationships and student's self-belief and self-efficacy (NCSL, 2005).

MacBeath, Sutherland and their colleagues have shown that there are few limits to student participation other than those imposed by our own closed minds. Their ongoing project where students from all over the world evaluate schools and classrooms involves these students in sophisticated data gathering, analysis, interpretation and feedback which, as well as offering a rich student perspective, is a life-changing experience for the students (Learning School, 2005: 6). The students participate as equals, and indeed as leaders, in the international school improvement discourse (MacBeath, Sugimini et al., 2003; Learning School, 2005).

One of the authors has piloted student research as an AS level Sociology teacher, as illustrated in Example 4.3 below. Here, a relatively small-scale and manageable project has had an impact not only in identifying issues and putting forward recommendations for improvement, but also in making a move towards a more open school culture in which students' views and agendas are given credence in school improvement processes and their research is taken seriously rather than viewed tokenistically.

Example 4.3

Students as researchers: a pilot project

When I moved to a new school in September 2001, an opportunity arose to introduce my AS level Sociology students to the techniques and methods of qualitative research by encouraging them to carry out empirical enquiry into aspects of sixth form (post-16) provision at the school. This enabled them both to fulfil the demands of their syllabus and to help address an important element of the school development plan.

The students split into four groups and, following a presentation about the purpose and potential for the research led by a colleague from the university, participated in a workshop where they began to identify issues and devise action plans for enquiry.

The topics chosen were:

- How do sixth formers use their study periods?
- How could provision for independent learning be improved?
- How effective is the current system of 'release' in promoting good study habits?
- How effective do students find post-16 guidance arrangements in the school?

In order to gather their evidence, the students used semi-structured interviews and questionnaires and devised a variety of strategies to analyse the resulting data.

Each group then prepared a five-minute presentation in which they identified their research question, outlined their methodology, presented their findings and made recommendations for future improvements. The presentations were given to an audience made up of the headteacher, the head of sixth form and the assistant head of sixth form. The members of staff took the students' findings very seriously, and more work will take place this summer to incorporate some of their perceptions into plans for next year. The fact that their views were supported by evidence made these more credible. In their evaluations, the students all felt that they had made important progress and contributed to school change.

Next year, I intend to involve the student representatives on the school council more fully. I propose to train a further group of sixth formers in simple research methodology. Then, having administered a school self-evaluation survey to the members of the school council, we will use the data to agree on a small number of issues to pursue further, inviting the sixth formers to become lead researchers, with school council members acting as research assistants.

Sometimes it is helpful to involve an external researcher in gathering evidence from student voices on behalf of teachers and their schools. This serves to build initial confidence in the value of student voice and to give the evidence gathering more time and attention than might be possible if teachers were trying to do this themselves. Although it is no substitute for dialogue between teachers and their students about learning, it may be the start of such a dialogue, as shown in Example

3.6 in Chapter 3 where a head of Mathematics developed a week-long 'conversation' with an external critical friend whilst gathering a range of evidence in relation to learning and teaching. Describing this experience as '… the best INSET [professional development] I've ever had in my life,' she noted amongst other benefits that she

> … spent a day this week talking to students as a direct result of what [the reviewer] said. It's become what we do on a regular basis … They were remarkably forthcoming. You have started something, we'll carry it on now … (Durrant et al., 2004: 164).

Talking to students has become a priority for her department to the extent that teachers now build it into their everyday practice. A further example (Example 4.4) shows the power of the external researcher when acting as a catalyst:

Example 4.4

The external researcher as catalyst

A secondary school wanted to carry out a review of its sixth form (16-19) provision and employed an external team from a university to carry out observations, look at a range of evidence and talk to staff and students in order to support the school's self-review. The team comprised an experienced inspector, an academic specialising in 16-19 provision and a head of sixth form from another school. As the team began to gather evidence over several visits, it was soon obvious that students had a great deal to say. Reviewers were taken with the high degree of pupils' engagement. One said: 'they were full of stuff … kept collaring me'.

At this school the pupils were invited to lunch with the reviewer from the university and gave a passionate 'Powerpoint' presentation in which they compared the promise of the sixth form brochure with their own experiences and perceptions. Action points were derived from this, typed up by the reviewer and put up on the sixth form noticeboard. Through observations and further conversation, the visitor was able to state with confidence 'I knew those students' understandings about what it was they were supposed to be learning,' and was therefore able to feed this back in a report to the whole school staff.

However it was noted that interpretation was not straightforward, for example it was felt that 'the cleverer pupils were more critical.' Any data gathering involving survey tools was treated with caution, recognising that weighted responses and box ticking need to be analysed with understanding supported by dialogue. One reviewer commented, 'Tick boxes don't tell the truth. *Pupils* tell the truth.'

Some reviewers felt that training was needed in how to hear and communicate student voices; these skills must not be taken for granted amongst teachers. Teachers sometimes expressed anxiety about what students might say and clearly there are ethical issues around any dialogue of this kind in which the interests of both staff and pupils need to be protected.

(Durrant et al., 2004)

Other voices

Whilst pupil voices are increasingly part of the school improvement dialogue, it is interesting to consider the extent to which other voices and wider participation are encouraged. The 'ladder of participation' could equally be applied to teachers, teaching assistants, other support staff, parents and so on, in terms of the extent to which they are participants, decision makers and evaluators within school-based enquiry and development processes, school self-evaluation and school improvement planning. MacBeath (1999) makes the case for school self-evaluation in which schools are able to 'speak for themselves', offering a wide range of tools and strategies to support this. An interesting feature of MacBeath's work is the focus on analysis through gathering different perspectives and setting them against each other to note similarities and differences in values and priorities. For his project team, the research highlighted that there was marked agreement about core values and purposes between parents', pupils' and teachers' perspectives and that differences tended to be of degree and emphasis. Importantly, MacBeath places learning at the centre of his philosophy, learning that is enhanced through mediation by other people and that 'is social and emotional in origin and thrives in a supportive, gregarious climate' (MacBeath, 1999: 105). By inviting and engaging a discourse of many voices, learning about learning takes place through vibrant dialogue.

There is no reason to suppose that *full* involvement of *everyone* at *every* stage is the most effective approach, since this depends on people's circumstances, knowledge and stake in the process, and also on time and resources, but in planning enquiry and development processes it is helpful to map involvement and to be explicit about why different groups and individuals are participating in different ways.

Teachers – forgotten voices?

Despite the recent emphasis on pupil voice, there has not necessarily been a corresponding movement towards greater participation in school improvement dialogue by teachers and other members of staff. Yet it is important that schools listen to teachers' voices. Recent research involving interviews with teachers aged 45 or more (Kelly, 2005) shows the value of asking experienced teachers for their ideas and opinions. This research found, unsurprisingly, that they derived satisfaction where their schools valued career flexibility and professional development. However, it also revealed that experienced teachers relished the opportunity to 'spread their professional wings' through good links with the community, including working with families and other schools.

These teachers wanted their experience to be valued and respected and their voices to be heard; they wanted to be trusted, not over-directed. There was a general feeling that attention tends to be given to those in early career at the expense of looking after long-term career development. The teachers gave examples of how they have opportunities to use their expertise and extend their professional learning and influence, showing that while they might not think of themselves as leaders, they do in fact exercise leadership – supporting colleagues, creating and sharing professional knowledge and making complex connections within schools, between schools and in local communities. Voices are not necessarily heard most effectively through data gathering and discussion activities. Teacher leaders' voices may have enormous impact in conversations, relationships and day-to-day ways of working, with an emphasis on developing practice, supporting one another's professional learning and leading change, as shown in Figure 4.7 below.

Within school by:

- Mentoring, training and supporting colleagues and support staff
- Swapping classes to deploy expertise
- Fostering innovation and risk taking
- Maintaining an organisational culture in which people have their assumptions challenged
- Devolving responsibility
- Allowing time for school-based research (for example, by sabbaticals from pastoral work)
- Having involvement in voluntary working groups

Beyond school by:

- Liaising with families, including long-term relationships with local families
- Working with multidisciplinary agencies
- Supporting teachers in other schools and working on collaborative projects
- Tutoring in initial teacher education
- Offering consultancy to local businesses
- Creating international links

(drawn from Kelly, 2005)

Figure 4.7: How can schools recognise, encourage and value experienced teachers?

However, despite this wealth of experience the research also showed that teachers can feel marginalised and their voices can be stifled even as highly skilled professionals. One teacher explained why she responded to an open invitation to take part in the research:

> I wanted the voice of an older, more experienced teacher to be heard. Sometimes it's only the loudest voices that are heard. (Kelly, 2005: 12)

Another said

> No-one gives you a platform on which to speak about the research or other work you have done – say in teaching English as a foreign language. But you can bring these things to bear in the classroom, if you're allowed to get on with it. (Kelly, 2005: 12)

Comparing this with the experience and professionalism represented in Figure 4.7 gives considerable cause for concern. If these teachers, confident in the action of their own professionalism, do not feel they are listened to then how can schools gain the benefit of that experience? Furthermore, what breadth of experience and different understandings and perspectives could be contributed by the parent governor, the experienced teaching assistant, the newly qualified teacher or the playground supervisor? Clearly, even where schools are providing opportunities and support for teacher leadership, there may still be considerable potential and scope for developing a true and inclusive pedagogy of voice.

Voices across the school boundaries

Increasingly, schools are involved in multi-agency working. It is intended that Extended Schools in England will provide 'a range of activities and services, often beyond the school day, to help meet the needs of [their] pupils, their families and the wider community' (DfES, 2005c). Key principles of current DfES policy include the following:

> Greater personalisation and choice, with the wishes and needs of children's services, parents and learners centre-stage.

and

> Partnerships with parents, employers, volunteers and voluntary organisations to maximise the life chances of children, young people and adults. (DfES, 2005c)

Such policy emphasis makes it imperative that enquiry and development find a space for dialogue, providing opportunities for an intermeshing of different disciplines and therefore of languages of profession and practice as well as experience (see Ranson, 2000). An enquiry approach that values every voice is all the more essential here in contributing to a dialogue that seeks to illuminate issues and dilemmas and to cross barriers of language, experience and understanding. Discrete research projects should take place in the context of continued discussion through which roles, relationships and identities can be continually reconstructed. The foundation for collaborative working is a developing understanding of the values and perspectives of different groups and individuals.

Teachers, headteachers and other education professionals involved in leading change are extremely well placed to identify issues and areas worthy of exploration and also to learn from multidisciplinary enquiry. As well as giving voice to different groups and individuals and enabling them to learn from each other, this allows teacher leaders to explore their own roles within complex networks. In this way, insider enquiry complements external evaluation in order to provide accurate representations and interpretations of a complex reality.

Some cautionary thoughts

Fielding (2004) has challenged researchers to consider the problems and pitfalls which are inherent in other people's viewpoints. He points out that while there is a continued increase in 'student voice initiatives', the theoretical aspect has not been discussed widely. If it is seen as a 'fad' then expectations will be unrealistic and the integrity of the work will be compromised, as it eventually becomes marginalised and overtaken by other fashions and agendas. If students are invited to voice their opinions without coherent planning or a deeper belief in the value and purpose of the process, then they

> will soon tire of the increasing number of invitations a) to express a view on matters they do not think are important; b) framed in language they find restrictive, alienating or patronizing; and c) that seldom result in actions or dialogue that affects the quality of their lives. (Fielding, 2004: 306–7)

This is essentially an ethical dilemma: do the methodologies we advocate enable us to move towards greater democracy, creativity and justice?

There are many caveats in research and development work which involves making voices heard. Amongst many others, Fielding (2004) suggests that if the incorporation of student voice is to be transformative, it needs to 'rupture the ordinary' – to change what it means to be a teacher and what it means to be a student. He suggests a series of problems or questions that might be applied by teachers who involve students in research and development work. These are set out in Figure 4.8 as a checklist to apply in the planning stages and as the work progresses. These concerns do not apply only to pupils; the circumstances and power relationships may suggest they are most important in that regard.

---

1 Can people say what they want to say, or is what they want to say saturated with the values and assumptions of those who are structuring questions and reporting responses?

2 Are the voices we seek to represent reported accurately? Do we understand them sufficiently?

3 Are the circumstances sufficiently taken into account? Meanings and interpretations are dependent on who says what and to whom.

4 Are there some voices we wish to hear and others we do not? Are we listening to comments that make immediate sense and disregarding those that don't? What do we do with spoilt returns? What would happen if students interpreted the data?

5 Do participants understand the political, social and moral climate within which the dialogue is taking place? Will they feel badly let down if their ideas are not taken up?

6 Is there unwitting disempowerment as voices are put into one place such as a questionnaire, and therefore considered as heard? Does this prevent activism in other places?

(drawn from Fielding, 2004)

Figure 4.8: Some challenges to those making voices heard

By adopting an inclusive approach to improvement in which all those involved are invited to shape agendas and contribute their authentic experiences and perspectives, schools ensure that mutual learning happens through dialogue around change. Teacher leaders are often the most influential in this process, working directly with students and parents and developing trustful relationships with various stakeholders through an unremitting focus on improving student learning. Schools and the wider educational community, in turn, need to provide opportunities for teachers' leadership to be recognised in this respect and to make teachers' voices heard.

Enquiry Section 6
Exploring Stories, Selves and Identities

If school improvement is to involve the whole school community as leaders and learners, schools need to be especially sensitive to, and affirmative of, individuals making meaning within their own professional situations. This is important both because individuals need to be valued and supported in their growth and learning and because leadership of change requires a high degree of 'situational understanding' (Elliott, 1993b), which is about more than understanding the context within which we live and work; it is also about roles and relationships within that context. It depends on individuals' identities as seen by others and as understood by themselves. An enquiry approach helps teachers to draw out people's stories and their implications along with understanding of themselves as leaders of change.

Struggling selves

Somekh and Thaler (1997) believe that we need to look at the concept of multiple, overlapping selves and identities if we want to understand the complexity of roles and relationships in organisations. This might include, for example, the actor or problem solver (the 'I'), the way others see us and we see ourselves (the 'me') and an identity derived from the culture and norms of the group (the 'generalised other') (Somekh and Thaler, 1997). We engage all three together to develop a true or complete self, constructing and reconstructing continually through 'reading and writing ... talking, teaching and living' (Somekh and Thaler, 1997: 144). Inevitably, as we enact our 'multiple selves', we experience role conflicts and uncertainties and these may cross the boundaries between our professional and personal selves as well as between different aspects of our professional identities.

To a teacher leader adopting an enquiry approach, the image of multiple selves is both comforting and disturbing to confront. Somekh describes the self as

> a ... fragile concept, made up of multiple selves who respond differently to different people in different situations. These multiple selves hold conflicting values and beliefs and speak different languages in the sense of employing different discourses dependent upon context and relationships – yet they are wrapped up in a single body, in tension with one another, sometimes in strife like cats in a bag. (Somekh, 1995: 348)

Acknowledging these tensions and, most importantly, working *with* them are helpful in determining directions, making decisions and forging professional and personal relationships for effective leadership of learning. The lessons learnt from such enquiry can stay with us, as Example 4.5 suggests.

Example 4.5

Exploring 'multiple selves' in reflective writing

I felt uncomfortable that I was a teacher distancing myself from classroom practice, a researcher with negligible experience, an action researcher still seeking definition of the practice I sought to improve. I have learnt that reflecting upon these and other dilemmas is part of my stance as a researcher – that I can now abandon the 'mission to explain' in favour of a journey of exploration. I reject the 'solemn obligation to keep intact the purity of the singular self' (Haraway, 1991, in MacLure, 1996: 284) and instead value insights drawn from multiple perspectives within complex situations. Yet through my narrative, I have shown how the 'self undergoes change but … remains in some essential sense, "itself"' (MacLure, 1996: 275). I do not need to resolve conflicts and contradictions, since inhabiting the 'boundary zone' is enriching, inspiring and empowering.

(Durrant, 1997: 88–9)

Teachers' research and professional action are superimposed onto a fast-changing mosaic of local, regional and national policy. Excellent and ambitious new teachers follow a 'fast track', while leadership is distributed into cross-curricular roles such as co-ordinators of literacy, assessment and out of school hours learning, as well as heads of subject and those with pastoral responsibility. Teachers may have high levels of responsibility with multiple and continually changing roles, even in very early career.

This can be most marked in highly challenging schools, where promotion is used as a strategy for retention. Space to make sense of these extremely complex professional contexts and to reflect on one's work-life balance and well-being is a necessity, not a luxury, both where teachers have limited experience upon which to draw and where they have more experience, including headship. This can help them to explore the tensions and conflicts between maintaining and developing excellent classroom practice, keeping abreast of day-to-day management tasks, assuming responsibility for curriculum development, attending to pastoral issues and connecting with different initiatives, networks and the wider community.

Beyond 'technical' reflection

Day et al. suggest that

> teachers' work in many countries is increasingly being directed by closely monitored government policy initiatives, suggesting that only 'technical' reflection – a relatively simple form of practice evaluation – is necessary. (2000: 174)

Their own research concludes that school leaders must develop the capacity to reflect more widely, beyond the instrumental, about their own and others' beliefs, values and practices, about the position and progress of their schools in relation to policy contexts and also about school conditions. Day et al. (2000) conclude from their research that recognition of the power of the heart and the development of emotional intelligence are crucial for effective leadership, a theme followed up in Day's later writing:

> Teachers with a passion for teaching are driven by hope rather than optimism. They are hard working, practical people who know their craft and like their pupils. They are sustained as active learners by their own sense of moral purposes to do the best they can under all circumstances, and by the sense of common purposes shared with colleagues ... They understand that teaching is emotional as well as intellectual and practical work. They are not heroes and heroines but they are heroic. (Day, 2004: 177)

This resonates with Hargreaves and colleagues' recent research on teaching as 'emotional work' and on the importance of the affective dimensions of change (Hargreaves et al., 2001). Day et al. (2000) consider the development of the self through the interaction of technical, practical and emancipatory reflection to be as essential a characteristic of leadership as the development of capacity building in others. For teachers, the first stage is often an acknowledgement of the emotional dimension and social complexity of their work through sharing experience, which provokes feelings of relief, and sometimes surprise, when shared for the first time: relief that other people are experiencing similar pressures and conflicts, and surprise that it is considered valuable to be given 'permission' to talk about their everyday lives in this way. Activity 4.9 is a powerful initial exercise.

Activity 4.9

Exploring professional identity

Read the above passage from Day (2004), or another suitable passage expressing the nature of a teacher's work, and reflect individually on the questions. Share thoughts first in pairs, then choose thoughts to share with the group.

1 With which part of this do you identify most strongly?
2 What do you find most challenging in this statement?
3 Is there any part of it that you would like to reject?

This exercise is valuable in supporting individuals' reflection as part of their development as teachers and leaders. It also serves to explore common purpose and the ensuing discussion will give a strong indication of the nature of teachers' professional development needs.

This kind of exercise may seem to teachers, at first glance, to be indulgent and individualistic, but an opportunity to reflect in this way and the valuing of what they say are the beginning of a deeper dialogue in which people's stories emerge and unfold over time. As Lambert (in Sergiovanni, 2000) suggests, stories provide us with a sense of purpose and direction, with anchors that help us with questions of identity and with ways to make sense of our lives and create meaning. Schools that are good at helping members construct meaning and craft common purposes are likely to be highly skilled in building capacity and developing broad participation among members. Lambert makes the powerful claim that this combination promotes learning and encourages acceptance of a collective responsibility for the success of the school.

It is therefore important to allow opportunities not only for appraisal of professional development related to targets framed by accountability requirements, but also for a more profound consideration of roles and relationships to revisit the values and purposes that brought teachers into the profession and to rearticulate these as they evolve over time. Much has been written about these incentives and values which, as we have noted before, can generally be reduced down to the notion of wanting to 'make a difference' to children's lives (for example Fullan, 1993). This gives teaching its commitment and passion.

Handy (1997) coins the term 'proper selfishness' to describe the importance of the search for identity – who we are and what we stand for. He links this to self-respect and then to responsibility, arguing that in order to control our own lives and destinies, we need to shift our view of life towards self-expression of our talents and beliefs, balancing concern for society with attention to personal growth, self-fulfilment, sensibility and the quality of our own and other people's lives. This 'proper selfishness' spreads beyond oneself, involving our innate sense of justice and morality. It is not entirely rational; it involves listening to our emotions and our instincts, aspects which for teachers in the busyness of school life can become buried, tacit, acknowledged only informally or when there is a crisis.

Rekindling the passion

Day asserts that sometimes experienced teachers, while still working very hard on the core acts of teaching, may lose 'the levels of enthusiasm, emotional and intellectual commitment necessary for achieving excellence' (Day, 2004: 160). The following were found to be sources of satisfaction for primary teachers: sense of competence, pleasure in children's progress, working with colleagues, intellectual satisfaction, continuing personal challenge, variety and feeling in control. Physical and emotional exhaustion, lack of control over work, poor working conditions and stress were sources of dissatisfaction (Nias, 1989, in Day, 2004: 161). While it is obviously important to work to remove teachers' sources of dissatisfaction, this cannot substitute for emphasis on the satisfying factors. Schools need to do both.

In order to re-energise a passion for teaching, Day suggests that we need:

- An understanding of self and an ability to be reflective
- Empathetic leadership

- Openness and collegiality among staff
- Professional learning and development opportunities integral to the progress of individuals as well as organisations.

None of these are possible without providing a safe and trusting forum and sensitive facilitation of individual reflection, collaborative working, talking and sharing, planning and review in order to connect individual with organisational development. Many schools require a radical shift in priorities in order to make time genuinely available; valuing such activity takes courage in a climate of performativity and short-term targets. Yet where students are encouraged to develop thinking skills, self-knowledge and assessment for learning, teachers need support for their learning too, to take them beyond training for implementation, beyond 'technical reflection', to engage in journeys of developing understanding of self, role and identity. This is powerful in support of teachers' self-confidence and self-efficacy both in classroom practice and in leading change.

Stories of enquiry, learning and change

Storying, as suggested above, is an important dimension of the school-based enquiry that supports leadership of change. Research is often expressed as a journey and narratives of change serve many purposes; they enable individual professional and personal learning, structure analysis chronologically, provide a way of capturing the many complex factors involved in development work and offer 'ways in' for others seeking to understand 'what it felt like' as well as 'what I did'. Moving from a plain narrative or description to a critical or analytical narrative is part of the research process in itself. Example 4.6 expresses the importance of a narrative approach for the teacher researcher.

Obviously not all teachers will analyse their use of narrative like this, but any teacher may share these benefits. Stories may be used to identify issues for further investigation (as in the critical incidents in Enquiry Section 4), to explore work in progress and for summative reflection. The basic story can be deepened and structured to look for meanings and insights in relation to the instance in question and those that may be transferable to other themes and contexts. Sometimes it is difficult for teachers to know where to start, therefore this may need expert and sensitive facilitation. Teachers may also need to be convinced of the value of telling and writing if there is no explicit requirement such as an assignment for accreditation. Individual or paired reflective exercises such as the ones described in Example 4.1 (p. 85) build initial confidence because listening gives value to the story. It is worth progressing from talking to writing, since more consideration and care is usually involved in committing thoughts to paper or screen and documented thoughts can be returned to. Use of imagery or prompts may be helpful, as in Figure 4.9 below.

Writing unlocks many possibilities but whether on a staff development activity, engaging in a school study group or participating in a Masters programme, it is important not to be constrained by the tyranny of perceived academic conven-

Example 4.6
Reflecting on the value of narrative in teacher research

In adopting a narrative method I have to recognise the complexity of my subject matter, which is in essence my self. My roles and responsibilities have undergone considerable change over the past three years and my story is one of conflict and attempted reconciliation between my personal focus and different aspects of my professional life …

I have found that it is only through *telling* my story that I have become aware of its importance; my experiences and interpretations provide rich information for the research … As Pope recognizes,

> The telling of and reflection on an autobiographic narrative … can be emancipatory in the sense that the telling of the story liberates an understanding of its power. (Pope, 1993: 25)

Pope demonstrates a further importance of the narrative approach, in that through expressing tacit knowledge there is an opportunity for critical appraisal (Pope, 1993), for example the biases and assumptions underlying interpretations might be challenged more readily through articulating the narrative and exposing it to scrutiny by those less directly involved. The 'evaluative, argumentative or explanatory component' of narrative (Kelchtermans, 1993: 214) lifts it beyond the level of 'just a story' into the realms of criticality. In addition, the narrative gives the author agency since it is written selectively (Diamond, 1991). The writing of a critical narrative is a research method in itself.

(Durrant, 1997: 10–12)

My classroom is a …

I am on a journey …

I hate …

It is wonderful when …

Dear class,

Figure 4.9: Prompts for reflective writing

tions. Many teachers may not have done any creative writing since their own schooldays and may need considerable encouragement to build confidence and sensitivity as they make themselves vulnerable. Bolton describes the intensity of experience that fictional reflective writing can create, as people work on their drafts to filter experience, respond to their own thoughts and clarify their understanding:

> One practitioner likened it to a long refreshing swim, another to a deeply dreaming sleep. I remember overhearing someone whisper

'disgusting' as she wrote, hunched over her page. She was so deeply *there* – where she was writing about – we had all disappeared from her consciousness. (Bolton, 2001: 135)

The development of inspiring work in reflective practice (see for example Moon, 1999) including 'patchwork writing' (Winter, 2003) has enabled people to experiment and to develop different writing forms, which could include poetry, fictional analogy and word pictures. Although these are valuable in their own right, some higher education institutions have developed flexible assessment frameworks; portfolios accompanied by critical commentary are standard both here and for wider professional recognition (Field, 2003; DfES, 2005a) and more creative and innovative approaches can be accommodated where teachers seek further qualifications.

'Passionate enquiry'

Dadds (1993) argues that it is impossible to separate teachers' thinking from their beliefs, feelings, attitudes, values, beings and sense of self. In the 'passionate enquiry' in which they engage, teachers need to develop the skills of developing understanding and awareness of this and to build it into their inter-

Activity 4.10
The importance of the 'I' in teacher-led enquiry supporting leadership of change

Teachers can use this set of statements to explore the implications of their involvement in the situations they are investigating and seeking to change. This can provide a framework for paired discussion or verbal or written analysis. It might be organised as a SWOT analysis (exploring strengths, weaknesses, opportunities, threats, using a simple 2×2 grid).

1 Teachers and headteachers are key players in the situations that they are investigating. This must be taken into account in planning methodology and writing accounts of enquiry and development.

2 Leadership, teaching, learning and research need to take account of the 'affective' (feelings, emotions and so on) because they are all about people and relationships.

3 Each person has a wealth of 'situational understanding' that helps in interpreting data and analysing the complex contexts of classrooms and schools.

4 Acknowledging the 'I' enables reflection and personal professional learning, leading to greater understanding of self and professional identity.

5 Reflection and analysis of personal role and action in processes of change enables personal professional learning leading to greater efficacy in other situations.

6 A greater understanding and articulation of our selves and our roles can help to reconcile the tensions between individual and institutional priorities and concerns.

pretations and analysis; research involves the personal. Recognition of this is vital so that teachers can problematise their research, to consider its context, validity, political and ethical implications and the values and beliefs underpinning it. A structure for systematic consideration of these factors by teachers engaging in enquiry and leading change is given in Activity 4.10.

In any school-based enquiry, teacher and researcher are inseparable, as are the personal and professional selves, since it depends on the researcher, the researched and the context for the investigation (Shacklock and Smyth, 1998). This is all the more important where enquiry is overtly used to support leadership of change, since it becomes part of the fabric of an institution. Where this is encouraged as part of the organisational culture, a 'research-engaged school' can become a tangle of people, processes, evidence and analysis from which very little coherence or change emerges. Where individuals are engaged in dialogue with a sense of common purpose and professional action to pursue linked agendas for change, the threads of individual effort can begin to be woven into a tapestry with a discernable pattern. The headteacher's role is crucial in drawing this activity together to achieve coherence and synergy (Frost and Durrant, 2004).

Writing, while valuable for the individual, can also be an equally valuable means of sharing and building confidence in schools and networks in order to develop this pattern and purpose, as the following example shows.

Example 4.7

Sharing accounts of practice, enquiry and leadership of change: **The Enquirer**

The Enquirer journal (CANTARNET, 2005; Frost et al., 2000) has for 25 editions over eight years published teachers' accounts of their research and development work in progress. It has an archive of hundreds of articles by teachers on the themes and processes of school development, teacher leadership and school-based enquiry. It emphasises the belief that what teachers are doing is worth sharing, whilst exposing the ragged edges of school improvement and charting a course through the often confusing waters of professional development and school improvement policy. Teachers' authentic stories and voices have been captured in a simple photocopied format and published on the network website in a way that is impossible through publications with less academic freedom and more marketing constraints.

Attempts to formalise this publication with an editorial board and glossier presentation have met with resistance from teachers. The journal is recognised for what it is within trustful relationships between schools and higher education facilitators, and perversely its lack of finesse and polish give it greater credence, ownership and practical value amongst readers, who are also its contributors. Some schools are thinking of launching similar internal journals, not as information bulletins but to provide a forum for sharing developments in progress, professional learning and invitations into developmental discussions and collaborative work.

Some schools are experimenting with websites but these depend on the development of a culture in which teachers make time to access them. However, writing a short paragraph is not onerous and can be done in a teacher's own time and emailed so that publication is a simple task of compiling into a pre-designed format and photocopying. It does take time but more than this, it requires encouragement. It is an investment in raising the level of professional dialogue, making connections and building confidence in teachers' practice and leadership.

Stories to tell and how to tell them

If activity and orientation of discussion around the stories or 'lifeworlds' (Sergiovanni, 2000) of teachers and other members of a school community are essential in building leadership capacity then it is worth considering the extent to which there are opportunities for *everyone's* stories, views and experiences to surface and be shared in the day-to-day life of a school. Aspiring headteachers and those who are new in post have opportunities to explore their developing roles, values and identities, with training, mentoring and expert facilitation, but equally do headteachers with long experience have a chance to tell their stories, and what messages might these hold for schools and society? Are children's voices only heard through the constraints of the limited channels and opportunities offered to them, or are their authentic experiences, values and concerns part of the picture? What are parents' stories of schooling, are they relevant, and if so, who is listening? Do governors have stories to tell? Activity 4.11 could follow on from the more individually focused Activity 4.10, or could be a separate activity as part of a development day or team meeting.

Activity 4.11
Building capacity through sharing of stories

Discuss these questions and the implications for your school.

1 How does the school create opportunities for people to tell their own stories? Who listens?
2 What is 'building capacity' and how does storytelling help?
3 Who matters in all this? Who might get left out?

There are provisos attached to the use of discussion and writing to explore identity, describe professional journeys, illuminate experiences and account for the self in research. The importance of ethical care must be stressed, in discussion, in offering critical friendship and listening to accounts of practice and in reporting and writing (see Enquiry Section 3). Conducting research and supporting personal and professional learning through narrative involves developing individual analytical perspectives on people, situations and relationships and then in some way making this public. If this is to be of benefit and to enhance leadership of change then it must be constructed so as to contribute positively to understanding, avoiding unwitting damage to relationships and trust.

This kind of activity must also have a clear purpose that feeds back into enquiry and development. It is important to ensure that issues and emotions are not exposed in discussion and then left in mid-air with no process or follow-up. By using frameworks such as those in Figure 3.1 (page 35), reflection and narrative act as threads that can run through a supported process of leadership of change, from clarification of values and concerns to evaluative reflection. Peer coaching and mentoring also involve listening to each other's stories in a structured and focused way.

The research and experience upon which this section draws have important implications for schools and for teachers leading change, as shown in Figure 4.10 below.

- Schools need to take note of the stories of all members of a school community in order to discover hidden talent, energy and creativity. It may be worth paying particular attention to those who are often silent, who might say 'I'm just a teacher'; this requires considerable encouragement and the creation of special opportunities for discussion and sharing.

- In telling their stories, people gain confidence and feel that they have something valuable to say. Telling your story builds personal capacity. Listening to each other's stories builds interpersonal capacity. The interweaving of these stories is part of the social capital which provides a foundation for sustainable improvement.

- Teachers leading change may be in a strong position to provide encouragement and support for dialogue, in both formal and informal situations, particularly through collaborative working within teams and in their immediate spheres of influence.

- Teachers should be aware of the power of telling their own stories, in different forms and to different audiences, to support their leadership of change. Modelling and empathy, revealing dilemmas and vulnerabilities, sharing experiences and problems, may be extremely effective alongside directing, monitoring and evaluating.

- Recounting and reflecting on experiences to enhance understanding of self is a crucial part of leadership development.

Figure 4.10: The importance of stories and dialogue in school improvement

As West (2004) points out, we need to understand the pressure of dominant agendas in the telling of stories. These influence our views about which stories matter; where, how and why they are told; who listens and in what way. Teacher leaders can consider how they might communicate with others to support their own learning through narratives, while they might also have an important role in making other people's voices heard. In addition, schools must consider how learners tell their stories and how these fit not only into the school context but also into whole lives.

Enquiry Section 7
Gathering and Using Evidence

Teachers draw on information, ideas and evidence from a range of different sources in order to inform their professional knowledge and practice. This section explores some of the issues in gathering and using evidence, which can be used alongside the many excellent methodological texts available. Here, we discuss what constitutes evidence and how teachers and headteachers might use it to direct and evaluate change and improve individual and organisational knowledge and self-knowledge. In this discussion it is important to free schools to take a broader view than that imposed by external accountability demands, but it is helpful to start with the notion of evaluation as this is something in which all schools are already engaged.

Learning through enquiry

The English inspection regime of the 1990s has been widely criticised for its judgemental approach and punitive effect on schools. Learmonth (2000) summarises conclusions from research at the end of the decade that point to the inflexibility of the process, to the lack of consistency and reliability in methodology and to the weakness of links between inspection and school improvement. He argues that as the image and process of inspection sharpened and hardened, the subtleties of teaching, learning and school improvement and the creativity and 'artistry' of teaching were in danger of being trivialised and undermined. Recently, the harshness of the inspection process has begun to mellow and schools are becoming more confident in learning how to harness the process to serve their own purposes, supported by designated school improvement partners (DfES, 2004a). David Hargreaves notes the 'resuscitation' of self-assessment to complement the broad-brush assessments of OfSTED that 'rarely catch the fine detail' (2003: 45). Schools are required to undergo self-review, gathering evidence for self-evaluation to inform the inspection process, moving in Alvik's terms from 'parallel' (often disconnected) evaluation to 'sequential' evaluation (in Learmonth, 2000). Evaluation forms can be used by headteachers to determine the extent to which they and their staff know their own schools. This is mirrored by processes of individual self-review (see for example DfES, 2005a).

Andy Hargreaves (2003) emphasises that a continuous process of learning is needed in order to develop speed, cleverness, creativity and innovation for progress in the 'knowledge society'. Teachers need to gain new *instrumental* knowledge about how learning takes place, much of which they can acquire by accessing wider educational and social research. There are many excellent texts, digests and internet resources available for this (for example see CUREE, 2005; GTCE, 2005b; Pollard, 2002b). They also need a high degree of school and individual *self*-knowledge and the ability to adopt a critical and questioning approach, as promoted by school self-evaluation, mentoring and coaching. This enables them to develop innovative and flexible approaches to change as the basis for finding a sustainable way to move forwards (Bentley in D. Hargreaves, 2003; A. Hargreaves, 2003). This kind of knowledge is predominantly context specific, dependent on the interrelationships between people; it therefore needs to be generated in situ and allowed to evolve as relationships and dynamics change.

The importance of learning *through* enquiry as well as learning *from* enquiry cannot be over-estimated. This kind of knowledge is not easily transferred; it is a 'living theory' in which teachers and headteachers, in the best traditions of action research, are both researchers and researched, actors and evaluators (Somekh, 1995; Dadds, 1993; Whitehead, 1989). Clarke points out that the complexity and uncertainty of such activity are also its strengths in seeking to represent something as ambiguous as a school; members of a school community are participants aiming for 'emerging, uncertain, more holistic comprehension' (Clarke, 2000: 5–6, after Claxton, 1997), interpreting through the wisdom of local knowledge. Thus knowledge shared, built and made explicit need not be used in a mechanistic way but becomes part of an organic and inclusive process, growing as the school grows, to build organisational capacity for improvement. Inevitably, this is more likely to involve predominantly qualitative evidence gathering and the kind of discursive approaches discussed in previous sections, alongside quantitative methods that offer a different kind of perspective.

Enquiry to support teacher leadership

Teachers' engagement with evidence is vital because this supports their capacity to exercise leadership (Crowther et al., 2002; Katzenmeyer and Moller, 2001; Durrant, 2003; Frost and Durrant, 2003; Frost and Harris, 2003). As Bascia and Hargreaves argue

> It is about time that teachers were pulled back from the sharp edge of change and moved towards its leading edge – intellectually, emotionally and politically. (Bascia and Hargreaves, 2000: 20)

If teachers are to be involved in setting agendas and pursuing strategies for change, this should be supported by valid evidence to give them the power of argument and to provide opportunities for engagement. Through research both as teachers and as leaders, they can develop their agency as well as their action.

Elliott (1998) notes that while an external academic facilitator may help to provide the discourse conditions under which 'discursive self-awareness' can begin to develop, as shown in many of the illustrations in Chapter 3, ultimately the responsibility for change and the legitimacy of that change rest with the teachers themselves. Simons writes powerfully of an 'educative and emancipatory' role for evaluation, linking evaluation with action to facilitate 'reflective agency at all levels of the system' (MacDonald, cited in Simons, 1987: 53–4). Cordingley et al. (2003) in their review of collaborative professional development found that processes which encourage, extend and structure professional dialogue are most effective in terms of positive learning outcomes for students.

Teaching and learning can be improved through school-based and practice-focused learning in which teachers have an element of choice, building on their existing professional expertise and offering peer support. All these processes of professional learning are most powerful and most focused for teachers when overtly based upon evidence, particularly where it concerns their own students.

Where mutual suspicion can become rife as schools are forced into competition or are trapped into cycles of low performance according to external indicators, it is important to cultivate attitudes within these communities that enable dialogue where risk can occur without penalty (Clarke, 2000), but where there is sufficient challenge, direction and support to enable teachers and headteachers to develop new knowledge and act upon it, built on sound evidence, not supposition. This requires the balancing of both training and professional learning and support that Andy Hargreaves suggests is appropriate for strong professional learning communities, where 'information is turned into knowledge through shared learning and improvement' (2003: 183). These communities operate through teamwork, enquiry and continuous learning. Hargreaves contends that

> their success depends on continuing support from outside the school, compatibility with external reform imperatives, strong support in terms of instructional materials and leadership, and a staff with sufficient levels of knowledge, competence and skill to share with colleagues. (A. Hargreaves, 2003: 186)

Through parallel leadership and the encouragement of teacher enquiry, leadership and voice (Frost and Durrant, 2003; 2004; Crowther et al., 2002), schools even in the most challenging circumstances could aspire to become

> self-critical communities within high walls – groups who risk enough in collective self-reflection to be spared the added risk of continuous exposure to outside observation. (MacDonald, 1978, in Simons, 1987: 243).

We would argue that external perspectives afforded by outside observation are necessary, but are most helpful where they provide an additional source of evidence and while power and motivation for change arise from within. This kind of learning does not offer a quick fix and, while obviously requiring effective and appropriate external support, also relies on certain levels of motivation and expertise within the school. This work may aspire to the process described by Elliott, where changes of practice and linked systemic change involve a restructuring of individuals' 'practical consciousness' through reconstruction of their knowledge by using discourse about practice and its effects (Elliott, 1998: 188). School is acknowledged as 'a place of relationships, connections and contexts understood through practice, principles and spirit' (Clarke, 2000: 10) where teachers can develop instrumental knowledge and self-knowledge for improvement through enquiry to support their professional action. So how do teacher leaders undertake appropriate gathering and use of evidence in the impossibly complex environment of a school?

Strategic planning for enquiry

After finding a focus and establishing enquiry questions and intentions for change (see Enquiry Section 1), a systematic approach to teacher research or school-based enquiry demands a clear action plan that includes explanation of the ways in which evidence will be collected, processed, analysed, interpreted and reported (Frost et al., 2000). This provides the necessary structure within which more fluid, dialogic processes, as described above, can occur. It is extremely difficult for busy teachers focused on change to make this planning a priority, however it is necessary not only to achieve a high quality of method-ological process with due regard to validity and ethical principles, but also to ensure that the process is manageable and effective in supporting school improvement. This is not to say that the whole enquiry can be mapped out in detail since there may be unexpected developments or changes in circumstance and context and there are likely to be outcomes that are not envisaged. Nevertheless, detailed strategic planning enables teachers and their schools to ensure that, where time, opportunities and resources are in short supply, evidence gathering and interpretation are valuable and realistic rather than spurious, misplaced or over-ambitious.

What kind of evidence?

There is already a wealth of evidence available in schools that can be used to inform change. Often this evidence is statistical information such as pupil performance data which may be accessible, but is seldom used for internal enquiry, having been used for other purposes. There may also be information that has not been used simply because it has not been recognised as evidence, for example students' work and teachers' assessments. Yet gathering a group of teachers around students' work and discussing this evidence and its implications is one of the most powerful ways of engaging teachers in discussion about learning. Simple strategies are often the most effective.

The enquiry strategies that are usually considered first by teacher researchers are interviews and questionnaires. Observations may already be taking place so these may also prove easier to build into teachers' thinking than additional, specially constructed methods.

Questionnaires tend to be the 'first resort' in many investigations. They can yield data from whole groups or samples. The information can be more easily processed if closed questions, boxes and categories are used. Questionnaires can be useful to raise issues, gain an overview and provide factual information; MacBeath (2003b) likens them to 'tin openers' since they are more of a starting point than a finishing line in research. They are less useful for finding out detailed information and investigating the more 'affective' aspects – feelings, opinions, perceptions and preferences. If using questionnaires it is therefore important to recognize their limitations, although there are some extremely sophisticated tools based on the survey format that can be more revealing and valuable for more detailed analysis (see for example MacBeath, 1999; 2003a; 2003b). It is all too easy to type out a quick list of questions without proper consideration for the kind of information required and the conditions within which the survey is administered, but where there is opportunity for people's views to be sought, this should be taken seriously to make the most of their time as there are no second chances. Following detailed planning, for example using checklists such as those in Bell (1999) and Wilkinson and Birmingham (2003), it is helpful to pilot or at least gain some feedback on a draft before embarking on a full survey.

Interviews can take many forms, from the very formal and structured to the more conversational, as discussed fully in other methodological texts (see for example Altrichter et al., 1993; Bell, 1999; Wilkinson and Birmingham, 2003). The number of interviews a teacher researcher can carry out is limited and they yield large amounts of data to be sorted and analysed. However, the interview is one way to explore issues in depth, often with a small number of 'key informants'. Group interviews can involve more people within the same timescale. It is important to think carefully about how to record the interview data and about the ways in which the relationships between those involved affect the process. Ethical considerations are particularly important in planning and conducting interviews to ensure that people's interests are protected and confidentiality is respected (see Enquiry Section 3). As with questionnaires, it is easy for busy teacher researchers to list some questions quickly before embarking upon a series of interviews, but in order to make the most of people's time and to use the research opportunity to the full, careful preparation is needed including some methodological reading.

Observation enables teachers to gather detailed evidence about what actually happens in the classroom, as opposed to deriving evidence for this through the secondary sources of interviews and questionnaires. Again, this needs careful planning to ensure that observations are structured and focused. The purposes of the observation must be clear to all those involved, especially as observations are also used for inspection, internal review and professional mentoring. Since there is likely to be expertise in observation within the school, for example trained mentors for newly qualified and student teachers, these people can provide critical friendship for other teachers who wish to conduct observations. Planning, with the use of supporting literature (see for example Montgomery, 2002; Wragg, 1994) can include design of proformas and record sheets to set the agenda for observation and to enable the outcomes to be negotiated and noted down. It is important to allow a time and place for a follow-up discussion between observer and observed as this is likely to yield rich additional information and to enable both individuals to discuss implications and ways forward.

These familiar methods of gathering evidence are not necessarily the best. While they may be entirely appropriate, some of the most fruitful, powerful and creative pieces of teacher research use innovative methods for evidence gathering: annotated photographs, drawings by staff, student emails, 'graffiti walls', card sort exercises, journals and so on. Whether tried and tested or more unusual methods are used, teacher leaders may decide to carry these out themselves or to involve others (colleagues, students, governors, an external researcher) in gathering information and evidence. This has the advantage that this person is probably less directly involved in the situation and can therefore be more dispassionate and elicit more accurate responses. However, it may be the case that the opposite is true, that students and teachers will talk to a trusted teacher or mentor with a visible role and purpose more readily than responding to a stranger or someone with less perceived authority.

Given this range of strategies available it is essential that time is allowed for planning and discussion before deciding which methods to adopt. A teacher research group, considering the evidence available to them and the additional evidence they might gather to support their enquiry-based development work, derived the following lists (Figure 4.11).

Evidence that already exists	Additional ways of collecting evidence
● Pupil performance data	● Records of discussion – notes, tapes, flipcharts
● Minutes of meetings	● Observations in class, in playground and so on
● Specifications (say from manufacturers making claims for equipment and materials)	● Photographs annotated by different groups
● Baseline data	● Observations of tutorial/mentoring work and follow-up conversations
● Policies and other documentation	● Observations and conversations in other schools
● Children's work	● Video or audio recordings (digital cameras and camcorders can be used by students to present their own perspectives)
● Other people's evidence – the web, reading, journals, conferences and so on	● Interviews – parents, pupils, teachers …
● Marking and assessment	● Classroom journals or research diaries – paper, computer, Dictaphone …
● School self-evaluation data	● People's reflections expressed verbally, in writing (poetry, story, analogy and factual) and in pictures or diagrams
● Professional development documentation (performance management summaries, notes from workshops, courses, mentoring)	● Conversations – recorded as notes
	● Critical incidents (analysis based on incident log)
	● Questionnaires, audits and surveys
	● Email and discussion board correspondence

Figure 4.11: Types of evidence in school-based enquiry

When embarking upon leadership of enquiry-based development work, it is helpful to follow a format such as the one below (Figure 4.12)to plan for evidence gathering, which can be completed individually but is best used in a workshop situation to allow peer support for reflection, discussion and planning and to allow appropriate time for the activity. It is also worthwhile if critical friends who have expertise within the school or external advisors or tutors can be involved in discussing draft plans to ensure that they are realistic and appropriate for the focus and timescale of the investigation.

Information needed	Type of evidence to be collected	From where/ from whom/by whom	How evidence will be recorded	How evidence will be processed and analysed	Dates and timescales

Figure 4.12: Planning evidence gathering

When planning evidence gathering, the opportunities for collaborative working and integrating with everyday classroom practice and school life should be seized wherever possible, as discussed in Enquiry Section 8. Once a draft plan has been constructed, the design of the enquiry should be refined to ensure that it is fit for purpose, is achievable within the context of a teacher's everyday practice without disrupting teaching and learning and is part of a *managed change strategy* (Frost et al., 2000). It is then important to raise methodological awareness and reflexivity in order to make sure that the investigation is rigorous and ethical (see Appendix 6 (www.paul chapmanpublishing.co.uk/resource/durrant.pdf). An exercise such as that outlined in Activity 4.12 can be used to explore methodological issues in a less threatening and more engaging way than by handing out reading material or making a presentation.

Activity 4.12
What counts as evidence

This exercise is for teachers who have identified their development priorities and focus for enquiry and are ready to think about gathering evidence. It can be applied to a draft plan for enquiry as in Figure 4.12 above.

- In small groups, make lists of existing evidence that may be helpful and any additional evidence that could be collected. Make a definitive list for the whole group on a flipchart. (This could then be compared with the list in Figure 4.11.)
- Open up discussion while compiling the list, about what counts as evidence.
- Distribute cards on which are printed words that raise methodological issues such as: validity, reliability, bias, qualitative data, quantitative data, objectivity, subjectivity, ethics, sample, triangulation. Ask each person to attempt a definition of their word or words. Depending on the group's understanding, some prompt material may be provided such as a reading, picture or cartoon. During feedback, the meaning of the words should become clear.

- Hand out the cards again in a different order and ask participants to offer to the whole group an explanation of their term in relation to their own situation and enquiry dilemmas.

- Each person should then be in a position to revise their draft plan according to what they have learnt.

  The facilitator of this exercise needs to be sufficiently familiar with these terms to be able to explain them clearly in relation to teacher enquiry. A background knowledge of the wider context for educational research is helpful and methodological texts can be used to explore aspects of particular interest to members of the group, depending on the nature of their enquiries. People will need further discussion of issues as they subsequently emerge.

Use of this evidence and the gathering of new evidence can become part of the strategy for change by adopting approaches such as those discussed in Enquiry Section 8, where different groups engage with data and work collaboratively to pursue development priorities. There are many creative, interesting and enjoyable ways to use evidence and teacher leaders should be confident in applying their judgement and pedagogical skills and expertise in supporting adult learning. Exercises such as workshops to discuss obstacles and opportunities for change and different leadership strategies that teacher leaders can employ (Frost and Durrant, 2003) are helpful to place the discussion of evidence in the context of school improvement and to maintain a clear focus on different aspects of learning.

Powerful enquiry

It is vital that teachers engaged in enquiry-based development work and leading change have appropriate support. Workshop scenarios or one-to-one critical friendship (preferably a combination of both) are most appropriate for this kind of work (Frost et al., 2000; Frost and Durrant, 2003). Whether this is arranged internally or through external arrangements and partnerships, the value of this should not be underestimated. Although enquiry can be set in motion on a development day or one-day course, it is ongoing support that ensures that teachers sustain momentum and that they not only have opportunities to discuss their dilemmas and problems but also have encouragement and someone interested in their progress. Comments from teachers leading enquiry-based change demonstrate the importance of the headteacher's role and the school culture; teachers' leadership and effective use of evidence founders where the context is unsupportive or indifferent (Frost and Durrant, 2002; 2004; see also Appendix 4 (www.paulchapmanpublishing.co.uk/resource/durrant.pdf)). By showing interest, giving the enquiry a high profile and offering discussion opportunities, time and resources, the impact is likely to be greater and teachers better motivated, as well as practically supported in sustaining their enquiry and development work.

Teacher leaders should be encouraged to develop the confidence to design a methodology that is most appropriate in order to find out the necessary information and to support and engage people in the change process. The quality and rigour of the process are achieved by justifying the methods and strategies used through adopting a critical perspective throughout. A checklist such as that in Figure 4.13 can be used at different stages of the enquiry, challenging teachers to ensure that evidence gathering is fully planned, justified and fit for purpose. Questions can be adapted depending on the circumstances, to emphasise different stages of the enquiry process or to highlight particular issues. Again, a discussion in a workshop or tutorial/mentoring situation is likely to be more helpful than using this for individual reflection, enabling peer support in context and allowing teachers to compare each other's ideas and processes.

---

1 Can you justify your enquiry in school improvement terms?

2 Can you justify the processes and techniques you have planned to gather data, analyse, interpret and apply it? Are they fit for your purposes?

3 Will your enquiry fit reasonably into your own practice and does it avoid disrupting other people's learning and teaching?

4 Does your enquiry rely on several sources of data? If so, how do they relate? If not, what are the implications of this?

5 Is your enquiry ethically sound – have you considered consent, confidentiality, power relationships?

6 To what extent will you be able to provide evidence to support your argument for change?

7 How is the nature of the evidence and its interpretation affected by your own involvement?

8 How will you ensure that your conclusions are valid (an accurate interpretation of what you are investigating)? Are they reliable (applicable in different circumstances)? To what extent is it important that they are valid and reliable?

9 Where are the planned audiences for your enquiry and leadership of change? Who needs to be involved or informed? How will you communicate with them?

Figure 4.13: Challenges for enquiry to support school improvement

Teachers have previously suggested how to introduce the gathering and use of evidence into school-based development work (Frost and Durrant, 2002), as shown in Figure 4.14 below. More detailed 'principles of procedure' (see Frost et al., 2000) can be negotiated by individual teachers to suit their particular context.

● Build data gathering into the development process at the planning stage

● Agree criteria against which to assess the efficacy of any changes being made

● Involve other people (researcher, advisor, senior manager as mentor and so on)

● Develop a system to collect and organise evidence (portfolio, log, database)

● Plan regular reporting and discussion to prompt analysis and interpretation.

Figure 4.14: Integrating enquiry with everyday practice

At the start of this chapter, we suggested an aspiration to raise the level of professional dialogue in schools and to develop situational understanding and reflective agency amongst teachers working towards a more holistic comprehension of their practice and its context. Schools that learn to work with evidence can become more effective self-critical learning communities; if enquiry is an engine for change then it is evidence that fuels the fire. Teachers working with evidence are confronted with the direct questions and challenges that motivate them to make improvements. The starting point is often to engage people more fully in the strategies that are already being used for school and individual self-evaluation as shown in the examples in Chapter 3. Headteachers and teacher leaders working in parallel can use evidence formatively and powerfully to build capacity for change throughout the system.

Enquiry Section 8
Impact through Interaction

School improvement is effective if it is enquiry-based, not only because evidence is used to determine the nature and direction of change but also, crucially, because enquiry provides a vehicle for managing change and developing the organisational culture:

> It has the potential to empower people by enabling voices to be heard, perspectives to be articulated and proposals to be debated.
> (Frost et al., 2000: 49)

This view of school change places particular importance on the interactions and relationships between different stakeholders and on the value and power of professional discourse. However, even where circumstances in schools allow and funding and practical support are available, teachers are often reluctant to take time away from their classes. They therefore need to find ways of integrating this with their normal work, adopting an enquiry stance to their leadership of change and basing collaborative activities around evidence from the school context.

New ways of working together

This is easier said than done; teachers need to develop a repertoire of approaches and techniques to embed these into their practice and that of their schools, teams and departments. Success in this respect largely depends on initial confidence in breaking the mould to try new ways of working, different patterns and structures of meetings and interactions. There is often considerable risk in trying out new activities with colleagues, particularly in well-established groups, but encouraging discussion, consultation and debate around evidence can enliven meetings and improve relationships, which helps to involve and engage colleagues in the change process.

The following are two illustrations (Examples 4.8 and 4.9) where heads of subject departments in secondary schools have begun to adopt a more creative approach to the development of assessment strategies, simply through using their meeting time in a different way.

Example 4.8

Using 'de Bono's hats' to develop new assessment policy

Dave is head of mathematics in a comprehensive school. Although his department were happy to accept his leadership and he was confident in decision making, his reading about school improvement suggested strongly that a more collaborative approach would be beneficial in his management of change. His priority for develop-

---

ment within the department, as highlighted by self-evaluation, was student assessment. Staff were prepared to spend hours on marking but Dave's reading had suggested that this has limited effect. Having already carved out part of each department meeting for discussion and development of practice (as opposed to administration), Dave decided to use a technique that he had encountered on a training day – 'de Bono's Hats' – at one of the meetings.

This technique involves using six 'thinking hats' to structure discussion and include all perspectives (de Bono, 1986). The hats, symbolically chosen to indicate different roles and also because hats can be taken on and off easily, represent different viewpoints. A black hat emphasises difficulties and problems; yellow is for positive points and benefits; red involves feelings, intuition and emotions; green indicates new ideas; white is about information and a blue hat is for the facilitator. The idea can be used in various ways, including the development of thinking skills in children, but in this case each member of the department assumed a different perspective from which to contribute to the discussion on assessment.

The team used the hats method to discuss the pros and cons of their existing policy. Under the pros (yellow hat) were comments that the current method was 'quick and easy' and 'every student gets a level every two weeks'. The cons (black hat) were that students were not getting any guidance as to how they were progressing mid-unit and targets were not being set at Key Stages 4 and 5. Information (white hat) included wider research evidence (see Assessment Reform Group, 1999) as well as students' work. Staff did not feel particularly strongly that current policy was either good or bad (red hat). They shared ideas about what might work better (green hat). As facilitator (blue hat), Dave wrote up the full discussion into a draft policy and circulated it to gain further suggestions and fine tune the detail into a new policy based on their own evidence linked to wider research.

Dave concluded that the conversations they had on that day were very balanced and, more importantly, resulted in a policy that everyone now agreed with. The theory facilitated an extremely useful conversation and it is a technique that they will return to in the future.

(Watkins, 2004)

The following example shows a different response to the same issue.

Example 4.9

Using a card-sorting exercise to develop new assessment policy

Kieran is head of English in a secondary school, leading a well-established department but with a recent influx of new staff. He wanted to open up discussion about assessment and to challenge traditional practices. Each member of staff was marking every piece of work out of 10, with inconsistency between classes and limited additional feedback to students.

Kieran wrote a set of definitions of assessment on cards and asked staff to rank them in order according to the extent that they agreed with them. The definitions included 'assessment is important to indicate how well students are doing in relation to each other'; 'assessment is important to indicate to teachers how well students are doing'; 'assessment is marking'; 'assessment is of value mainly to parents'; 'assessment is to help students know what they need to do to improve'; 'assessment is meaningless unless it has a grade', and so on.

Staff explored their current practice and understanding through the cards and with Kieran's support began to reach a common understanding of the purpose of assessment. At this point Kieran was able to introduce some current literature that provided research evidence about the effectiveness of different forms of assessment.

As a result of this and further discussions, Kieran began to move his department towards more individualised, consistent and formative assessment for learning. This included replacing grades with written comments for many assignments and introducing much more peer assessment.

These examples highlight the effectiveness of processes that encourage, extend and structure professional dialogue. This work may aspire to the process described by Elliott, where changes of practice and linked systemic change involve a restructuring, of individuals' 'practical consciousness' by reconstruction of their knowledge through discourse about practice and its effects (Elliott, 1998: 188). Through appropriate support, expertly provided by teacher leaders, the 'hard questions about practice' (Elmore, 2002) can be confronted.

Seeking discourse, building capital

We have already argued the importance of involving people and listening to their voices and have shown how teachers are at the fulcrum of interactive and collaborative school improvement processes. David Hargreaves's theory of school effectiveness and improvement (2001) suggests that the development of organisational capacity involves an increase in both intellectual and social capital. Social capital concerns the levels of trust between people, the extent to which they work collaboratively, are mutually supportive and are tied by strong relationships and networks. Intellectual capital grows through the creation and transfer of knowledge between situations and people and is therefore strengthened by high levels of social capital. Teacher leaders can increase social capital through developing their individual agency directly and by providing support for their colleagues, finding new ways of working and learning together. This provides fertile ground for the development of intellectual capital with the creation and transfer of professional knowledge through leadership within their own school communities and sharing between schools and across networks. They develop process knowledge in ways of working that can achieve maximum effect on the learning of students, schools and organisations, through working and learning together. In other words, both individually and collectively they enhance their capacity for leadership of learning.

One powerful way of achieving collaboration, avoiding the pitfalls of contrived collegiality (Hargreaves, 1994) is to use evidence and enquiry as a catalyst. In Example 3.4 (p. 45), Ruth as headteacher engaged her whole staff in discussions with students about their learning which led to a more creative curriculum, greater involvement of students in their own learning and an improved learning culture. Teacher leaders can use evidence strategically to raise issues and identify development needs, then to monitor progress and to measure success against criteria agreed beforehand. It can also be used in a more exploratory way as developments progress organically. The anticipation of evidence alone can immediately excite the interests of those who are already involved in the situations from which it has been collected. Teachers can become adept at gathering evidence as a basis for evaluation, reflection, planning and action, sometimes integrating this entirely within their normal practice. Ideally this should be systematised since lack of time easily results in marginalisation of this aspect of development work.

There are many different groups that can be consulted with or reported to in the course of any teacher's professional practice. When planning research, there may be obvious sources of support or circles of involvement and there can be a requirement to present and discuss the work in progress and report the outcomes to particular individuals or groups. A teacher conducting research into aspects of her professional practice would need to negotiate first with a line manager or senior teacher to ensure that the work was relevant in the context of the school's development priorities as well as her personal professional responsibilities. The senior colleague concerned would be likely to continue as an important point of reference throughout the study. Beyond this, in planning any enquiry strategies, it is helpful to take a broad view of the groups and individual contacts that should or could be involved. Often the most valuable interactions with members of a school community are those that involve pupils directly, not merely as objects of the investigation, but as consultants, collaborators, researchers and agents of change (see Enquiry Section 5). While most teachers need to work with existing teams and lines of communication, there may be much to be gained from collaboration with colleagues working in other areas of the curriculum or in different teams, or from forming a new team or focus group. There may also be less formal but equally influential groupings of staff providing mutual professional support and a focus for dialogue.

Interactive enquiry

Having established the groups and individuals to be drawn into the enquiry and development, there are many different ways in which they might be involved, as shown in Figure 4.15 below.

1 Testing initial ideas about the change and enquiry processes and seeking feedback
This can be done in discussion with a critical yet supportive group or with a tutor, mentor or colleague familiar with the school context.

2 Gathering information
This can be arranged specifically for the purpose, e.g. a staff development day could be used to carry out an audit of departmental or individual practice in relation to a particular theme. Meetings can offer rich opportunities for further evidence gathering, as in Examples 4.8 and 4.9.

3 Analysing and interpreting data
Collaboration in interpreting evidence relevant to people's practice offers much potential in providing insights for those involved, raising awareness not only of themes but also of issues, and increasing the level of professional discourse around learning. Ethical codes are particularly important where evidence is shared (see Enquiry Section 3).

4 Making a 'positional statement' to represent a particular stage of development
In seeking an audience, teacher leaders make enquiry and development work public – an important step. Drawing together the results of an investigation for presentation to any audience clarifies ideas and points the way forward. Presenting a coherent argument requires considerable confidence but also builds confidence. Inviting interaction may feel threatening but will yield rewards as the insights, ideas and opinions of others are expressed and respected.

5 Subjecting findings to peer scrutiny for validation
Teacher research usually involves small-scale studies and individual interpretation of situations and practice. It is therefore important to provide other perspectives against which these interpretations can be tested and challenged or supported using others' knowledge and experience.

6 Increasing criticality and reflexivity
Teacher researchers need to maintain a level of criticality as a continual process that underpins enquiry, so that each stage of the investigation has a rationale and a strategic process. This is best achieved through dialogue.

7 Being co-researchers
Drawing colleagues, students and others into collaborative research in which they are not restricted to respondents or data gatherers, or simply consulted, but are actively involved from the planning stage, is a powerful way of managing change. Involvement becomes infectious, enabling different people and groups to access the activity on their own terms according to their own perspectives, levels of commitment and individual circumstances.

Figure 4.15: Involving others in working with evidence and effecting change

As well as consulting and reporting within the school, there are usually opportunities to widen the scope of the enquiry beyond this. Conferences provide a forum for sharing ideas, reporting findings and gaining useful feedback, while the potential for web-based discussion is being explored in a variety of contexts. It is particularly worthwhile investing time in developing critical friendship, mutual sharing and collaborative working with colleagues from other schools. There is much emphasis on networks and clustering of schools in current government policy in England which presents interesting dilemmas in encouraging shared leadership and collaborative working while ensuring that self-run networks remain sufficiently well organised. Lieberman and McLaughlin note that while these may be 'free from the constraints of the cultures of university and school-based educators', they also warn of the dangers of falling 'prey to the myopia of familiar practices and the misdirection of unchallenged assumptions' (1996: 67). Networks as well as institutions and individuals need to adopt a critical stance which may require some external support, structuring and critical friendship. They set out the characteristics required of such network leaders who need to be

> visionary, multicultural [comfortable in different settings], at ease with ambiguity and flexibility, knowledgeable about different forms of organizations, action-orientated and able to nurture emergent talent. (1996: 71)

However, the success of a network or cluster depends greatly also on the extent to which it is genuinely a community of practice (Wenger, 1998), engendering a sense of belonging, loyalty and common purpose and enabling members to enact shared leadership (Durrant, 2003). If this can be achieved

> the effects may be not only an expanded conception of teacher development but also the accomplishment of significant and lasting school change. (Lieberman, 1996: 86)

Those involved in discussions within and beyond the school need to have some insights into the enquiry process, but realistically it falls to the teacher leader to take responsibility for the methodology of the work. Stenhouse points out that clarity and precision of definition are often required of those engaging in research and development work but that certainty can communicate prescription. In a climate of research, uncertainty and provisionality are surely part of the exploration but without an understanding of that climate they can be associated with vagueness (Stenhouse, 1975: 212). It is therefore important to communicate not only the substance of the work but also the research stance and the nature of the evidence and information presented, so that those involved can judge whether the work bears out their own experience and whether, in their own professional judgement, it is valid (Somekh, 1995).

Mapping involvement

Having considered the full range of possibilities it is helpful to map people's involvement either over time as the work gains momentum, or as a series of circles of involvement with some people only peripherally involved or concerned with one particular aspect of the work, while others may be centrally involved throughout. It is then important to ask how change processes can become more genuinely collaborative to achieve greater impact, where change and enquiry go hand in hand.

The framework earlier in Figure 3.2 (p.38) helps teachers to consider the range of potential impact that their leadership could have, during the planning stage and as the development work progresses. It is a good starting point for thinking about the possible opportunities for collaboration to maximise impact on pupil, teacher and organisational learning. The framework has been used to design workshops and planning exercises for teachers to plan, track and evaluate impact, making their leadership of change more powerful through collaboration (Frost and Durrant, 2003). A more detailed version of the framework is included in Appendix 3 (www.paulchapmanpublishing.co.uk/resource/durrant.pdf), where the sections are expanded to prompt teachers' thinking about the range of possible outcomes for their work. Activity 4.13 could be used to focus on the links between involvement and impact.

Activity 4.13

Who is going to be involved in development work?

● Use the framework for impact (Appendix 3 (www.paulchapmanpublishing.co.uk/ resource/durrant.pdf) or a summary) to think about the range of possible outcomes for the work you are planning to do.

● Against this, map the different individuals and groups that you will need to work with (this could be done using a flipchart diagram):

   1 Who will be involved in or affected by the changes you are making?

   2 Who needs to be kept informed?

   3 Who else might benefit from ideas and information arising from your enquiry (in school and beyond)?

   4 Who could provide data, information, ideas and opinions to support and inform your development work?

   5 Are there any whole groups that you do not normally work with who may have a stake (for example support staff including teaching assistants, lunchtime supervisors, librarians, parents, sponsors or employers from local businesses, governors, youth workers and so on)?

● Work with a colleague or in a small group to plan how you will use existing links and groups and how, where necessary, you will go about making new links and developing a wider web of communication.

One of the most powerful, yet surprisingly rare, forms of collaboration around evidence is the use of student work as the focus of discussion. Clements (in Head, 2000: 1) suggests that we ask three questions: 'What do we see particularly?'; 'What do we not see?'; 'What are the needs?', as shown in Activity 4.14 below.

These three questions applied to one poem by a Year 9 student produced a whole hour of animated discussion in a conference workshop. They could be applied equally to a series of pieces of work to determine progress, for example in developing creativity in boys' writing or in improving strategies for supporting history assignments. This brings colleagues immediately to the heart of learning and teaching and is likely to be a much more interesting and relevant use of their time than discussion of the school's learning and teaching policy in the abstract. Furthermore, policies can be built on the ideas generated in such discussions.

Activity 4.14

Looking properly at student work

● Choose one piece of student work relevant to the team, for example a poem or piece of creative writing, a mathematical investigation, a drawing or painting, a video of a dance routine or a group history project.

● Apply these questions in individual reflection and then discuss together in small groups:

1 What do you see particularly?

2 What do you not see?

3 What are the needs?

● If you have found this valuable, discuss the implications for staff development. Could such activity be shared more widely? Could it become a regular feature of department meetings?

This exercise may be used by teachers with a range of different subject specialisms. Discussing student work in different curriculum areas is as intriguing as staying within subject specialisms.

Teacher leaders can use such discussion as a vehicle for highlighting issues, expertise and inconsistencies in current practice and in shaping and critiquing policy.

Where schools are working in partnership, teachers can begin to gather data across a network so as to present and discuss information with a wider basis than the individual school but which is still context-specific, offering a more powerful basis for change. The impact on schools and teachers can be profound (see Frost, 2005). Sharing and discussion of this evidence through networks and clusters, often supported by LEAs, universities or other educational agencies, can provide more opportunities for building leadership capacity, thus strengthening the foundation for development and increasing professional confidence and individual agency amongst the teachers involved.

Enquiry Section 9
Making Sense and Making Meaning

Although the gathering of evidence is an important part of school-based research, the planning of this aspect can sometimes threaten to take over. It is equally important to plan what happens to the evidence after it has been collected. Teachers using enquiry to support change need to take into account the fact that their role is different from that of an 'outsider researcher' who usually has to produce a summative research report. As we have seen from the examples in Chapter 3, the boundaries between research and professional action are not clear-cut. It is extremely limiting and sometimes unhelpful to think in terms of reporting 'findings'. We need to look carefully at the notion of 'dissemination', to see what is actually happening. We may need to acknowledge that writing and presenting reports and case studies or posting them on the internet may, in fact, have negligible value for colleagues in schools. Analysing and interpreting evidence are an integral part of leadership of change, so as we have noted in Enquiry Section 3, it is important to build into this a sense of *audience* as well as *purpose* (Frost et al., 2000) to underpin the whole process of enquiry and development.

Engaging with evidence

This is not to say that there is no place for such formalised reports. Through writing, authors have to clarify what has been achieved, while through publication this achievement is celebrated and valued. This gives confidence that the work is worthy of consideration by a wider audience within and beyond the school, something that may need continual reinforcement.

It is also important that evidence, experience and ideas from school-based research and development are communicated within the wider discourse to contribute to knowledge about learning and teaching in different contexts and to provide a basis for comparison. The process of sharing stories of enquiry, change, leadership and learning generates excitement and builds capacity within networks since there is mutual interest in what other teachers and other schools are doing. The Networked Learning Communities conferences and publications through the National College for School Leadership (NCSL, 2005) emphasise 'learning with, from and on behalf of one another' and celebrate the considerable achievements of many groups of schools whose energy and enthusiasm are evident as they present their work. The National Teacher Research Panel activities and conferences have a similar vibrancy (NTRP, 2005). Workshops and networks enable teachers and students, along with advisors, academics and consultants who support them, to critique and challenge one another's practice.

Arguably, though, these activities may be most valuable for those presenting their work in their gaining feedback from diverse audiences, growing in confidence and feeling part of something bigger. For someone who has a passive role in this as a listening, observing member of an audience, their imagination may be captured and they may also pick up some 'tips' but the real learning happens when they decide to engage fully and systematically in leading learning through enquiry, experimentation and collaboration.

It may therefore be helpful to think in terms of *engagement* with evidence, widening beyond a teacher's normal sphere of influence. This requires information to be processed so that it is accessible and can support the development of thinking, understanding and planning. Stimulating discussion of challenges, problems and dilemmas arising from the enquiry as it progresses excites interest and gains different perspectives on managing change. It is helpful to establish an interactive forum where some real 'work' can be done, perhaps as part of an additional data gathering exercise in response to the data, perhaps raising awareness through individual or group reflection, perhaps sharing different experiences through thinking stimulated by the evidence in order to reach a more sophisticated understanding of a complex situation, perhaps responding to the information by drawing up a plan to take the development forward. We therefore need to think in terms of multiple stages of analysis leading to further questions and actions, rather than of a summative process where analysis is simply written up into a report or document, often for accountability purposes to demonstrate what has been achieved.

Working interactively with complex evidence

The methodology of teachers' school-based research that we have discussed in previous sections has implications for analysis and interpretation. Its characteristics are summarised in Figure 4.16 below.

- Collection of information from a wide variety of sources as a continuous process

- Use of data that already exists as well as additional data specific to the enquiry

- Teachers' engagement with the data while investigating their own practice

- Analysis taking place all the time, directly or indirectly feeding back into practice

- Cycles of planning, reflection and action operating over different timescales and overlapping with each other

- Adoption of a reflexive approach, monitoring the research process and maintaining criticality through dialogue with self (for example, in a journal) and with others

- The collection of predominantly qualitative data

Figure 4.16: Characteristics of teacher research methodology

These characteristics show the continual back and forth process of enquiry-based school improvement and the direct relationship with professional practice. As explained in Enquiry Section 2, the teacher researcher has to select evidence to compile a case study from the case record in its entirety. The first stage of this might be to compile a portfolio of evidence, organising it perhaps chronologically or in themed sections, so as to provide a basis for study. This may in some cases be the basis of an assignment for an academic or professional award (Frost et al., 2000; Frost and Durrant, 2003; Field, 2003).

Evidence may include that which is already available in the school and that which has been collected specifically for the purpose of the enquiry (see Figure 4.11, p. 115). There may be time to adopt the technique of *theoretical sampling* to home in on subjects likely to reveal the most significant information or a relevant perspective on the most problematic issues, for example certain members of staff may be interested in commenting on particular issues raised through a questionnaire. *Progressive focusing* enables us to concentrate on the most helpful types of data collection and to discard others, for example a survey might raise issues that can then be followed up with classroom observations. Decision making about selection of evidence and the development of a responsive methodology are part of the analytical process.

From informal to formal analysis: what counts as research?

Stenhouse famously defined research as 'systematic enquiry made public' (1980: 1). This has proved to be an excellent opening definition for teacher researchers but it also holds the key to leading change. It is only when teachers communicate with others that the work they are doing progresses beyond a 'research project', which might be for the author's own gratification or effective only in improving practice in a narrow sphere of individual influence. Altrichter et al. (1993) reinforce this, suggesting that the everyday analysis which we carry out as reflective practitioners deserves the title of 'research' when:

● It is more *systematic* (using theoretical and methodological knowledge)
● It is more *critical* (tested against conflicting data and interpretations)
● It is more *communicative* (process and results are made public)

This provides both a helpful set of aims for more formal analysis and a set of criteria against which the work can be assessed as the enquiry progresses. It could be argued that planning systematic, critical and communicative enquiry-based development work from the start is bound to increase its impact. Teachers could use a simple analytical framework for reflection and planning as in Activity 4.15 below.

Facilitators should note that practical support may be needed to make the enquiry and development work more powerful. Often teachers do not feel they have the status or time to command an audience within school and may need to be encouraged to offer their ideas for wider consideration, or to approach the headteacher to ask for allocated time on a meeting agenda. Simple suggestions may not have been considered before because they are not part of everyday practice, but with some support could have much wider influence, as Example 4.10 illustrates.

Activity 4.15

Is this research and is it supporting school improvement?

Use this activity when participants are in the process of enquiry-based development work.

● Display the Stenhouse definition of research as 'systematic enquiry made public' and the three criteria for research from Altrichter et al., (1993): systematic; critical; communicative. Discuss what each of these terms and statements really means and the challenges these present to teachers.

● Consider how these notions of research might make the link with leadership of learning and school change.

● Individuals (or groups if working collaboratively) should then consider their responses to the questions below:

1 What is your focus for enquiry and development?

2 How have you tried to make your work systematic?

3 How have you tried to make your work critical?

4 How have you tried to make your work communicative?

● Think together about how to make the enquiry more powerful to support leadership of student, professional and organisational learning. (The impact framework in Appendix 3, www.paulchapmanpublishing.co.uk/resource/durrant.pdf or summary in Figure 3.2 (p.38) may help.)

● Allow time for rewriting plans to include any new ideas.

Example 4.10

Improving motivation and learning

Carolyn is a Year 4 teacher (pupils' age 7–8) in her second year of teaching. She wants to improve learning in a challenging mathematics class with very wide ability range and a number of disaffected students. She brings this to a meeting of the school's Learning and Teaching group.

Her colleagues suggest that she could talk to the SENCo (Special Educational Needs Co-ordinator), the headteacher and other trusted and more experienced colleagues. These critical conversations provide some starting points for leading change. The discussion in the group also raises this formally as a school issue; Carolyn finds that others are wrestling with the same difficulties of behaviour management and differentiation. She and her teaching assistant are already keeping a log of some lessons to identify strategies that work well and things that are less successful, using a format to structure observations so that they can make independent comments for comparison. She also arranges some ten minute conversations with students to ask them what helps and what hinders their learning. She displays a summary of their comments and improving the learning ethos and environment becomes an aim for the class. She realises that that this might encourage *all* students, rather than just the most attentive and well-motivated, to see themselves as learners and hopes that it will give them a new 'learning vocabulary'. She suspects that they may need to work on aspects of the classroom environment and introduce more peer support.

Colleagues in the Learning and Teaching group ask Carolyn to feed back to them on progress and agree to meet in her classroom next time to view the display, inviting the teaching assistant to participate. Everyone agrees to bring strategies from their own practice to this meeting. This generates discussion about the school's learning and teaching policy and areas needing development are fed by the deputy headteacher into school improvement planning. The idea of displaying children's 'comments about our learning' is adapted by several colleagues and leads to a display in the foyer for an open evening. Meanwhile, Carolyn's investigations reveal that students find teacher inputs too long and they do not have time to consolidate and practise their learning. She introduces much shorter starts to lessons on some days, followed by activities, games and exercises. On the other days students work at their own pace in groups. This has markedly improved behaviour, attentiveness and learning.

Carolyn's story not only demonstrates that evidence, enquiry, action and improvement are interlinked but shows how, by sharing and working strategically and collaboratively beyond her classroom, impact on the whole school has been achieved. There is no clear sequence of evidence gathering, analysis, reporting and action, but the elements of systematic enquiry, criticality and communication are all included and have been made more powerful through group discussion and peer support. Significantly, Carolyn has started with an issue derived from her own immediate concerns, something she was losing sleep over, and through skilled facilitation she may eventually influence school policy. She is leading school developments to improve learning.

From informal to formal analysis

While we have presented enquiry-based development as quite fluid and organic, there are points where teachers have to stand back and make some sense of the evidence in its entirety, moving from informal analysis to formal analysis (Hitchcock and Hughes, 1989: 74). As we begin to focus more closely on the analysis stage, Walker suggests that analysis of data is generally viewed as the technical application of manipulations in order to process information so that it can be interpreted. This could result in the raw information being 'cooked', in other words organised, verified, processed and presented without necessarily achieving understanding (Walker, 1980).

It is improved understanding that is the purpose of enquiry to support change and as explained in previous sections, understanding of self and identity, other people's perspectives and complex situations and processes of leadership and school change are as important as understanding the specific aspects of practice under investigation and solving practical problems. In such analysis, Walker draws a useful parallel with documentary film making, an analogy that can be helpful in thinking about selection and interpretation, as in Activity 4.16 following. An editor 'reassembles reality'. Theoretical and moral judgements are needed in order to select materials to use in the final story. There is a lot of wastage, but there may still be a need for more information. Eventually the editor makes the best of what is known. Therefore meaning does not simply present itself – sense has to be made of the information. It is not the data that tells the story, it is the researcher.

Activity 4.16
Which story needs telling?

Having reached the stage where formal analysis is required:

- If someone had been filming your enquiry and development work for a year and had access to all the evidence and experience gathered along the way, what would their reels of film contain? Map or list all the possible elements and strands of the work.
- What is your interpretation of the story and what message should the finished film convey?
- Which audience(s) will watch the film?
- What are the key elements that need to be included? Highlight these on your list or map.
- What will the critics say? Check the design for your finished film against the comments below – might any of them apply?

... I got the feeling that only part of the story had been told....
... ducks the problematic issues – looks a little too slick..
... I couldn't see the purpose in this film...
... somehow it doesn't ring true...
... the main character is missing...
... fragmented story, chaotic camerawork, difficult to make sense of the whole ...
... rather an epic, didn't really hold my attention ... it was simply too long
... skimped on the detail...
... lots of factual information but I wanted to know how the people felt ...
... where were the children in all of this?

- Draw up a list of criteria for judging the quality of an account of teacher-led enquiry and change (whether it be a presentation or written account). To what extent should this be qualified for different audiences?

It could be that more than one story needs to be told. Teacher leaders may need to distinguish between analysis and interpretation for the purposes of feeding back into their own practice and the additional selection and processing required for communication to various audiences. A more reflective account may be needed to support and express personal learning, while a report with recommendations may be requested by the school. A more analytical account with reference to theory and policy could be required for an academic assignment, while a short summary of the work completed and key learning points might be useful for a network website or bulletin. Most importantly any communication must engage the audience, so creative and interactive alternatives to written reports or 'talks' should always be considered. It is helpful if this is part of a *managed process of change,* rather than an event that leaves the onus on the audience to take new steps unsupported.

Analysing the evidence

When starting the formal analysis it is helpful according to Altrichter et al. (1993) to view it in two stages:

● *The constructive stage*: read, select, present, interpret and draw conclusions.
● *The critical stage*: critically examine the analytical process to check the validity of the findings.

In practice these often merge or overlap, but by considering analysis in this way teacher researchers can think more carefully about exactly what their purposes are and plan to make them more effective. Adopting a critical perspective makes the enquiry more powerful.

There are many different techniques that can be used at each stage of the analysis, which are well documented in the methodological literature. These range from summaries and written studies constructed by combing manually through the evidence, through to statistical analysis and 'coding' of data under a set of headings. There is no substitute for exploring alternatives and making choices with reference to more detailed explanations of different techniques in the methodological texts, thereby choosing realistic strategies as a teacher researcher.

It is important to develop a personal style even within prescribed techniques, using methods of sorting, recording, categorising, viewing and representing that are 'comfortable' for individuals and will help them better to understand the information. As part of the change process, to develop confidence and to achieve a higher level of understanding it is valuable to involve colleagues, pupils or others in analysis and interpretation. Some teachers choose to ask someone less directly involved with the evidence (such as a student, teaching assistant or administrator) to analyse and interpret, with the aim of achieving a greater degree of objectivity as well as sharing the workload. This leaves them with the task of re-engaging, particularly if it includes detailed qualitative information such as interview data, but it does provide the basis for a critical conversation. Teachers interpreting their own data for the situations in which they are intimately involved find this a powerful experience, although it is obviously important to aim for a high degree of self-awareness and reflexivity at the critical stage of the analysis, to take account of bias and perception in the interpretation.

Struggling with interpretations

Ball (1991) describing his analysis of interview data from research on educational policy, shows his methods to be time consuming, low-tech, idiosyncratic – largely a matter of familiarisation with the data. He likens it to a detective solving a murder mystery: look for clues, form hunches and a picture emerges; look for evidence for and against; reorganise the facts so that they connect, with as few contradictions as possible. However, elsewhere (Ball, 1994) he notes that by using this intensive approach, researchers are faced with complexity and have to recognise incoherences as well as patterns in the evidence.

Ball suggests that an inexperienced researcher achieves confidence and security through struggling with the process, and that much of this is to do with the physical organisation of information. Therefore experimenting with methods of analysis is as valuable as experimenting with methods for evidence collection. Teachers must expect analysis to be complicated and time consuming and should plan for this within the enquiry process. He suggests a series of stages for interview analysis:

- Read and re-read
- Indulge in some writing about the data
- Code and categorise
- Map concepts and relationships using diagrams
- Test out relationships through more data gathering
- Make decisions about progressive focusing and theoretical sampling.

(drawn from Ball, 1991)

These stages should be straightforward for teacher researchers since there is no particular methodological mystique involved, yet they represent a systematic and sophisticated process that can be adapted according to purpose and circumstance. All analysis requires the application of the developed understanding of the researcher in order to find meanings and interpretations. It could not be analysed in the same way by somebody else as enquiry is centred upon the researcher's own situation and understanding, as argued in previous sections. Teachers leading change need to think continually about an added dimension: how can the information be used strategically to support learning and school development, both as enquiry is in progress and as each phase comes to a conclusion? During the analysis there is often a wealth of 'tacit knowledge' that comes to light. It is perhaps best revealed in discussion with others who will ask questions we may not ask ourselves. We are

> telling a story which we invent and criticize and modify as we go along, so that it ends up being, as nearly as we can make it, a story about real life. (Medawar, 1969, in McNiff ,1988)

The story is not simply an interpretation of a situation but has the added dimension of being a story of leadership of change. Teachers bringing notions of scientific research into their investigations of their own practice are often disconcerted that they do not seem to be finding answers, clear conclusions or 'findings', but should be encouraged that at the analysis stage, the importance of stories and selves, the artistry of case study and the value of voice, as discussed in previous sections, are brought together into an interpretation of real situations and dilemmas. At concluding points in the analytic process, it should be possible to answer the questions in Figure 4.17 below.

---

1   What has been learnt from the enquiry and development process?

2   What evidence is there to support these interpretations?

3   How has the analytical process been subjected to scrutiny and critique?

4   Who has been involved in the analysis and interpretation?

5   How has understanding of the particular situation or theme under scrutiny been improved?

6   What questions remain?

7   How will this work influence future practice?

Figure 4.17: Summative questions for teacher-led enquiry

Throughout this book we have argued that enquiry at its most powerful becomes part of a managed change process led by the teacher involved. While it is important to break away from limited notions of 'research projects', teachers must also resist the temptation to focus on change at the expense of rigorous and systematic enquiry processes. It is important to allow enough time for interpretation of evidence at every stage, following cycles of interactive enquiry to support change. It is teachers as both researchers and leaders who are best placed to enable enquiry to drive change, by placing evidence and its interpretation at the heart of discussion, planning and professional action. Often the timescales for research and development are externally set, for example where the work fits within a structured programme, is based around a particular year group over a given timescale, or is required to feed into policy development or implementation of initiatives. Within these structures, allowing time for interpretation, the development of understanding and the individual and collective making of meaning always pays dividends.

Enquiry Section 10
Improving Practice

All the previous sections in this chapter endeavour to explain how enquiry can become integrated with teachers' practice and inform leadership of learning. It is therefore rather academic to separate professional action into a separate section. However, the processes by which teachers translate professional knowledge into practice are far from straightforward. In order to explore this we need to consider the relationships between leadership and learning, research and action.

Research and action: a false divide

In discussing the unique characteristics of action research, Somekh (1995) points out that research and action are integrated rather than being a two-stage process in which research is carried out first by researchers and then applied by practitioners. The validity of such research depends on developing increased 'practical wisdom' or 'situational understanding' in unique contexts and testing these in spirals of data collection, interpretation and action. Action research is grounded in the culture and values of a researcher's social group; Somekh notes that its momentum is towards collaboration, contributing further to the development of shared values and social cohesion. This means that it is highly pragmatic in orientation. Researchers may be limited in research skills and knowledge but they have the power and ability to use the research process strategically to bring about change. It is therefore important to examine the nature of practice as the context for intervention in classrooms, experimentation with different ideas and implementation of new learning and teaching strategies.

The creative nature of practice

In considering the relationships between enquiry, leadership and practice it is important to remember what teaching and learning look like from close quarters. Teaching is not clinical and analytical work, it is emotional, challenging, joyous, chaotic, hard, unpredictable work. Saunders (2002) draws together some valuable insights:

> Maingay ... argues that there is much more to effective teaching than the effectiveness of planning, procedures, routines; sound subject knowledge and good but flexible routines are necessary, yes, but not sufficient. He talks convincingly about the 'generally uncodified skills and abilities that teachers possess to some degree' which he calls 'teaching intelligence' (p. 167). These skills and abilities are to some extent instinctive: things like improvisation, grace, tact, humour, rapport, rhythm, timing, empathy, being 'in flow' – what some people now call 'emotional intelligence'.

Maingay's train of thought … equates this intelligence with 'tact' in the classroom, which he says involves:

- Being personally present
- Being open and not over-planned
- Creating and using an appropriate tone
- Genuine interest
- Humour
- Being on good form
- Being well enough prepared
- Being confident but not too confident
- Being relaxed – but alert
- Being the right you for that situation.

(Saunders, 2002: 11–12)

Saunders is also captivated by Humphreys and Hyland's analogies between the performances inherent in teaching and in jazz music, where 'technical competence provides the requisite basis for the exercise of artistry, intuition, improvisation, dynamism and expressiveness'. She observes that this is not necessarily what teachers learn when they are trained, although they are 'certainly implicitly judged on these attributes' (Saunders, 2002: 12). Holly (1989), similarly, notes the importance of creativity in teaching that involves playfulness, the juxtaposition of the everyday and the novel and the ability to withhold judgement.

Holly notes that 'the more opportunity the teacher has to create and adapt the lesson, the more chance there is to engage the spirit and strengthen self-affirming aspects of the self (or selves)'. She links this to psychological maturity and health, noting that effective teachers are risk takers, embrace diversity, have a differentiated view of the world, are 'cognitively complex … self-accepting … compassionate … personally adequate … and flexible' (Holly, 1989: 74). She goes on to explain the importance of making explicit that which is already known, which might hitherto be tacit, sensed, intuitive knowledge, to support the development of such attributes. Activity 4.17 is a group activity that helps teachers to recapture what one teacher has called the 'glittery bits' that often go unremarked, and helps them to define practice beyond a set of competencies.

The results of one such exercise when used with a group of teachers in early career are shown in Figure 4.18. This is not definitive but shows the richness of ideas that can be derived from a small group whose only evidence here is their own practice.

While such observations are not new, they are always, as Saunders (2002) notes, refreshing to revisit. This is particularly true when teachers and their students inhabit a tick-box, content-laden world, where the 'performance training sect' threatens to engulf the 'professional learning community' (A. Hargreaves, 2003). How, as leaders of learning, can teachers use enquiry and artistry to enhance these attributes which would be widely acknowledged to characterise excellence in teaching?

Activity 4.17
Exploring the nature of practice

This exercise is similar to exercises elsewhere in this book, for example the critical incident analysis in Activity 4.7, but teachers never tire of talking about their classrooms, whether they are newly qualified or highly experienced. Adapt the exercise to use different 'ways in' (writing, talking, video and so on).

- Individually, identify one really good lesson or part of a lesson that you remember. Alternatively, watch a video clip of a successful lesson.

- In pairs or threes, make notes to answer the question 'What does good learning and teaching look like?'

- Gather ideas together, allowing plenty of time for discussion. Type up for distribution to members of the group and for sharing more widely.

- Making work personal to the student

- Flexibility and adaptability within the specified learning outcomes

- Students and teachers looking in detail at students' work

- Good planning, clarity of instruction and differentiation

- Students engaged and interested in the topic, it is fun, they like learning

- Humour and relationships being important

- Knowing your students

- Teachers having their own style but maintaining a professional approach

- Teachers as advocates for the students

- Teachers sometimes needing to admit they get things wrong or don't know the answer

- Modelling learning: teachers are learners as well as their students

- The importance of setting boundaries and establishing an ethos over time.

Figure 4.18: How can good teaching and learning be recognised? Results of a discussion based on teachers' accounts of 'good' lessons

Tate reflects on his contrasting experiences of a school development day on 'the effects of the information technology revolution on children's learning' compared with the Oxford Education Conference which has the rationale that 'good teachers are those who remain intellectually curious, enthusiastic about their subjects, and alert to wider philosophical, cultural, social and political issues' (Tate, 2005: 22). He concludes that good professional development involves challenging teachers' minds beyond narrow professionalism, enabling them to reflect on their experiences as learners. Of course there is always the need for training, but there is a strong case for more of a balance with wider learning experiences and deeper scholarship. The relationships between learning and leadership, professional learning and student learning are not linear. It may take a long time for teachers to understand and develop the use of their wider learning to enhance their practice.

Leading learning through inclusive leadership

We have argued in earlier chapters that schools must take account of teachers' agency and support their leadership of change in their own professional situations. It is interesting to note that the kinds of attributes that teachers feel characterise excellent teaching and learning, listed above in Figure 4.18 could be applied to leadership too, as suggested in Figure 4.19. In other words, in cultivating excellence in classroom practice, teachers may at the same time be improving their leadership skills.

The analysis below is particularly significant in that it is derived from teachers' own ideas of what excellent teaching and learning looks like, even while they may not necessarily think of themselves as leaders. Leadership, if not yet actively exercised, is latent in all teachers and it can be 'awakened' (Katzenmeyer and Moller, 2001), or unleashed, by unlocking the structures and cultures that constrain it and by offering appropriate encouragement and support.

Excellent teaching	Effective leadership of change
Build personal experiences into learning	Build on colleagues' and others' experience to lead change
Be flexible and adaptable within clear goals	Be flexible and adaptable within clear goals
Use evaluation of student work as a focus for learning and development	Use evaluation of school processes, activities and outcomes as a focus for improvement
Good planning and clarity of instruction	Good planning and clarity of vision
Students are engaged and interested	Staff are enthusiastic and well motivated
Humour and relationships are important – teaching is emotional work	Humour and relationships are important – leadership is emotional work
Know your students	Know the members of the school community
Teachers have their own character and style and a professional approach	Leaders have their own character and style and a professional approach
Good to model learning – the teacher is a learner too	Good to model learning and leadership – everyone can be a learner and a leader
Set boundaries and develop ethos towards a culture of learning	Set boundaries and develop ethos towards a culture of learning and inclusive leadership

Figure 4.19: Suggested comparisons between excellent teaching and effective leadership of change

Taking action

Since the action that teachers will take depends on their priorities for development, their professional situations, the evidence they have gathered, its interpretation and the supporting school context, it is impossible to offer a blueprint for the change process (Fullan, 1993). Sometimes it is appropriate to experiment on a small scale, perhaps with one class, one unit of work, one lesson or one staff development day. Trials or pilots may pave the way for more widespread intervention or implementation. In other cases, teacher leaders may be interested in evaluating and refining changes they are required to make, for example the English National Curriculum prescribes certain subjects that must be taught; the OfSTED action plan requires particular improvements to be made; Literacy and Numeracy Strategies apply across the curriculum. In this case, although change may be prescribed, there is choice about the ways in which it happens.

How can teachers approach this experimentation and innovation? All too often it is done in a haphazard way because of the lack of time for planning and preparation; it is not much more than the 'tinkering' which Hargreaves suggests is a ubiquitous feature of classrooms, citing Huberman's definition of a trial and error process using 'a variety of new and cobbled together materials' (in Hargreaves, 1998: 8). A more systematic approach is needed if change is to be managed, evaluated and co-ordinated effectively; falling short of this may provide hunches about 'what works', but does not enable teachers to contribute knowledge, validate claims and build upon their learning with colleagues and others in such a meaningful way. Action planning is best done collectively if several teachers are then going to be involved in the implementation. Formats and supporting workshops (see Frost and Durrant, 2003) can be adapted to concentrate on any aspect or scale of change, from classroom intervention to school-wide initiatives. Particular attention must be given to the ethics of experimentation, for example it is not equitable to introduce with some children a practice that is thought to improve learning when others do not have that opportunity. Finally, changes need to be carefully evaluated using the techniques previously discussed, preferably involving the voices of as many of those involved in the changes as is feasible.

Choosing to change

Craft points out that 'the teaching profession, whilst demanding creativity, does not foster it in its members' (Craft, 1997: 84, following Woods). She goes on to examine the nature of the creative self:

> One of the key aspects of the creative self is that there are no rules …
> we make it up …

and

> implicit in creativity is the conviction that one can choose to change.
> This contrasts with the educator literature … which emphasises the

adherence to responsibility and ways of behaving which conform to 'oughts'. (Craft, 1997: 85)

Perhaps this idea comes closest of all to the essence of teachers' leadership of change and to describing the dilemmas they face. There is sometimes tension between making changes because they accord with your values, are directed by evidence and are believed to improve learning, compared with making changes because they are what you have been told to do. Sometimes these are the same thing; often they are not. If the concept of teacher agency is to be taken seriously, teachers have to have some choice about whether to change and if so how. They have to be able to exercise genuine leadership.

Activity 4.18 below enables teachers to focus more effectively on what they can change instead of expending energy on becoming frustrated at what cannot be changed.

Activity 4.18
Choosing to change: where does your influence lie?

- In relation to one *aspect of improvement* you are leading, make lists of a) things you are able to change, and b) things over which you have no influence.
- Considering your various *roles* within the school, make lists of a) things you are able to change, and b) things over which you have no influence.
- In relation to development work you are leading, write or revise an action plan to focus on changing the things you *can* change.
- Discuss in a group or with a colleague the extent to which you feel able to influence school and wider education policy and contribute to school improvement processes such as self-evaluation and school improvement planning. How great is your influence? What is your strategy for improving your influence?

This activity fits with exploring notions of teacher professionalism, for example it might help in reviewing a school's approach to professional development.

As we have argued earlier, building a culture that supports teachers' capacity to experiment and introduce changes in practice needs to be divorced from the hierarchical structures and role cultures (Hargreaves, 1994) that still pervade most schools. Frost argues emphatically that

> if schools are to develop their organisational capacity to the maximum, all teachers need to be encouraged to exercise leadership. It is not simply a matter of developing 'middle leadership' or 'emergent leadership'; these terms reflect an assumption that the function of leadership should continue to be limited to those who take on management roles ... . A more productive view of teacher leadership is a more inclusive one ... All teachers can participate in the leadership of learning-centred development work ...

There is a growing body of evidence to suggest that it is through the leadership of such development work that teachers can make a major difference to the personal and interpersonal capacities of themselves and their colleagues, to pupils' learning, and to the organisational structures and cultures of their schools ... (Frost, 2004: 2)

Interviews with experienced teacher leaders (Frost and Durrant, 2002; Frost, 2004) have shown the importance of supporting the development of such a culture. Appendix 4 (www.paulchapmanpublishing.co.uk/resource/durrant.pdf) provides a set of 20 key strategies that teacher leaders suggest headteachers (and others with greater power and authority in schools) might use in support of this kind of inclusive leadership. Within such a climate, teachers feel confident that they can not only experiment with their practice but also contribute to the school's knowledge creation and transfer in order to build greater and more sustainable capacity for learning and improvement.

It is vital that in action planning for change, the creativity, energy and artistry of teachers are not lost. Headteachers, co-ordinators and facilitators can capture some of the attributes and enthusiasm described earlier in this section through imaginative approaches, applying their pedagogic expertise to their work with colleagues. Collaborative working is effective and enjoyable; sharing ideas about practice is helpful but can also be fun. Activity 4.19 below helps teachers to explore what it feels like to be a learner and also to hold a mirror up to their teaching.

Activity 4.19

Exploring experiences of learning and assessment

- Ask selected individuals (or everyone if a small group) to prepare a simple exercise where they spend no more than five minutes teaching colleagues a new skill (this can be anything where at least some progress will be made, for example juggling, sugarcraft, speaking Cantonese, hair braiding, balloon modelling or playing the spoons).

- After the first few 'learning experiences', colleagues could be asked to reflect on how they felt as successful/unsuccessful learners, collecting words and phrases on a flipchart.

- For the rest of the 'learning experiences', ask the 'teachers' to set targets in advance and then to assess colleagues against these. Again discuss the learning experiences and consider how the targets and assessment affected the learning.

- What implications does this discussion have for learning and assessment?

This could be linked to some reading and further discussion on learning (for example Claxton, 1999; Carnell and Lodge, 2001; Stoll et al. 2003). It might be useful as a prelude to reviewing the learning and teaching policy for the department, subject or school.

Teachers reflecting on their own learning are often surprised at the range of emotions they have experienced. Sometimes there is a fine line between perseverance and despair. Teachers describe fear and embarrassment, frustration, anger, disillusionment, determination, excitement, delight and pride. They talk about the inner motivation that helps them to succeed and the support they need to call upon. They contemplate what it is like to struggle and to fail, and what makes them react positively or negatively. Sharing such reflections in a supportive environment can make them look at their classrooms in a new way.

In school improvement, a theory of 'what works' is not enough. Enquiry, leadership and action are interlinked because teaching is about self, complexity, identity and relationships. It is involvement in the process of enquiry, not knowledge of the results of enquiry, that fuels creativity and creates the confidence which enables teachers to change practice and lead change that has impact beyond their own practice. Seeking a better understanding of learning is central to this journey. Reflection and enquiry both in and on action (Schon, 1983; Saunders, 2002) can create the conditions for artistry, innovation, experimentation and evaluation that can help teachers to meet the challenges of their day-to-day work. Through this they can feel comfortable with their own learning, alongside their leadership, to build greater capacity for change.

5   *Teachers' stories of change*

There is a danger that in championing the cause of teacher leadership, we over-simplify and glamorise teachers' attempts to make a difference in their schools. It is easy to present dialogue and collaboration as straightforward and self-evidently desirable aspects of professional practice. The reality of school life, however, is complex and messy. Teachers labour under multiple demands on their time, skills and energy and it can be immensely difficult to find opportunities to engage in collaborative activity.

The following accounts provide an insight into some of the dilemmas experienced by teachers who lead change. All three were participants in the school-based Masters programme (see Chapter 3) at St. James's Roman Catholic 11–19 Comprehensive School. The school-based programme is well-established and was set up in partnership with Canterbury Christ Church University College in 1994 (Frost et al., 2000). Since then around 20 teaching and support staff have obtained qualifications at Certificate and Post Graduate Diploma level with some progressing to the full Masters degree. The culture of the school, therefore, is supportive of teacher action research and the school has worked hard to create opportunities for participants to work collaboratively, to share their work with relevant audiences within the school and to contribute to whole school developments. Despite this, all three teachers represented here had to overcome obstacles to their attempts to lead change. What they have in common is that in order to initiate and sustain this change, they had to engage with the school culture through collaboration, dialogue and a willingness to listen.

The quotations included here are either extracts from teachers' written accounts in the form of their Masters dissertations (Rylatt, 2000; Parsons, 1997; Fryer, 2000) or statements from interviews conducted for doctoral research (Holden, 2002a).

Gloria's story: Teacher leadership to improve the learning culture in the school's sixth form

We have previously reported on aspects of Gloria's school development work in an earlier publication (Frost et al., 2000). Here we explore other dimensions of her enquiry work as Head of Sixth Form at St James's School. Shortly after taking up her post, she decided to focus on the issue of student guidance and support, and made use of Whitehead's (1989) formulation 'How can I improve my practice...' as a starting point for an action research project. Her question was:

> How can I, as Head of Sixth Form, effect an improvement in the quality of advice, guidance and support given to students in Year 12 and Year 13?

In the course of her investigations, Gloria highlighted two important issues concerning the relationship between teacher leadership and school culture. Although she reported that many colleagues were supportive of her work and had offered constructive criticism when she hosted an open meeting for staff to discuss the issue, others seemed to take some pleasure in making negative and unhelpful comments. She recognised that in undertaking this enquiry, she had laid herself open to such attacks. Culturally, not all staff were ready for the climate of openness and the mutual sharing of good practice that Gloria had hoped for. The other notable issue was Gloria's appreciation of the support provided by the other members of the school-based Masters group and the debate and professional dialogue that took place in their group sessions.

The focus for a subsequent phase of development work was on learning, and more particularly on 'learning relationships' (Young, 1998), which Gloria herself defined as 'a developmental, interactive process'. Where beforehand in her earlier work she had seized opportunities when they arose for this kind of dialogue, there was now greater recognition that for school improvement to be sustained over time, it had become necessary to formalise and institutionalise dialogue both for staff and students:

> There are many opportunities for teachers to become actively involved in school improvement if there is a commitment to staff development within the institution, and if real efforts are made to involve staff in collaborative planning. We also need to apply these considerations, and provide similar opportunities for students to participate in school development planning, and in the planning of their personal educational needs.

Gloria did not underestimate the scale of the task she fluently outlined here, and was keen to point out that while one person may describe the sharing of power and decision making as *empowerment*, another could see it as *exploitation* (Fielding, 1996). For change to be genuinely empowering, she argued that it must arise from ongoing and 'interactive dialogue' between all sections of the school community, rather than simply being imposed from above. In her writing she displayed an increasingly sophisticated understanding of the culture of the institution and of the nature of educational change:

> In essence, I have learnt to look at the whole picture, realising that issues which concern me have many dimensions and need to be viewed from many different angles ... I also know that I can be a successful change agent and that I am not totally at the mercy of outside influences.

This is a very powerful picture of a growing sense of personal efficacy and of what Fullan (2003) calls 'moral purpose'. Reflecting on the question of impact,

Gloria noted that it was not so much her *findings* that made the difference, but the process of enquiry itself, or as she put it later on, 'I have found that the process itself has had more intrinsic value than the "result" produced'.

Part of her ongoing development plan to improve the ethos of the sixth form included the introduction of Key Skills. She identified a youth award scheme as a useful vehicle for this. The scheme seeks to encourage students to develop a variety of skills by providing a framework for them to assemble evidence and present it for accreditation. Gloria saw similarities between the process of action planning, negotiation, action and review that the award scheme encourages and the action research framework that she was using for her own enquiry. She saw this as an important way to give students control over their own learning, but realised that it relied on the commitment of staff to 'sell' it to students:

> I was convinced that the scheme was a great facilitator of independent learning, action planning and student reflection. I felt, however, that there was a need to provide better staff training and to raise the status and profile of the youth award scheme.

In attempting to account for the impact of Gloria's work, it is interesting to note the way she went about this task of staff training and profile raising. Rather than arrange off-site training by an outside provider, she arranged for sixth form tutors to attend a presentation of their completed submission by a group of students who had just completed their youth award. Each candidate was required to make a presentation consisting of a talk and display followed by a question and answer session. Gloria felt that this would be an ideal opportunity for the students to 'sell' the scheme on its best points and would be a more effective way to alert the tutors to its nature and benefits. In order to emphasise the staff development potential of this strategy, she arranged for the presentations to take place during one of the five statutory staff development days. This demonstrates once more Gloria's growing ability to think strategically about how to disseminate good practice and, crucially, how the model of learning relationships described earlier might look in practice. It is instructive to reflect here on the degree to which this apparently simple strategy of having students make presentations to staff served as a vehicle to further teacher and student learning, as well as providing a valuable opportunity for dialogue between the two groups. In reflecting on the impact of her enquiry work on her leadership role, she concluded:

> I feel that I have gained the self-confidence to view my role as Head of Sixth Form as one concerned not only with the pastoral needs of students, but truly as a leader of a learning community.

Sarah's story: Dilemmas in improving the place and perception of technology in the curriculum

Sarah was head of the Design Technology department at St. James's School. She was concerned that her subject was not fairly represented in the school's curriculum, and was disappointed at the senior management's team decision to offer so-called 'short' courses as well as 'full' courses in GCSE. She saw the decision as short-sighted and timetable-led rather than forward-looking and curriculum-led, and felt that it was an example of how practical subjects fare less well than academic ones when parcelling up curriculum time. She felt that the argument that short courses would allow students to exercise greater curriculum choice was one motivated by timetable convenience rather than by a vision based on the needs of young people in the twenty-first century. She believed an opportunity had been missed:

> I felt the school should question the validity of preserving our traditional and elitist academic curriculum.

The language of this statement reveals Sarah's strength of feeling, in her characterisation of the school's existing curriculum arrangements as 'traditional and elitist' and her questioning of the 'validity' of these arrangements. This is an example of how involvement in teacher-led curriculum development activities can help to give teachers the confidence and language to question institutional practices. However, there is more than mere questioning here. The adversarial tone of Sarah's statement is indicative of the feeling that her subject area was being given insufficient status. Indeed, the processes by which decisions are made about curriculum historically, nationally and at St. James's, form a key theme of her enquiry. She pointed to a damaging and divisive attitude that she believed prevailed across the country concerning the role of practical and academic subjects in the curriculum. She felt that St. James's was clinging on to an outmoded view based on the primacy of the academic curriculum at the expense of disciplines like hers which, she believed, were more suited to the changing demands of the world outside school.

Although disappointed at what she took to be her managers' lack of understanding, she seized the opportunity to air her views in a public and formal way at one of the school's Curriculum 14–19 working group meetings. However, she described herself as 'despondent at the unsympathetic response' from fellow middle managers to her proposal that a 'full' GCSE in technology should be compulsory for all students. Sarah was asking for curriculum time, one of the most hotly contested resources in secondary schools (Ball, 1987). It is perhaps unsurprising that the heads of other departments would not voluntarily relinquish curriculum time to another department. However, it does suggest that there was a degree of 'balkanisation' (Hargreaves, 1994) in the culture of the school, where middle managers were thinking more about the political and power implications of decisions rather than about their potential value for pupil learning

This raises the vital question of how teacher leadership can help individuals overcome professional setbacks. Sarah chose to deal with her frustration by 'gathering evidence to persuade the management team that design and technology was worthy of a better deal'. We take this firstly to be proof of an enhanced sense of agency, a belief on Sarah's part that her voice is important and that those in management positions can be influenced. In addition, it indicates a certainty in the value of empirical data to support arguments.

The enquiry that she carried out involved a consultation with different groups within and beyond the school. She engaged in one-to-one conversations, carried out surveys, administered questionnaires and attended meetings to establish as wide a range of views as possible about the perceptions of technology held by students, staff and parents. It is interesting to note here that the process of carrying out this enquiry was itself a valuable strategy for raising awareness of the nature of technology as a discipline. It also allowed her to understand other views and helped her to articulate her arguments more coherently.

She concluded from this intensive phase of enquiry that across the school generally her subject was misunderstood and held in low esteem. However, she felt that the process of enquiry, gathering evidence and consulting with key stakeholders, had itself helped to raise the profile of her subject area. Therefore, she was pleased with the outcome of these negotiations and felt that Design Technology was achieving the recognition it deserved. This story is important because of the stress it places on conflict. Models of school improvement are often couched in terms of the structures and processes needed to manage change, but do not seem to recognise that for many practitioners this is deeply threatening and therefore to be resisted. These models lack both a recognition of conflict and a coherent strategy for its resolution. For us, Sarah's work reveals a vital feature of teacher leadership: in placing the focus on dialogue and collaboration, Sarah developed a framework for negotiation between herself and her managers that sought to find a common language – that is a set of shared values about curriculum change.

Not only did school-based enquiry allow her to find things out, it also brought about enhanced self-knowledge. Sarah realised at the end of her development work that 'there will be no instant results for my efforts in building an effective collaborative team' but looked forward to 'developing my own skills as an effective change agent and those of my team' in order to pursue her agenda in the long term.

Jonathan's story: Empowering A level biology students to become independent learners

Jonathan's development work over a number of years was concerned primarily with empowering students to become independent learners. He began this line of enquiry with a study of a group of students in their first year of Biology A level. He had noticed that students who had experienced success in GCSE science did not always continue to perform well in the first year of their A level biology course. He was keen to find out why this might be, and became interested in the problems students faced in the transition from GCSE to A level (that is into the post-16 or sixth form curriculum). In his enquiry work he sought to find ways to ease students' passage into sixth form science, and considered it important to find out how students themselves viewed the situation. Influenced by ideas about the role of reflective writing in learning (Holly, 1989; Altrichter et al., 1993), he decided to invite them to keep a journal, in which they were to record their thoughts about their learning, his teaching, difficulties they were encountering or any sudden moments of illumination. He then collected the diaries in after a period of time in order to analyse them. He found that overall students seemed to lack confidence in themselves and some even expressed fear of the subject and despair at their chances of success in it.

He began to reflect on his own role in creating this climate in his classroom, and concluded that he had focused too much on his teaching of the material at the expense of their learning:

> My failure to encourage good discussions or encourage students to openly question the work studied compelled me to read more on this issue, believing in the benefits of discussion over more than just lecturing.

We believe this provides excellent evidence of the impact teacher-led enquiry can have on student learning. Having identified a learning gap in his students, he had enquired further into the reasons for this, found evidence that his teaching style was over-directive, and with the help of relevant literature had sought to make changes in his practice. The particular change he wanted to implement concerned the use of oral and discussion work in his classroom. He became convinced that children learn best if they have had the chance to assimilate new material into their own language before writing about it.

Jonathan also found that the process of keeping a journal had become a powerful learning tool for some of his students. He quoted one student thus: 'I feel pretty chuffed when I look back and see what I didn't understand, but now I do'. Jonathan reflected that this kind of statement shows a 'step towards better self-management and independence in learning'.

However, like Sarah and Gloria, Jonathan found some resistance amongst colleagues to his ideas. He shared the teaching of his group with a colleague who made his opposition to Jonathan's experiments in teaching and learning clear both to Jonathan himself and to the students. Reflecting on this, Jonathan came to a similar conclusion as Sarah; that part of the problem arose from his failure to involve his colleague in the initiative from the start.

> More discussion might at least have informed colleagues enough to gain their support for my research, if not their total belief in my methods.

He set about working with his departmental colleagues in a more collegiate way, and was successful in gaining the other biology teacher's agreement to use journals as a routine classroom strategy and to devote more time to classroom discussion. As Jonathan himself put it:

> I have had confirmation that for effective learning to take place there must be dialogue. Teachers must be involved in talking with the students about their learning, giving them positive feedback about their work.

It is fascinating to see this word 'dialogue' appear again. Teachers who engage in school-based enquiry also engage in dialogue with managers, peers, and students in order to better understand the processes of learning in their institutions. It seemed that one of the main impacts, therefore, of this Masters programme at St. James's school was to increase the level of professional discourse that took place in the school.

Jonathan returned to the issue of dialogue:

> I asked students to reflect on past and present performance, attempting to build better awareness about themselves as learners, and with guidance, produce targets that encourage increased independence and more effective learning.

This is a remarkably crisp and clearly expressed vision of the kind of teacher Jonathan wanted to become. He wanted to build a bridge between learning and assessment so that students could have at their fingertips the tools they needed to monitor their own learning and would be able to set realistic targets for future development. In thinking these issues through, he came across Sergiovanni's (1994) ideas about learning communities, which stress the importance of 'commitments' rather than 'contracts' as the glue that binds members of a community together. In other words, it is personal relationships rather than structures that lie at the heart of successful learning communities. Jonathan worried that the language of league tables, raising standards and targets that characterises the public discourse about education was inimical to ideas of community. In his own practice he was determined to 'personalise' the teaching and learning process for his students.

It seemed to Jonathan that the setting up of a mentoring programme would be the best vehicle for him to try out these ideas. He was drawn to Elliott's (1991: 151) assertion that learning involves 'the active construction rather than the passive reproduction of meaning'. He believed that a mentoring scheme would require both the students and their teacher to reflect not only on what was learnt, but on how it was learnt also; that is, the focus would be on both cognition and metacognition.

It is instructive to see also how teachers who engage in enquiry over an extended period of time become more institutionally literate. In planning this round of enquiry, Jonathan, remembering the hostility of his colleague to his journal writing experiment, listed discussion with his head of department and co-teachers as his first action step. We therefore see Jonathan becoming more skilled in working with the culture of the school to achieve his objectives.

As he thought more about the mentoring programme, he came to see that not only could it facilitate learning, but it could also provide a channel whereby students could have a genuine voice in the design of learning experiences. Jonathan realised that the comments students made to him in one-to-one interviews would probably lead to his revising schemes of work to accommodate their perceptions, difficulties and strengths. He agreed with Rudduck and Flutter (2000: 85) that 'the more that regimes are changed to reflect the values that pupils call for ... the stronger pupils' commitment to learning in school is likely to be'.

Jonathan also devoted considerable time to devising success criteria for his project. How would he know whether the mentoring scheme was having an effect on student learning? He knew that it was very difficult to attribute any change in behaviour to any one input. While the setting up of the mentoring scheme could be seen as the impact of belonging to an award-bearing school development programme on his practice, the impact of that change in practice on students would be much harder to discern.

Jonathan's conclusion was that improvements were likely to be found in students' attitudes to learning and it was through a series of interviews with three students that he sought to track this. He found that where the mentoring relationship worked well there was a pre-existing good relationship between student and teacher. Equally, both parties had to be clear as to the purpose of the mentoring interviews so that neither teacher nor student had unrealistic expectations of what could be achieved. For example, some of his students expected Jonathan to simply give them an assessment of their current performance, and then set some targets for the future; they did not expect to have to lead a conversation based on their perception of how things were going. Herein lay one of the chief difficulties that Jonathan had to confront. Nothing in students' backgrounds or prior experiences in school had prepared them for such a fundamental shift in the relationship between teacher and pupil. Therefore, time became a critical factor in Jonathan's programme. It took time to establish the kind of atmosphere he wanted, and then as the year progressed, it became increasingly difficult to find that time to engage in the sort of reflective dialogue necessary.

As he thought through these issues, Jonathan realised that a key determinant of the success of the mentoring programme he had set up was the culture of the school. If students were not required to take responsibility for their own progress in this way elsewhere in their curriculum, then it would remain in students' eyes an enthusiasm of that particular teacher, rather than part of the school's vision of how their learning could be supported. However, it would not be true to say that the culture of the school worked against Jonathan. A working party was set up to review the induction procedures and policies for new sixth formers. The Teaching and Learning Post-16 Group met four times in all outside of school hours and was made up of volunteers from the staff who had a particular interest in post-16 issues. In the event, around 20 colleagues attended at least one of the meetings, the final result of which was a list of proposals for future good practice. One of these proposals was that all teachers of post-16 classes should devote one lesson out of every 12 to one-to-one mentoring. However, what the working party failed to do was to consider the staff development issues from this proposal. The result was that it was only partially successful, and Jonathan was particularly disappointed that there had been 'insufficient planning and not enough thinking regarding the mechanism of change'.

What this account reveals most powerfully is that teaching is much more than a set of techniques by which information is moved from one place to another. It is clear how much of himself Jonathan put into his work and how much becoming a certain type of teacher, and the impact that would have on student learning, were bound up with his own sense of identity.

Working with the culture: developing a model for teacher-led school change

From a close reading of all three stories it can be inferred that successful change comes about not only as result of changing policies, practices and procedures, but also as a result of modifying one's own attitudes, values and beliefs. There is, therefore, a kind of synergy that takes place when change happens successfully, which is not about one force acting upon another to alter it, but rather a subtle process of dialogue, negotiation and accommodation, which affects all those involved.

In addition, the case studies reveal that it is in the carrying out of development work itself that one sees the greatest impact on teachers' professional learning. In these accounts, there is persuasive evidence of a clear link between enquiry and a growth in teachers' capacity to plan, implement and evaluate change. In particular, their stories show teachers negotiating with managers, peers and students to clarify concerns, gather further evidence and plan future action. In our account of Gloria and Sarah's work, we noted their willingness to engage in dialogue with managers, colleagues and governors. We believe the ability to engage in dialogue with all members of the school community in order to address their professional concerns constitutes a highly significant impact on professional learning. This development of institutional literacy, that is, the capacity to make sense of the organisational world and act strategically to bring about cultural change within it, is vital to the growth of teacher leadership. In Jonathan's story, we saw him make significant and demonstrable changes in *how* his students approached learning. The key to this development of students' metacognitive awareness appears to be rooted in increased dialogue with their teachers. Importantly, in his discussions with pupils, Jonathan did not provide simplistic recipes for success so much as build students' capacity to improve their own learning skills.

So from what we have written so far, it seems that some important principles need to be in place before teacher leadership can take develop. The 'givens' necessary for teacher leadership at St. James's to take root were:

- A receptive school culture
- A supportive senior management team
- A recognition that it takes time for relationships and collaborative partnerships to develop if change is to be sustained and deep rooted
- Partnership with an external facilitator
- The challenge and support provided by internal facilitation.

The key indicators of impact on teachers' practice seemed to be:

- Enhanced self-esteem on behalf of teachers
- Increased collaboration with colleagues
- A willingness to listen to the student's voice
- Greater willingness to question own values and those of the institution
- Increased capacity to initiate and lead change.

The impact on the culture of the school was found in:

- Increased levels of participation in whole school decision making
- Increased levels of professional dialogue throughout the school.

The impact on student learning could be seen in:

- The development of metalearning/metacognition in students.

It became clear to us that while the partnership between the school and the Higher Education Institution (HEI) was a vital factor in encouraging the development of teacher-led change, more vital still was the culture of the school. We would argue that the school-HEI partnership at St. James's was instrumental in establishing a culture of learning amongst a sizeable group of teachers, and that this critical mass of individuals was able to influence the 'way we do things around here' (Deal and Kennedy, 1983).

What follows is an attempt to represent the impact of teacher leadership on school culture. Our preferred model takes the form of a web, an ideal shape to represent the importance of networking, but also to represent clearly the interdependence between the various aspects. Figure 5.1 shows the result of these reflections.

The model identifies five interrelated areas that amount to a map of the impact of teacher leadership at St. James's school. These areas are collaborative enquiry, leadership, learning, policies and practice. By 'collaborative enquiry', we mean the systematic and shared gathering and analysis of evidence about practice. By 'leadership', we do not mean simply the actions and policies of those in formal leadership positions, but also the way in which undertaking enquiry helped build teachers' capacity to initiate and lead change, as shown in their stories.

The case studies reveal that many of the most valuable changes were not in policy and practice, but in the attitudes of individuals and groups. We argue that sustained change is more likely to be evolutionary rather than revolutionary in form and that it arises from a process of collaboration and negotiation between teachers that takes place over time. Learning encompasses teachers' professional

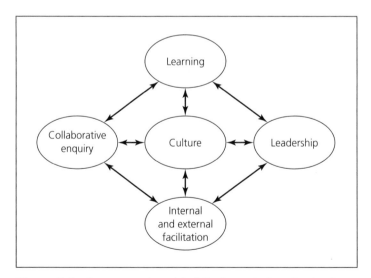

Figure 5.1: A conceptual model of the impact of teacher leadership on teacher, student and organisational learning

learning, organisational learning and student learning. The stories presented above provide evidence of all three types of learning.

This model provides a map of the processes involved in teacher-led change. Most importantly, however, the complementary nature of each of the elements involved is clear. The double-headed arrows represent the dialogue and channels of communication that exist between individuals and groups within an organisation. Culture is placed at the heart of the model to demonstrate how it both shapes and is shaped by teacher leadership. The model is, therefore, more than an example of top-down support for bottom-up change. Rather, there is a commitment in this model to distributed leadership (MacBeath, 2003a; Spillane, 2003). The complexity of schools and the accelerating rate of change mean that it is unrealistic to expect one or even a few leaders to sit at the apex of an organisation wielding total power. A more appropriate and sustainable model that enables schools to keep pace with this rapidly changing environment distributes leadership throughout the organisation in order to build the capacity of all to confront and control change.

Similarly, the transfer of new knowledge about what has worked in a school becomes less to do with providing opportunities for people to talk about their curriculum development work with others, important though this is, but more about the evolving practices of those teachers for whom dialogue and collaboration become integral aspects of how they work, rather than an additional task bolted on to the end of their enquiry.

Teachers as learners, teachers as leaders

How can these ideas be applied to education at the start of the third millennium? It is a key aim of any education system that children leave school having fulfilled their academic potential, while at the same time, having developed as individuals and as members of a community, ready to play a full part in the adult world. We have come to a view of school leadership as less about 'getting things done' or directing the work of others, and more about creating the optimum conditions for learning – student learning, adult learning and organisational learning. In the stories of change illustrated here, distributed leadership means more than the handing out of tasks or roles. In short, the purpose of leadership is to facilitate the growth of a learning organisation (Senge, 1993) or of a learning community (Wenger, 1998). This requires schools to move away from bureaucratic, linear and hierarchical approaches to management, to a more participative, flexible model of school development based on the principle of teacher agency. Such a model should grow out of a culture of reflective practice, criticality, professional dialogue and a commitment to shared decision making, involving all members of the school community.

6 Towards new ways of working

In previous chapters, we have argued for a more holistic approach to improving schools, emphasising leadership of learning by all teachers within their own professional situations and contexts. We have offered tried and tested strategies and frameworks for supporting teachers leading change, emphasising that enquiry can be used not only to inform change but to draw members of the school community into the processes of change. This is made more powerful by working with evidence derived directly from the school contexts within which teachers are working, enriched and informed by wider research evidence and educational discourse. We have provided many illustrations from our developing experience of using these approaches in different scenarios, which have implications for the kinds of internal and external support needed for individuals and for schools. The repertoire of activities along with the examples and checklists can be adapted for use within any school-based programme, project, initiative or development involving teacher enquiry and leadership, to build capacity for improvement within and between schools. The approaches can be applied within any policy context, although we know that policy influences school climates, limiting or liberating teachers' activities and professionalism.

Our research and experience has led to a strong conviction in the importance and enormous potential of teacher leadership through enquiry, as central to school improvement. While it is important to be directly concerned with the practical ways in which teachers and schools can be supported, the theoretical dimension to this work must also be driven forwards. As Frost and Harris (2003) have suggested, there is an urgent agenda for research into the concepts and processes underpinning teachers' leadership of change, as teacher enquiry and shared leadership gather momentum. Strands of this research agenda are scattered across different fields of interest and emphasis within the educational discourse and need to be drawn together, but this is a long-term aim. At this stage, through work which is still very much developmental, our experience and research suggest features and processes that schools might emphasise in working for deep and sustainable improvement. It is also possible to offer ideas that contribute to the construction of the research agenda surrounding teachers leading change.

Practically speaking, rather than presenting this as an opposite approach to that which already exists in schools, it is more helpful to think in terms of a 'movement towards' new approaches, as shown in Figure 6.1 overleaf.

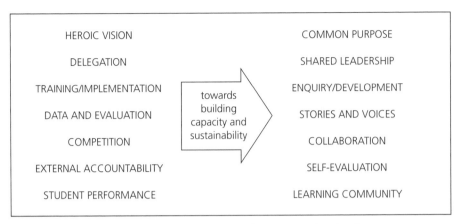

Figure 6.1: Moving towards building capacity for sustainable school improvement

These approaches emphasise people, relationships, enquiry and dialogue in building internal capacity for leadership of learning and enhancing children's educational experience. They are not alien to the current policies with which we are most familiar in England – the rhetoric is full of such language – but such approaches help to counteract the danger of being subsumed by a narrow agenda that still forces schools to concentrate on those aspects on the left-hand side of the diagram. Moving to the right-hand side, if these approaches are used mechanistically for the purposes of implementing initiatives, this may reduce their power. If used creatively, they can offer a framework for further development of school cultures in which teachers and their students can find more affirmation, encouragement and opportunity for learning. While this involves gradual and subtle changes in ways of working, it may require a radical shift in our ways of thinking because these characteristics take seriously notions of human agency, leadership and voice.

Considering each element of Figure 6.1, how can we move towards these more affirmative and sustainable ways of working?

From heroic vision towards common purpose

Headteachers on leadership training programmes often find a strong emphasis on providing a foundation for their schools based on their own clear personal vision and underpinned by their values, as in programmes such as 'New Visions' from the National College for School Leadership (NCSL, 2005). Headteachers are encouraged to involve members of the school community in sharing this vision. In conversation with them, it is evident that this rhetoric can gloss over the fundamental questions about how to arrive at, or even begin to move towards, a genuinely shared vision and common purpose for a school. Headteachers new in post may need to establish a particular direction for their schools; in order to do this they may gather allies by recruiting staff who share their ideas, in particular when appointing senior staff who will support them and whom they can trust. Clearly, while some headteachers have the opportunity to draw together a majority of staff who share their vision, others have to work with varying degrees of success with existing staff to bring them to a shared understanding about values and purposes, while in other schools tensions and ambiguities can lie beneath the surface to such an extent that the mission statements posted around the walls and the policy documents in the headteacher's office may have no chance to become embedded in everyday practice. On the rare occasions when there is time for discussion, usually at pivotal points such as on the appointment of a new head or to inform a new phase in a school's development, teachers may express cynicism. Perhaps this arises partly from the assumption that discussion about values and purposes is distant from the classroom and the business of learning and teaching and it may ultimately express teachers' overwhelming experience that what they say and feel will not make any difference.

It requires considerable patience, therefore, to draw out teachers' values and priorities that may never otherwise be articulated. For 'shared vision' to be formalised there must be time and space for such discussions. The role of informal discussion must not be underestimated, since spontaneous conversations in the staffroom connect with what happens in classrooms, but it is important to make more formal connections. Structured discussion may be easier to achieve in a small school or in sub-groups of staff such as subject departments or year teams. Joining this up across a large school or one with a less close-knit staff or scattered buildings needs careful and skilful facilitation; it is vital that the work of exploring values and building shared vision is meaningful and not contrived or coercive.

Many countries have a more democratic approach than in England and in some of these teacher unions and assemblies are much more prominent in decision-making processes both locally and nationally. Challenges include maintaining a focus on learning and enabling teachers along with other members of the school community to articulate their collective vision and to decide on their purposes as an organisation, as long as there is sufficient tension for rigorous debate. It is important to allow for dissonance and the airing of alternative viewpoints, as suggested in Enquiry Section 5. Through such discussions, teachers exercising leadership and working for change see their work as part of the bigger picture and are able both to use and to change their context.

From delegation towards shared leadership

Schools are traditional, hierarchical institutions where real change happens slowly and is normally resisted both actively and by sheer inertia and exhaustion with initiatives. Despite sustained emphasis on shared leadership, leadership tasks and responsibilities are still normally designated by role through the exercise of some higher authority, usually the headteacher working with a senior leadership team. Leadership is truly 'distributed' – handed out to people – therefore the extent to which the people to whom it is distributed can truly exercise leadership is arguable.

In Chapter 1 we suggested that leadership is a characteristic that exists in everyone and needs to be taken and nurtured rather than given. We have also emphasised the important influence of status and power in the exercise of teacher leadership, worked out through established school structures and cultures. Agendas for change are usually determined externally and imposed or decided internally by a small number of senior staff. In order to break out of this culture a headteacher has to take risks. The sense of timing is crucial; some schools where there is little capacity for leadership and growth may require strong direction in order to build confidence and create the conditions wherein leadership can be shared.

However, distributed leadership is not something that can be turned on and off as the situation demands. It is not a tool; it arises from a particular value position and therefore even where the headteacher may have to adopt a strong and clear stance, this can involve principles of parallel and shared leadership, for example in the making of decisions, in the sharing of existing expertise, in shaping school structures and processes to develop a greater sense of responsibility, to ensure voices are heard and to enable collaborative working to take place. The challenge is to make certain that school improvement processes take account of the role of all teachers, along with other members of the school community. This raises expectations about the contributions they can and do make as part of their normal professional responsibilities. Building capacity for leadership of learning and school improvement is about new concepts of professionalism, not about new models for structuring leadership.

From training and implementation towards enquiry and development

Despite the tensions in the current policy in England, there is a clear intention to build teacher enquiry into professional learning and the links with leadership development are more overt than previously (DfES, 2005a). However, traditional views of research are still latent in schools and while much progress has been made in small pockets and with individual teachers, teacher enquiry is still linked with academic courses – the ivory towers of the university, the mistrusted methods of white-coated scientists and the fanaticism of enthusiastic scholars.

We have shown through the many illustrations in this book that enquiry is not simply a source of information from which to make decisions about directions and strategies for change. It is integral to the sustenance of a critical and challenging approach to practice, a focus for collaborative working and a motivating and energising force. Involving teachers in processes of gathering and interpreting evidence is often the first step towards developing their capacity to exercise leadership; it provokes them to ask questions and seek new directions in their practice.

This requires new ways of thinking about professional development through leadership of learning, or even *as* leadership of learning. Where training and dissemination models persist and where simplistic notions of causality and impact pervade, these should be challenged. Where teachers' learning and professional support are low priority, for example in countries and cultures emphasising subject knowledge rather than pedagogy and where teaching is viewed more technically and less vocationally, the strategies we have described have to be introduced in a particularly subtle and gentle manner, to encourage and energise rather than to disturb and threaten, starting from where teachers are and moulding these approaches to their circumstances and contexts.

Where there is a shortage of time, resources and priority, many of the activities and approaches can be introduced using the minimum of equipment. There is a great deal that can be done with a circle of chairs, a flipchart and some pens. As momentum gathers, the value of providing more space and time for teachers to collaborate in development work becomes increasingly evident, particularly when working in networks and clusters of schools. This should result in a shift of emphasis towards the facilitation of teachers' leadership of enquiry-based development work, as opposed to bringing in expensive 'experts' and deluging teachers with training packs devoid of any supporting processes for introducing and embedding the information into practice.

Moreover, far from substituting for the huge range of excellent materials and resources available, the approaches suggested in this book can provide frameworks for selecting, comparing, trialling and developing these materials and adapting them to purpose – collaboratively, critically and in context. What we are advocating, therefore, is not an instrumental package or formula, but a different way of thinking and working, on the part of schools and also the institutions and agencies that support them. Professional development becomes individually tailored and is integral to processes of investigating practice and leading change.

From data and evaluation towards stories and voices

Schools are now far more used to evaluative processes through external accountability requirements and most enrich these observations and judgements through internal self-evaluation in its various forms. However, schools are still subject to the tyranny of the quantitative, forced to value what is more easily measurable and comparable, instead of ensuring that they measure what is truly valued. Schools are full of unused and under-used data; information that is provided for one purpose may not be made available more widely, in particular to those who might be able to relate to it and interpret it most effectively.

We have argued that it is people's stories, the combination of voices heard and shared, that moves schools forwards and draws individuals into communication and action leading to improvement. Providing opportunities for dialogue around evidence, carefully facilitated and with clear purpose, is essential for a learning community that wishes to grow, and narratives are an essential part of that evidence. The balances and checks that are afforded by analytical and critical dialogue, particularly through involvement of external support and critical friendship, are important but no more so than in the use of numerical data, statistical summaries of survey data and the like. Again the value and power of dialogic approaches are harnessed through a clear focus on improving learning.

The examples of teacher leadership in Chapters 3 and 5 are about teacher leaders' personal stories of learning and change interacting with those of their colleagues and students. Many teachers understand the importance of the voices around them and can work in sophisticated ways amongst them, crossing the boundaries of roles, classrooms, schools and communities and building bridges of understanding. This enables people to support one another in mutual learning, exploring each other's perspectives and seeing how each person's story influences another's. An enquiry approach that embraces these voices, conversations and stories, deepens and structures learning to support change.

From competition towards collaboration

Schools can be surprisingly uncollaborative places. Teachers with little time to spare fall back on their own resources and ideas in planning their classroom activity. They spend evenings and weekends preparing resources, making or collecting 'props' to furnish self-sufficient classrooms and planning in isolation lessons that may run in parallel with those of colleagues who are teaching the same age group according to the same curriculum. Where teachers do realise the value of collaboration on these practical matters and develop less isolated approaches, it is evident that there are other dimensions to the activity. The level of professional dialogue and sharing is raised, individuals are challenged to account for their own practices, ideas pass backwards and forwards, confidence is gained as everyday knowledge and information is shared, and there is great security in fellow feeling and experience which provide the basis for experimentation. As one teacher has explained:

> I think people feel safer knowing everybody's doing it and that for once we all know that we are being consistent ... that we are moving forward together on something we can achieve. (Frost and Durrant, 2002: 153).

Teachers' leadership of learning can spread beyond the school boundaries, supported by networks and collaborative links. In Example 3.8 (p.52) this started through government funding for one of the schools chosen as a 'Beacon School' and charged to share its excellence, which led into the establishment of a Networked Learning Community funded by the National College for School Leadership. The summary in Chapter 3 explains how teachers at every stage of their careers are supported in leadership development with a strong focus on improving learning for the whole *town's* young people rather than just those students within each school. An external evaluation of the network found that this purpose was widely shared amongst teachers and headteachers. By working together over a long period and by sharing activities and expertise, many of the town's schools have broken barriers down and learned to work together, predominantly in the primary sector but with some key links with secondary schools where appropriate.

In Ruth's case in Example 3.4, (p. 45) the former Education Action Zone (now an Excellence Cluster) provided a forum for sharing her school's story and she has also run a workshop for Masters students, tutors, advisors, researchers and consultants at a network conference. As a headteacher she is encouraging the teachers in her school to share their experiences of leading development based on enquiry, for example through NCSL programmes, and the school is now receiving many visitors as word of its success spreads.

Collaborative working seems to rely greatly on the attitude and drive of the headteacher who ultimately governs teachers' time, enabling them to work together in school time and creating conducive conditions for collaboration. This requires headteachers to exercise considerable generosity where invest-ment of time and resources relies on the integrity of teachers to make this worthwhile. It may also involve simple measures like rearranging furniture and rooms to encourage interaction rather than isolation. Headteachers are responsible not only for the practicalities, but also to a large extent for the bal-ance of ethos towards collaboration or competition. In secondary schools in particular, where subject leaders or team leaders are set against each other in a 'balkanised' culture (Hargreaves, 1994), with tensions over budgets, resources and territory and being called to account in comparisons of student perfor-mance data, this militates against the learning and sharing that is helpful in moving schools forward. Where teachers are comfortable with working together in their own schools, they feel more confident to cross the boundary into a wider arena.

From external accountability towards self-evaluation

As we have suggested in Chapter 1 and Enquiry Section 7, the relationship between self-evaluation and inspection, internal and external accountability, is a crucial one. Exploration of the issues and the development of tools and strate-gies to help to make this relationship effective have been spearheaded by John MacBeath's immensely influential work, which now informs school improve-ment worldwide (MacBeath, 1999; MacBeath et al., 2000; MacBeath, Sugimini et al., 2003; MacBeath, Demetriou et al., 2003; MacBeath and Oduro, 2005). Central to this work is the notion of voice, which we have previously discussed in relation to evidence and enquiry. Here the concern is not only in providing evidence and contributing to discussions about change but also in taking collec-tive responsibility. An over-emphasis on external accountability for schools removes responsibility, encouraging improvement to satisfy judgements from the outside, to tick the necessary boxes as established criteria are met. Schools developing competence and confidence in self-evaluation can use this as an ongoing process feeding continually into planning and improvement, develop-ing stronger internal accountability. Where teachers and others feel that they are 'evaluating' rather than 'being evaluated', the responsibility for striving for excellent learning and teaching becomes shared and accountability resides more firmly within each individual's professionalism.

Although we have placed considerable emphasis on teachers' individual and collaborative enquiry, school self-evaluation is an *institutional* enquiry process. Teachers should be encouraged to view their own investigations as contributions to a whole-school process, while headteachers need to explore how to make best use of these contributions. Documenting evidence and change is vital in order to provide a body of information that can be shared. This 'institutional archive' is often intangible and disconnected; in order to make self-evaluation effective, the processes by which the various strands of enquiry and sets of evidence are joined together need to be properly planned. This requires another layer of responsibility for teachers leading change, as their enquiry or research is conducted not only on behalf of their students, themselves and their colleagues but also on behalf of their schools. Where working in networks and clusters, this applies even more widely.

Obviously this is far from straightforward; there is no one model that can be used for this purpose. Most important is a willingness to adopt these challenges and provide the space for discussing and working them through. Headteachers in Example 3.8 (p. 52) in Chapter 3 have worked together on this issue. They have compared processes and frameworks for self-evaluation and school improvement planning in their schools, focusing particularly on ways of involving different groups of stakeholders and sharing responsibility. They have developed some evaluation tools and formats that are common across the network, collaborated on drawing up some guidelines for school improvement planning based on self-evaluation, and have discussed and developed their ideas about research, enquiry and the nature of evidence related to school improvement. They have also explored different ways of obtaining external perspectives on the learning taking place in schools and through network activity, including enlisting external support for self-review and conducting learning visits to make classroom observations and discuss issues in each other's schools. This is not expected to yield a 'solution' or 'model'; what is important is the *dialogue* around evidence, involvement and improvement and their collective responsibility for every child's learning.

From student performance towards a learning community

Teachers and headteachers would not dismiss academic standards as unimportant, but would also talk about 'educating the whole person', about different facets of learning, about social and emotional skills and personal growth, about children's self-esteem and confidence.

Following the distinct change in emphasis from teaching to learning that has already pervaded many schools, a further shift in thinking is required to make the concept of the 'learning community' a reality. As Riley and Jordan (2004) point out, this work is context and culture specific, but common elements such as collaboration, reflection, emphasis on learning, engagement and inclusivity are widely agreed. To develop these in practice, however, requires sophisticated understanding and development of complex processes of knowledge creation, transfer and application. As explained above, this may require new understandings of professionalism: teachers need to be drawn into learning and leadership and this requires a better understanding of the relationships between teachers' learning, organisational learning and student learning and of how these relationships might be developed. Furthermore, around this we need to build the learning of policymakers, advisors and academics as part of the wider educational learning community, with the common purpose of school improvement. Schools draw upon many different relationships and groupings, involving schools and the individuals within them in many overlapping communities of practice (Wenger 1998) serving interlinked purposes.

Teachers are at the very heart of this process, best placed to understand how organisational learning affects students in the classroom and best able both to inform and implement change. Where teachers are engaged in learning about their practice, motivated to ask questions, gather evidence, reflect and analyse in order to improve their students' learning, the effect goes beyond finding answers and developing strategies. Teachers who are modelling learning and communicating a love of learning generate an excitement that is in itself motivating and which conveys a powerful message, while headteachers in turn can motivate their staff in the same way.

Teacher-led development is not only appropriate for 'successful' or 'improving' schools but can be a means in itself to improvement. In challenging schools under pressure to raise standards, support and structuring by the headteacher and senior staff can create the conditions for building capacity for improvement through collaborative enquiry, enhanced professional discourse and teachers' leadership of change (Frost, 2005). Teacher leaders are instrumental themselves in building this capacity. The most effective leaders of learning, like Ruth, the headteacher in Example 3.4, (p. 45) are those who are enthusiastic about learning themselves and who cannot help but communicate this to others. A genuine learning community is one that captures this spirit.

An antidote

The approaches described in this book and encapsulated by Figure 6.1 offer some challenges to the current climate in both England and the USA, where performance targets pervade the rhetoric, thinly masked by the language of collaboration, creativity and capacity building. They help to balance current approaches to research and evaluation in schools that favour quick, quantified assessments of complex and changing phenomena. They also help to counteract the pressure upon headteachers and LEAs (districts) to deliver ever-improved performances within ever-shorter timescales.

Subjection to performative, judgemental, mechanistic regimes saps strength, crushes creativity, erodes relationships and denies humanity. Headteachers may, while keeping a weather eye on meeting the necessary demands, work hard to enable school communities to flourish, but with pressure to complete quality surveys, meet deadlines, attain targets and bid for funding, they are drawn into political games. In completing self-evaluation forms for external accountability: 'How do we show that we are aware of our limitations while not calling too much attention to them which might invite greater scrutiny?' In raising standards judged by public lists – league tables – of performance: 'How can we adjust the entry of pupils to the school to improve results?' and 'Should we focus teaching on the tests?' In bidding for specialised status or funding: 'What links with the community and with our feeder schools can we construct for the purposes of the bid?' These dilemmas are part of the conversation of headteachers who know that there are severe consequences for schools that are not deemed to be 'successful'. They are forced into competition – for funding, for status, for children – knowing that, in England at least, we have a system where parents who are ambitious, affluent and aware may move house to guarantee places in the 'right' catchment areas. This exacerbates the differences between 'good' and 'bad' schools, with perceptions fuelled by the media. The cost of becoming a 'named and shamed' school is greater prescription, performance training, scrutiny and pressure, so while few headteachers would argue against the importance of raising standards, it is also in schools' interests to play the performance game in order to give themselves the scope to develop their own preferred ways of working.

We are not advocating replacement approaches, but rather ideas to suffuse school communities with the values, processes and cultures that enable human beings to flourish, grow and enjoy learning together. These can be applied whatever the prevailing educational climate. Headteachers and teachers working in parallel to build capacity need more than piecemeal individual support. While individual teachers' lives can be changed through involvement in research or collaborative development work, more coherent strategies are needed to change school cultures, although a single project can be the catalyst (see Frost, 2005; Holden, 2002b). In practice, this should result in long-term improvement that includes, but is not restricted to, standards of pupil performance, enhancing school improvement and effectiveness by improving learning in sustainable ways and in many dimensions.

No soft option

The alternative approaches we are suggesting focus on the long term and on building teachers' and schools' capacity to sustain themselves, counteracting the 'quick fix' mentality and emphasising the collective rather than the competitive. They express a more sustainable possibility in which schools work together and hold themselves jointly accountable for improvement. Those who have developed such approaches stress that this is no soft option, as we demonstrated in Chapter 3. Trusting relationships, real dialogue and critical friendship encourage a kind of honesty that is difficult to express in questionnaires, surveys and snapshot observations, even if honesty is the intention of respondents and those observed. Collaboration and involvement enable people to work towards the heart of issues and seek real explanations and understandings. Use of evidence and frameworks for enquiry linked to change gives this a 'hard edge', bringing questions, issues and challenges to the surface and creating a critical and authentic dialogue around learning that fuels further learning. Teachers once initially engaged become committed, because as well as seeing the value in terms of school improvement, this kind of activity helps them to make meaning of their professional lives.

The teachers, headteachers and schools that have developed the approaches discussed in this book are subject to the same pressures and policy regimes as other schools, and English schools in particular, have had to adopt hard-headed and sometimes courageous strategies in order to meet external accountability requirements while building capacity for leadership and learning. They have taken risks in allowing enquiry and creativity to flourish and long-term processes to become embedded. Headteachers are bearing the brunt of the pressure, facing inwards towards their schools to ensure that learning and teaching measure up to standards externally imposed, while facing outwards to offer a measure of protection for a school community wishing to develop, learn and grow in its own way. Their schools have experimented with development of leadership of learning in ways that are rigorous and challenging but also interesting and imaginative, affirming and supportive, valuable and credible. They engage everyone in a collective endeavour to improve educational achievement and experience.

As we have evaluated these strategies, representatives of schools supported by one higher education partnership commented that the characteristic openness, trust and freedom of this work were different from their experience in working with their LEA, where information could be published outside of the school and outside the school's control, and where there was perceived to be more judgement involved (Durrant et al. 2004; see also Swaffield, 2003a). LEA staff are, of course, subject to pressure themselves. Headteachers were emphatic that they did not want to be scrutinised by their immediate peers, especially if they were working hard to improve standards but still, in terms of external targets, had some way to go (Durrant et al., 2004). It is worth noting that tension was heightened in this specific area by the differentiation and competition between schools caused by selection by ability. It was therefore extremely important that development work was carried out through trusting relationships and without setting up hierarchies where less successful schools learnt from 'good' schools. Schools need affirmation, confidence and support to create conditions whereby difficult questions and challenges to practice can be faced.

A learning disposition

University staff may have advantages in supporting this kind of work because of their freedom from the constraints of accountability (Frost and Durrant, 2003). However, it is important not to restrict the dialogue to academic concerns but to encompass also the strategic dimension. External facilitators and teams therefore need to be carefully chosen to involve people with practical experience of teaching and school leadership as well as methodological expertise, an ability to think critically and creatively and flexible, responsive ways of working. The most experienced facilitators and critical friends speak humbly about their own learning in these situations and indeed the success of the work depends on consultants or tutors adopting a learning approach themselves. For ourselves, we are more comfortable in learning alongside teachers rather than casting ourselves as experts (Holden, 2002b). Tentativeness in the role of consultant is expressed in this journal entry on arriving as an English consultant in Sicily (see Example 3.7, p. 50):

> On my first evening here I am wondering what we can all learn from this. How can two people from England contribute to school improvement in Italy? Will we even be able to have a conversation? Will the political and cultural differences be too great for us to understand one another or learn from each other? (Durrant, 2004)

As well as expressing a learning attitude, this journal extract illustrates the lack of prior knowledge and the extent of the risk that is characteristic of much partnership work using dialogic, investigative, capacity building approaches. The visit did result in powerful learning for all involved. This depended more on attitudes and long-term relationships based on shared values than it did on content and detailed planning. The learning focus was clear and the other key elements for sustaining improvement outlined in Figure 3.3 (use of evidence, collaboration, trust, dialogue, planning and leadership) were evident. We have found that a *disposition towards learning* is essential, something that can be modelled and enacted by teacher leaders, headteachers and all those involved in supporting their work. This is not an expression of uncertainty; the certainty comes from convictions about the common purposes and values, articulated through partnerships, relationships and dialogue, that underpin all our endeavours.

De-mystifying capacity building through teacher leadership

By careful use of enquiry techniques and strategies as explained in Chapter 3, teachers can involve colleagues, students and others in the development process. Teachers use existing relationships and situational understanding to bring about change through sophisticated processes that encourage wider ownership. They know what is likely to work, often employing a range of small approaches over time and as appropriate:
One teacher said,

> It's not very nice to be told that what you're doing isn't very good ... really I think people on the whole are very talented and I think we've lost some of the sparkle in people, in individual flair and skills. (Frost and Durrant, 2004: 321)

However, teacher leaders can offer ways forward:

> I've been chipping away, I have done it very gently and said it's not going to be a lot of extra work and this is how we'll do it. Every staff meeting I or the deputy head has made some mention of (the development work) and praised staff ... and so on. (unpublished teacher interview)

In seeking wider ownership of change, pseudo consultation – asking opinions and then presenting ready-made ideas – is damaging. Headteachers must employ a range of different strategies to support genuine leadership by teachers (see Appendix 4 www.paulchapmanpublishing.co.uk/resource/durrant.pdf).

An excitement about learning cannot easily be faked, planned for, or achieved through training. It can, however, be cultivated through giving support, 'space', permission even, to flourish and grow. It can certainly be spread or 'caught' and it suffocates through cynicism and exhaustion. Headteachers who wish to foster such a climate recruit teachers who will contribute to it, but on the inside, teacher leaders can have the understanding and patience to win less enthusiastic colleagues round. Teacher leaders embody capacity building, working strategically through small steps and simple, inexpensive approaches that build easily into existing practices, as shown in Appendix 5 www.paulchapmanpublishing. co.uk/resource/durrant.pdf. Precious commodities apart from time are imagination, confidence, empathy and situational understanding; these can only be acquired and exercised by working alongside people.

The role of teacher leaders: agency, authority and action

Earlier in this book, research, leadership and continuing professional development are presented as cul-de-sacs of activity that may divert us from the core purpose of improving student learning if they become aims in themselves. It is suggested that these areas of discourse can be bridged by engaging teachers in leading learning, of their students, themselves and each other, and of their schools as organisations. The current discourse in the field of teacher leadership (Crowther et al., 2002; Katzenmeyer and Moller, 2001; Frost and Durrant, 2003; Frost and Harris, 2003) supports the argument that teachers have the capacity to exercise leadership in a radical sense. As experts in their own practice, they need to escape the rhetoric of involvement, participation and team building that empowers them 'to do what they have been told to do' (Gunter, 2001: 144) and claim authority to contribute to the shaping of school structures, cultures and policies. This involves teachers encouraging leadership in their colleagues, so that shared or distributed leadership is not dispensed by the headteacher, used as an implementation tool or represented by a list of roles and tasks, but becomes a value underpinning the way in which schools work.

For 'authentic school improvement', Hopkins (2001) argues that we need to look beyond intervention to carry through a series of initiatives. We have instead to be developing strategies that enhance the learning of teachers as well as students, including collaborative research to create and share new knowledge about practice, schools and change. Most importantly, as shown in the examples in this book, encouraging teachers to reflect, challenge, plan and exercise leadership of learning enables a school to manage its own improvement processes. Policy that bypasses human agency, presenting teachers merely as implementers of policy and recipients of training, omits a fundamental dimension of professionalism; it eliminates the political dimensions of practice. Teachers can use enquiry powerfully to support their leadership, with uncompromising commitment to making a difference to children's learning and school experience, while also building capacity for school improvement through paying attention to the importance of their own and one another's learning and leadership. Thus their professional learning is not restricted to the themes of a particular enquiry, but embraces the transferable skills, strategies and sensitivity required for leadership in complex school environments.

As we have already noted, leadership involves not only *agency* (capacity to make a difference) but also *strategic action* to narrow the gap between the current reality and the vision of 'what could be and what ought to be' (Frost and Durrant, 2003: 2). Teachers' genuine engagement in leadership, rather than just the implementation of change, enables them to operate more effectively, intelligently and critically within changing policy contexts, working to high standards and 'responding creatively, imaginatively and with finesse' to changing situations (Elmore, 2004). Schools and external agents working together can provide frameworks and structures for practical support of teacher leadership and conduct research to develop further our understanding about the nature and effectiveness of teacher leadership (Frost and Harris, 2003). Together we must explore the issues of power, ownership, authority and involvement that need to be addressed in order to motivate and enable every teacher to take up their leading role in school change.

Sustainability within

Through the strategies explored and illustrated in this book, teachers can assume a central role in change not just as implementers and recipients but by being active in setting agendas and in providing the leadership to make changes work. Enquiry is essential in enabling them to assume control over their practice and to assimilate evidence to support the developments they are advocating. It develops both their personal capacity – skills, knowledge, understanding, confidence and self-esteem – and their interpersonal capacity – their ability to work collaboratively, to participate in dialogue and to lead and manage change.

Schools, working with external agents where appropriate, need to develop communities of practice that foster everyone's interest and excitement about learning. Through this, teachers' leadership of learning cements the relationships by which schools can improve. This is the only way in which we can realistically approach the notion of sustainability, that ability to maintain excellence through the shifting phases of policy; changing demography; the ebb and flow of staff and students; further developments in technology, information and communication; community, societal and political change. This certainty, not only of survival but of growth and flourishing, cannot be injected or imposed. It must be nurtured from within.

Bibliography

Ainscow, M., Hopkins, D., Southworth, G. and West, M. (1994) *Creating the Conditions for School Improvement: A handbook of staff development activities.* London: David Fulton.

Ainscow, M., Hargreaves, D., Hopkins, D., Balshaw, M. and Black-Hawkins, K. (1994) *Mapping Change in Schools: The Cambridge Manual of Research Techniques* (First Edition). Cambridge: Institute of Education.

Alcock, K. (2003) 'NQTs: Developing professionally in their induction year'. Paper presented at In-service Professional Development Association Conference, Birmingham, 31 October.

Altrichter, H., Posch, P. and Somekh, B. (1993) *Teachers Investigate their Work: An introduction to the methods of action research.* London and New York: Routledge.

Angus, L. (1993) 'New Leadership and the possibility of educational reform', in J. Smyth (ed.), *A Socially Critical View of the Self-managing School.* London: Falmer Press. pp. 63–92.

Arnot, M., McIntyre, D., Pedder, D. and Reay, D. (2004) *Consultation in the Classroom: Developing dialogue about teaching and learning.* Cambridge: Pearson Publishing.

Assessment Reform Group (1999) *Assessment for Learning: Beyond the black box.* Cambridge: School of Education, University of Cambridge.

Atkinson, P. and Delamont, S. (1985) 'Bread and dreams or bread and circuses? A critique of case study research in education' in M. Shipman (ed.), *Educational Research: Principles, policies and practice.* London: Falmer Press. pp. 26–45.

Ball, S. (1987) *The Micro-Politics of the School: Towards a theory of school organisation.* London: Methuen.

Ball, S. (1991) 'Power, conflict, micropolitics and all that!', In G. Walford (ed.), *Doing Educational Research.* London: Routledge. pp. 166–92.

Ball, S. (1994) 'Researching inside the state: issues in the interpretation of elite interviews', in D. Halpin and B. Troyna (eds), *Researching Educational Policy: Ethical and Methodological Issues.* London: Falmer Press. pp. 107–20.

Barber, M. (1996) *The Learning Game: arguments for an education revolution.* London: Gollancz.

Barth, R. (1990) *Improving Schools from Within.* San Francisco: Jossey-Bass.

Bascia, N. and Hargreaves, A. (eds) (2000) *The Sharp Edge of Educational Change: Teaching, leading and the realities of reform.* London: RoutledgeFalmer.

Bassey, M. (2003) 'If the power to pursue excellence in research in education were vested in teachers, research would have a key role', *Research Intelligence,* 83: 22–31.

Beare, H. (2001) *Creating the Future School*. London: RoutledgeFalmer.

Bell, J. (1999) *Doing Your Research Project: A guide for first time researchers in Education* (2nd edition). Buckingham: Open University Press.

Bennett, N., Crawford, M. and Cartwright, M. (eds) (2003) *Effective Educational Leadership*. London: Paul Chapman Publishing.

Bolton, G. (2001) *Reflective Practice: Writing and professional development*. London: Paul Chapman Publishing.

Bottery, M. (2004) *The Challenges of Educational Leadership*. London: Paul Chapman Publishing.

British Educational Research Association (2004) Ethical Guidelines: http://www.bera.ac.uk/guidelines.html (accessed 2005).

CANTARNET (2005) Canterbury Action Research Network: http://education-resources.cant.ac.uk/cantarnet/ (accessed 2005).

Carnell, E. and Lodge, C. (2001) *Supporting Effective Learning*. London: Paul Chapman Publishing.

Clarke, P. (2000) *Learning Schools, Learning Systems*. London: Continuum.

Claxton, G. (1997) *Hare Brain, Tortoise Mind: How intelligence increases when you think less*. London: Fourth Estate.

Claxton, G. (1999) *Wise Up: The challenge of lifelong learning*. London: Bloomsbury.

Connolly, F.M. and Clandinin, D.J. (1990) 'Stories of experience and narrative inquiry', *Education Researcher*, 20 (4): 2–14.

Cordingley, P., Bell, M., Rundell, B. and Evans, D. (2003) 'The impact of collaborative CPD on classroom teaching and learning', *Research Evidence in Education Library*. London: EPPI-Centre, Social Science Research Unit, Institute of Education: http//eppi.ioe.ac.uk/EPPIWeb/home.aspx (accessed 2005).

Costa, A. and Kallick, B. (1993) 'Through the lens of a critical friend', *Educational Leadership*, 51 (2): 49–51.

Craft, A. (1997) 'Identity and Creativity: Educating teachers for postmodernism?', *Teacher Development,* 1 (1): 83–96.

Crowther, F., Kaagan, S., Ferguson, M. and Hann, L. (2002) *Developing Teacher Leaders: How teacher leadership enhances school success*. Thousand Oaks, CA: Corwin Press.

CUREE (2005) Centre for the Use of Research and Evidence in Education: www.curee-paccts.com (accessed 2005).

Dadds, M.(1993) 'Thinking and being in teacher action research', in J. Elliott (ed.), *Reconstructing Teacher Education*. London: Falmer Press.

Darling-Hammond, L. and McLaughlin, M.W. (1995) 'Policies that support professional development in an era of reform', *Phi Delta Kappan,* 76 (8): 597–604.

Day, C. (1999) *Developing Teachers: The challenges of lifelong learning*. London: Falmer.

Day, C. (2004) *A Passion for Teaching*. London: RoutledgeFalmer.

Day, C., Fernandez, A., Hauge, T. and Moller, J. (eds) (2000) *The Life and Work of Teachers: International perspectives in changing times*. London: Falmer Press.

de Bono, E. (1986) *Six Thinking Hats*. London: Penguin.

de Botton, A. (2002) *The Art of Travel*. London: Penguin.

Deal, T.E. and Kennedy A. (1983) 'Culture and school performance', *Educational Leadership,* 40 (5): 140–1.

DfEE (1997) *From Targets to Action.* London: HMSO.

DfEE (1999) *National College for School Leadership: A prospectus.* London: DfEE.

DfEE (2000) *Professional Development: support for teaching and learning.* London: HMSO.

DfEE (2001) *Learning and Teaching: A strategy for professional development.* London: HMSO.

DfES (2003a) Best Practice Research Scholarships: http://www.teachernet.gov.uk/bprs (accessed 2003).

DfES (2003b) *Excellence and Enjoyment: A strategy for primary schools.* London: HMSO.

DfES (2004a) *A New Relationship with Schools.* London: HMSO.

DfES (2004b) *Pedagogy and Practice: Teaching and learning in secondary schools.* London: HMSO.

DfES (2005a) *Leading and Coordinating CPD in Secondary Schools.* London: HMSO.

DfES (2005b): http://www.teachernet.gov.uk (accessed 2005).

DfES (2005c): Standards Site: http://www.standards.dfes.gov.uk (accessed 2005).

Diamond, C.T.P. (1991) *Teacher Education as Transformation: A psychological perspective.* Milton Keynes: Open University Press.

Durrant, J. (1997) 'Reflective action planning for professional and school development: An investigation through collaborative action research'. Unpublished M.A. dissertation. Canterbury: Canterbury Christ Church College.

Durrant, J. (2003) 'Partnership, leadership and learning', *Professional Development Today,* Spring: 6–12.

Durrant, J. (2004) 'Self-evaluation and shared leadership for school improvement: Seminario Internazionale sull'Autovalutazinoe d'Istituto per il Miglioramento della Qualita: Aspetti di Una Leadership Diffusa – learning from a Sicilian experience', *The Enquirer,* Summer: 28–34. Canterbury: Canterbury Christ Church University College.

Durrant, J. (forthcoming) 'Teachers leading change: frameworks and key ingredients for school improvement', in *Leading and Managing* (Special Edition on Teacher Leadership), 10 (2): 10–29.

Durrant, J., Dunnill, R. and Clements, S. (2004), 'Helping schools to know themselves: Exploring partnerships between schools and higher education institutions to generate trustful, critical dialogue for review and development', *Improving Schools,* 7 (2): 151–70.

Edmonds, D. (2004) 'Leading development work'. Unpublished M.A. portfolio. Canterbury: Canterbury Christ Church University College.

Elliott, J. (1991) *Action Research for Educational Change.* Buckingham: Open University Press.

Elliott, J. (1993a) 'Professional education and the idea of a practical educational science', in J. Elliott (ed.), *Reconstructing Teacher Education.* London: Falmer Press, pp. 65–85.

Elliott, J. (ed.) (1993b) *Reconstructing Teacher Education.* London: Falmer Press.

Elliott, J. (1996) 'School effectiveness research and its critics: Alternative visions of schooling', *Cambridge Journal of Education*, 26 (2): 199–224.

Elliott, J. (1998) *The Curriculum Experiment: Meeting the challenge of social change.* Buckingham: OUP.

Elmore, R. (2002) 'Hard questions about practice', *Beyond Instructional Leadership*, 59 (8): 22–5.

Elmore R. (2004) 'The hollow core of leadership practice in education'. Paper presented at 2nd International Summit for Leadership in Education: 'Integrity and Interdependence', 4–6 November, Boston, USA.

ESRC (2001) 'Communicating ...', ESRC Network Project Newsletter No. 1, May: http://www.consultingpupils.co.uk (accessed 2005).

ESRC (2005) Consulting pupils project website: http://www.consultingpupils. co.uk (accessed 2005).

Essex County Council (2003) *The Research Engaged School.* Chelmsford: Essex County Council.

Field, K. (2003) *Portfolio of Professional Development: Structuring and recording teachers' career development.* London: Optimus Publishing.

Fielding, M. (1996) 'Empowerment: emancipation or enervation?'. *Journal of Education Policy.* 2 (3): 399–417.

Fielding, M. (1999) 'Communities of learners. Myth: Schools are communities' in B. O'Hagan, (ed.), *Modern Educational Myths.* London: Kogan Page: pp. 64–84.

Fielding, M. (2001) 'Beyond the rhetoric of student voice: new departures or new constraints in the transformation of 21st century schooling'. *Forum* 43 (2): 100–109.

Fielding, M. (2004) 'Transformative approaches to student voice: Theoretical underpinnings, recalcitrant realities', *British Educational Research Journal*, 30(2): 295–311.

Fielding, M. and Bragg, S. (2003) *Students as Researchers: Making a difference.* Cambridge: Pearson Publishing.

Fink, D. (1998) 'Confronting complexity: A framework for action', *Improving Schools,* 1 (3): 54–8.

Frost, D. (2003) 'Teacher leadership: towards a research agenda', paper presented within the Symposium 'Leadership for Learning: the Cambridge Network', International Congress for School Effectiveness and Improvement, Sydney, 5–8 January 2003.

Frost, D. (2004) 'What can headteachers do to support teachers' Leadership?', *Inform* No.4. Paper produced for Leadership for Learning: the Cambridge Network, University of Cambridge.

Frost, D. (2005) 'Resisting the juggernaut: Building capacity through teacher leadership in spite of it all', *Leading and Managing* (Special Edition on Teacher Leadership) 10 (2): 70–87.

Frost, D. and Durrant, J. (2002) 'Teachers as leaders: Exploring the impact of teacher-led development work', *School Leadership and Management,* 22 (2): 143–61.

Frost, D. and Durrant, J. (2003) *Teacher Led Development Work: Guidance and support.* London: David Fulton.

Frost, D. and Durrant, J. (2004) 'Supporting teachers' leadership: What can principals do? A teacher perspective from research', in J. Chrispeels (ed.), *Learning to Lead Together: The promise and challenge of sharing leadership.* Thousand Oaks, CA: Sage Publications. pp. 307–26.

Frost, D. and Harris, A. (2003) 'Teacher leadership: Towards a research agenda', *Cambridge Journal of Education,* 33 (3): 479–98.

Frost, D., Cullen, J. and Cunningham, H. (2003) 'Making a difference: Building a research community of practice', *Professional Development Today,* 6(2): 13–20.

Frost, D., Durrant, J., Head, M. and Holden, G. (2000) *Teacher-Led School Improvement.* London: RoutledgeFalmer.

Fryer, J. (2000) 'Mentoring for improvement: The role of mentoring in post-16 science education'. Unpublished M.A. dissertation. Canterbury: Canterbury Christ Church University College.

Fullan, M. (1991) *The New Meaning of Educational Change.* London: Cassell.

Fullan, M. (1992) *Successful School Improvement.* Buckingham: Open University Press.

Fullan, M. (1993) *Change Forces: Probing the depths of educational reform.* London: Falmer.

Fullan, M. (1999) *Change Forces: The sequel.* London: RoutledgeFalmer.

Fullan, M. (2003) *Change Forces with a Vengeance.* London: RoutledgeFalmer.

Fullan, M. and Hargreaves, A. (1992) *What's Worth Fighting For in Your School?* Buckingham: Open University Press.

Furlong, J. (2003) 'BERA at 30: Have we come of age?'. Presidential address, British Educational Research Association Annual Conference, Heriot-Watt University, Edinburgh, 10–13 September.

Giddens, A. (1984) *The Constitution of Society: Outline of the theory of structuration.* Cambridge: Polity Press.

Giddens, A. (1991) *Modernity and Self-Identity: Self and society in the late modern age.* Cambridge: Polity Press.

Gray, J., Hopkins, D., Reynolds, D., Wilcox, B., Farrell, S. and Jesson, D. (1999) *Improving Schools: Performance and potential.* Buckingham: OUP.

Gronn, P. (2003) *The New Work of Educational Leaders: Changing leadership practice in an era of school reform.* London: Sage.

GTCE (2005a) General Teaching Council for England website: http://www.gtce.org.uk (accessed 2005).

GTCE (2005b) 'Research of the Month': http://www.gtce.org.uk/research/romhome.asp (accessed 2005).

Gunter, H. (2001) *Leaders and Leadership in Education.* London: Paul Chapman Publishing.

Hadfield, M. (2003) 'Building capacity versus growing schools', in A. Harris, C. Day, D. Hopkins, M. Hadfield, A. Hargreaves, and C. Chapman (eds), *Effective Leadership For School Improvement.* London: RoutledgeFalmer. pp: 107–19.

Hall, J. (2004) 'Improving transition from Key Stage Two to Key Stage Three'. Unpublished M.A. dissertation. Canterbury: Canterbury Christ Church University College.

Hammersley, M. (ed.) (1993) *Educational Research, Current Issues*. London: Paul Chapman Publishing.

Handscomb, G. and MacBeath, J. (2004) 'Professional development through teacher enquiry', *Professional Development Today* 7: (2) (Spring): 6–12.

Handy, C. (1997) *The Hungry Spirit: Beyond capitalism – a quest for purpose in the modern world*. London: Hutchinson.

Handy, C. and Aitken, R. (1986) *Understanding Schools as Organisations*. London: Penguin Books.

Hargreaves, A. (1994) *Changing Teachers, Changing Times: Teachers' work and culture in the postmodern age*. London: Cassell.

Hargreaves, A. (2003) 'Professional learning communities and performance training sects: The emerging apartheid of school improvement', in A. Harris, C. Day, D. Hopkins, M. Hadfield, A. Hargreaves and C. Chapman (eds), *Effective Leadership For School Improvement*. London: RoutledgeFalmer. pp. 180–95.

Hargreaves, A. (2004) 'Inclusive and exclusive educational change: Emotional responses of teachers and implications for leadership', *School Leadership and Management*, 24 (2): 287–308.

Hargreaves, A. and Fullan, M. (1992) *Understanding Teacher Development*. London: Cassell.

Hargreaves, A. and Evans, R. (1997) *Beyond Educational Reform: Bringing teachers back in*. Buckingham: Open University Press.

Hargreaves, A., Earl, L., Moore, S. and Manning, S. (2001) *Learning to Change: Teaching beyond subjects and standards*. San Francisco: Jossey-Bass.

Hargreaves, D. (1996) 'Teaching as a research-based profession: Possibilities and prospects', Teacher Training Annual Lecture. London: TTA.

Hargreaves, D. (1998) 'The knowledge-creating school'. Paper presented to symposium on Educational Research – New Directions? Annual Conference of the British Educational Research Association, Queen's University, Belfast, 27–30 August.

Hargreaves, D. (1999) 'Helping practitioners explore their school's culture', in J. Prosser (ed.), *School Culture*. London: Paul Chapman Publishing. pp. 48–65. .

Hargreaves, D. (2001) 'A capital theory of school effectiveness and improvement', *British Educational Research Journal*, 27 (4): 487–503.

Hargreaves, D. (2003) *Education Epidemic: Transforming secondary schools through innovation networks*. London: Demos.

Hargreaves, D. and Hopkins, D. (1991) *The Empowered School*. London: Cassell.

Harris, A. (2000) 'What works in school improvement? Lessons from the field and future directions', *Educational Research*, 42 (1): 1–11.

Harris, A. (2004) 'Successful leadership in schools facing challenging circumstances: No panaceas or promises', in J. Chrispeels (ed.), *Learning to Lead Together: The promise and challenge of sharing leadership*. Thousand Oaks, CA: Sage Publications. pp. 282–304.

Harris, A. and Lambert, L. (2003) *Building Leadership Capacity for School Improvement*. Maidenhead: OUP.

Harris, A., Day, C., Hopkins, D., Hadfield, M., Hargreaves, A. and Chapman, C. (eds) (2003) *Effective Leadership For School Improvement*. London: RoutledgeFalmer.

Head, M. (2000) Editorial, *The Enquirer*: The CANTARNET Journal (Summer): http://education-resources.cant.ac.uk/cantarnet/ (accessed 2005).

Helsby, G. (2000) 'Multiple truths and contested realities: The changing faces of teacher professionalism in England', in C. Day, A. Fernandez, T. Hauge and J. Moller (eds), *The Life and Work of Teachers: International perspectives in changing times*. London: Falmer Press. pp. 93–108.

Hitchcock, G. and Hughes, D. (1989) *Research and the Teacher: A qualitative introduction to school-based research*. London: Routledge.

Holden, G. (2002a) 'Changing stories: The impact of teacher-led development work on teacher, school and student learning'. Unpublished PhD thesis. Canterbury: Canterbury Christ Church University College / University of Kent.

Holden, G. (2002b) 'Leading learners: The role of teacher-led development work in building capacity to lead and manage educational change', *CELSI Occasional Paper No.7*. Canterbury: Canterbury Christ Church University College.

Holly, M.L. (1989) 'Reflective writing and the spirit of enquiry', *Cambridge Journal of Education*, 19 (1): 71–80.

Hopkins, D. (1996) 'Towards a theory for school improvement', in J. Gray, D. Reynolds, C. Fitz-Gibbon and D. Jesson (eds), *Merging Traditions: The future of research on school effectiveness and school improvement*. London: Cassell. pp. 30–50.

Hopkins, D. (1997) *Improving the Quality of Schooling*. Lewes: Falmer.

Hopkins, D. (2001) *School Improvement for Real*. London: RoutledgeFalmer.

Hopkins, D. and Ainscow, M. (1993) 'Making sense of school improvement: an interim account of the "Improving the Quality of Education for All" Project', *Cambridge Journal of Education*, 23 (3): 287–304.

Hopkins, D., Aiscow, M. and West, M. (1994) *School Improvement in an Era of Change*. London: Cassell.

Hughes, M. (2002) *Tweak to Transform*. Stafford: Network Educational Press.

Joyce, B. (1991) 'The doors to school improvement', *Educational Leadership*, 48 (8): 59–62.

Joyce, B., Calhoun, E. and Hopkins, D. (1999) *The New Structure of School Improvement: Inquiring schools and achieving students*. Buckingham: OUP.

Katzenmeyer, M. and Moller, G. (2001) *Awakening the Sleeping Giant: Helping teachers develop as leaders,* 2nd edition. Thousand Oaks, CA: Corwin Press.

Keating, I. and Roberts, I. (2003) 'Teachers as researchers: Working in higher education partnership', *Professional Development Today* (Spring): 28–35.

Kelchtermans, G. (1993) 'Teachers and their career story: A biographical perspective on professional development', in C. Day, J. Calderhead and P. Denicolo, *Research on Teacher Thinking: Understanding professional development*. London: Falmer Press. pp. 198–220.

Kelly, P. (2005) 'Fifty not out', *Teaching: The GTC Magazine* (Spring): http://www.gtce.org.uk/newsfeatures/92825/spring2005/105548 (accessed 2005).

Kelly, R. (2004) Remit letter, National College for School Leadership Priorities: 2005–6: www.ncsl.org.uk (accessed 2005).

Learmonth, J. (2000) *Inspection: What's in it for schools?* London: RoutledgeFalmer.

Learning School (2005): http://www.learningschool.org/ (accessed 2005).

Leithwood, K., Jantzi, D. and Steinbach, R. (1999) *Changing Leadership for Changing Times.* Buckingham: Open University Press.

Lieberman, A. (1996) 'Practices that support teacher development: Transforming conceptions of professional learning', in M. McLaughlin and I. Oberman (eds), *Teacher Learning: New policies, new practices.* New York: Teachers' College Press.

Lieberman, A. (2000) 'Networks as learning communities: shaping the future of teacher development', *Journal of Teacher Education*, 51 (3): 221–7.

Lieberman, A. and McLaughlin, M. (1996) 'Networks for educational change: powerful and problematic', in M. McLaughlin and I. Oberman (eds), *Teacher Learning: New policies, new practices.* New York: Teachers' College Press. pp. 185–201.

MacBeath, J. (1999) *Schools Must Speak for Themselves: The case for school self-evaluation.* London: Routledge.

MacBeath, J. (2003a) *The Leadership File.* Glasgow: Learning Files Scotland.

MacBeath, J. (2003b) 'Consulting through questionnaires', *Communicating: Consulting Pupils Project Newsletter* No.9, May.

MacBeath, J. (2003c) *'The Alphabet Soup of Leadership'* Inform No. 2. paper produced for Leadership for Learning, The Cambridge Network, University of Cambridge.

MacBeath, J. and Oduro, G. (2005) *Inspection and Self-evaluation – A new relationship?* Report commissioned by National Union of Teachers examining the changing relationship between inspection and self-evaluation. London: NUT.

MacBeath, J., Demetriou, H., Rudduck, J. and Myers, K. (2003) *Consulting Pupils: A toolkit for teachers.* Cambridge: Pearson Publishing.

MacBeath, J., Schratz, M., Meuret, D. and Jakobsen, L. (2000) *Self-Evaluation in European Schools: A story of change.* London: RoutledgeFalmer.

MacBeath, J., Sugimini, H., Sutherland, G. and Nishimura, M. (eds) (2003) *Self-evaluation in the Global Classroom.* London: RoutledgeFalmer.

MacGilchrist, B., Myers, K. and Reed, J. (1997) *The Intelligent School.* London: Paul Chapman Publishing.

MacLure, M. (1996) 'Telling transitions: Boundary work in narratives of becoming an action researcher', *British Educational Research Journal*, 22 (3): 273–86.

McKernan, J. (1996) *Curriculum Action Research: A handbook of methods and resources for the reflective practitioner.* London: Kogan Page.

McLaughlin, M.W. (1997) 'Rebuilding teacher professionalism in the United States', in A. Hargreaves and R. Evans (eds), *Beyond Educational Reform: Bringing teachers back in.* Buckingham: Open University Press. pp. 77–93.

McNiff, J. (1988) *Action Research: Principles and practice.* London: Macmillan Education.

Micciche, G. (2005) 'An example of school improvement and active citizenship by engaging students in taking on responsibility', *The Enquirer*, (Spring): 6–9. Canterbury: Canterbury Christ Church University College.

Middlewood, D., Coleman, M. and Lumby, J. (1999) *Practitioner Research in Education: Making a difference.* London: Paul Chapman Publishing.

Mitchell, C. and Sackney, L. (2000) *Profound Improvement: Building capacity for a learning community.* Lisse, The Netherlands: Swets and Zeitlinger

Montgomery, D. (2002) *Helping Teachers Develop Through Classroom Observation*, 2nd Edition. London: David Fulton Publishers.

Moon, J. (1999) *Reflection in Learning and Professional Development*. London: Kogan Page.

Morrison, K. (2002) *School Leadership and Complexity Theory*. London: RoutledgeFalmer.

National College for School Leadership (2003) *Tackling In School Variation*. NCSL: http://ncsl.org.uk (accessed 2005).

National College for School Leadership (2005), Networked Learning Communities: www.ncsl.org.uk (accessed 2005)

National Teacher Research Panel (2005) website: www.standards.dfes.gov.uk/ntrp (accessed 2005).

O'Sullivan, E. (1999) *Transforming Learning: Educational vision for the 21st century*. London: Zed Books.

Parsons, S. (1997) 'Managing to make things happen'. Unpublished M.A. dissertation. Canterbury: Canterbury Christ Church College.

Pollard, A. (2002a) *Reflective Teaching*. London: Continuum.

Pollard, A. (ed.) (2002b) *Readings for Reflective Teaching*. London: Continuum.

Pope, M. (1993) 'Anticipating teacher thinking', in C. Day, J. Calderhead and P. Denicolo, *Research on Teacher Thinking: Understanding Professional Development*. London: Falmer Press, pp. 19–33.

Prosser J. (ed.) (1999) *School Culture*. London: Paul Chapman Publishing.

Prosser, J. (1999) 'The evolution of school culture research', in J. Prosser (ed.), *School Culture*. London: Paul Chapman Publishing. pp. 1–14.

Ranson, S. (2000) 'Recognizing the pedagogy of voice in a learning community', *Educational Management and Administration*, 28 (3): 263–79.

Reed, J. and Learmonth, J. (1999) 'From reflective practice to revitalised accountability: Can school improvement help?'. Paper presented at International Congress of School Effectiveness and Improvement. San Antonio, Texas, 3–6 January.

Riley, K. and Jordan, J. (2004) '"It makes sense to me": Reforming classrooms from the bottom-up', *Improving Schools*, 7 (3): 227–42

Rudduck, J. and Flutter, J. (2000) 'Pupil participation and pupil perspective: Carving a new order of experience', *Cambridge Journal of Education*, 30 (1): 75–89.

Rudduck, J. and Flutter, J. (2004) *How to Improve Your School: Giving pupils a voice*. London: Continuum.

Rylatt, G. (2000) 'Learning together: A study of student participation and empowerment in post-16 learning'. Unpublished M.A. dissertation. Canterbury: Canterbury Christ Church University College.

Sachs, J. (2000) 'Rethinking the practice of teacher professionalism', in C. Day, A. Fernandez, T. Hauge and J. Moller (eds), *The Life and Work of Teachers: International perspectives in changing times*. London: Falmer Press. pp. 76–89.

Sammons, P., Hillman, J. and Mortimore, P. (1997) 'Key characteristics of effective schools: A review of school effectiveness research', in J. White and M. Barber (eds), *Perspectives on School Effectiveness and School Improvement*. London: Institute of Education. pp. 77–124.

Saunders, L. (2002) 'What is research good for? Supporting integrity, intuition and improvisation in teaching', *The Enquirer,* (Summer):. 5–22. Canterbury: Canterbury Christ Church University College.

Schon, D. (1983) *The Reflective Practitioner.* London: Temple Smith.

Scottish Office, The (1996) *How Good is Our School? Self-evaluation using performance indicators.* Audit Unit, Edinburgh.

Senge, P.M. (1993) *The Fifth Discipline.* London: Century Business.

Sergiovanni, T. (1994) 'Organisations or communities? Changing the metaphor changes the theory', *Educational Administration Quarterly,* 30 (2): 214–26.

Sergiovanni, T. (2000) *The Lifeworld of Leadership: Creating culture, community and personal meaning in our schools.* San Francisco: Jossey-Bass.

Shacklock, G. and Smyth, J. (1998) *Being Critical in Educational and Social Research.* London: Falmer Press.

Simons, H. (1987) *Getting to Know Schools in a Democracy: The politics and process of evaluation.* London: Falmer Press.

Simons, H. (1996) 'The Paradox of Case Study', *Cambridge Journal of Education,* 26 (2): 225–40.

Slater, J. (2005) 'Staff loath to stray from strategies', *Times Educational Supplement,* 25 February, 2.

Smyth, J. (1991) *Teachers as Collaborators.* Milton Keynes: Open University Press.

Smyth, J. and Shacklock, G. (1998) *Re-Making Teaching: Ideology, policy and practice.* London: Routledge.

Somekh, B. (1995) 'The contribution of action research to development in social endeavours: A position paper on action research methodology', *British Educational Research Journal,* 21 (3): 339–55.

Somekh, B. and Thaler, M. (1997) 'Contradictions of management theory, organisational cultures and the self', *Educational Action Research,* 5 (1): 41–160.

South, R. (2004) 'Developing pupils' independent learning skills', *The Enquirer,* The CANTARNET Journal, (Summer): 9–12. Canterbury: Canterbury Christ Church University College.

Spillane, J. (2003) 'Framing school leadership: A distributed perspective', Centre for Study of Learning, Instruction and Teacher Development website: http://litd.psch.uic.edu/initiatives/speakers/spillane (accessed 2005).

Stenhouse, L. (1975) *An Introduction to Curriculum Research and Development.* London: Heinemann.

Stenhouse, L. (1978) 'Case study and case records: Towards a contemporary history of education', *British Educational Research Journal,* 4 (2): 21–39.

Stenhouse, L. (1980) 'The study of samples and the study of cases', *British Educational Research Journal,* 6 (1): 1–6.

Stenhouse, L., (1981) 'What counts as research?' *British Journal of Educational Studies,* XXIX (2): 103–14.

Stenhouse, L., (1985) 'A note on case study and educational practice', in R.G. Burgess, (ed.), *Field Methods in the Study of Education.* London: Falmer Press. pp. 263–72.

Stoll, L. (1999) 'School culture: Black hole or fertile garden for school improvement?', in J. Prosser (ed.), *School Culture.* London: Paul Chapman Publishing. pp. 30–47.

Stoll, L. and Fink, D. (1996) *Changing Our Schools: Linking school effectiveness and school improvement.* Buckingham: Open University Press.

Stoll, L., Fink, D. and Earl, L. (2003) *It's About Learning (and it's About Time). What's in it for schools?* London: RoutledgeFalmer.

Swaffield, S (2003a) 'The local education adviser as critical friend: Superman/woman or Mission Impossible?' Paper presented within the Symposium Leadership for Learning: the Cambridge Network, 16th International Congress for School Effectiveness and Improvement, Sydney, 5–8 January.

Swaffield, S. (2003b) 'Critical friendship', *Inform* No.3. Paper produced for Leadership for Learning: the Cambridge Network, University of Cambridge.

Tate, N. (2005) 'Challenge your mind and keep on growing', *Times Educational Supplement,* 25 February, 10.

Teacher Training Agency (1996) *Teaching as a Research-based Profession: Promoting excellence in teaching.* London: Teacher Training Agency.

Teacher Training Agency (2004): Career entry and development profile: http://www.canteach.gov.uk (accessed 2005).

Tripp, D. (1993) *Critical Incidents in Teaching: Developing professional judgement.* London: Routledge.

United Nations (1989) Convention on the Rights of the Child: http://www.cirp.org/library/ethics/UN-convention/ (accessed 2005).

Walker, R. (1980) 'Making sense and losing meaning: Problems of selection in doing case study', in H. Simons (ed.), *Towards a Science of the Singular.* CARE: Norwich. Occasional Publication No.10.

Waller, R. (2004) 'Learning dialogues'. Unpublished M.A. dissertation. Canterbury: Canterbury Christ Church University College.

Watkins, D. (2004) Untitled, Unpublished M.A. dissertation. Canterbury: Canterbury Christ Church University College

Wenger, E. (1998) *Communities of Practice: Learning, Meaning and Identity.* Cambridge: Cambridge University Press.

West, L. (2004) 'The learner's voice: Making space? Challenging spaces?' Keynote address, CANTARNET conference, Canterbury Christ Church University College, 20 November.

West-Burnham, J. (2003) 'Leadership for learning'. Keynote address, at CANTARNET conference, Canterbury Christ Church University College, 22 March.

Whitehead, J. (1989) 'Creating a living educational theory from questions of the kind, "How do I improve my practice?"', *Cambridge Journal of Education,* 19 (1): pp. 41–52.

Wilkinson, D. and Birmingham, P. (2003) *Using Research Instruments: A guide for researchers.* London: RoutledgeFalmer.

Winter, R. (2003) 'Contextualizing the patchwork text: Addressing problems of coursework assessment in higher education', *Innovations in Education and Teaching International,* 40 (2): 112–22.

Woodhead, C. (1998) 'Blood on the tracks: Lessons from the history of education reform', Annual Lecture, H.M. Chief Inspector of Schools. London, March.

Woodward, W. (2004) 'You'll do it our way', *The Guardian,* 9 November: http://education.guardian.co.uk/ofsted/story/97348,1346360,00.html (accessed 2005).

Wragg, E. (1994) *An Introduction to Classroom Observation*. London: Routledge.

Wrigley, T. (2003) *Schools of Hope: A new agenda for school improvement*. London: Trentham Books

Yep, M. and Chrispeels, J. (2004) 'Sharing Leadership: Principals' perceptions', in J. Chrispeels (ed.), *Learning to Lead Together: The promise and challenge of sharing leadership*. Thousand Oaks, CA: Sage Publications. pp. 163–92.

Young, M.F.D. (1998) *The Curriculum of the Future: From the new sociology of education to a critical theory of learning*. London: Falmer.

Index